The New White Nationalism in Politics and Higher Education

The New White Nationalism in Politics and Higher Education

The Nostalgia Spectrum

Michael H. Gavin

LEXINGTON BOOKS
Lanham • Boulder • New York • London

Published by Lexington Books
An imprint of The Rowman & Littlefield Publishing Group, Inc.
4501 Forbes Boulevard, Suite 200, Lanham, Maryland 20706
www.rowman.com

6 Tinworth Street, London SE11 5AL, United Kingdom

British Library Cataloguing in Publication Information Available

Library of Congress Cataloging-in-Publication Data

Names: Gavin, Michael, 1976- author.
Title: The new white nationalism in politics and higher education : the nostalgia spectrum / Michael H. Gavin.
Description: Lanham : Lexington Books, [2021] | Includes bibliographical references and index.
Identifiers: LCCN 2021016303 (print) | LCCN 2021016304 (ebook) | ISBN 9781793629678 (cloth) | ISBN 9781793629685 (ebook) ISBN 9781793629692 (pbk)
Subjects: LCSH: Racism in higher education—United States. | White nationalism—United States. | Education, Higher—Social aspects—United States. | United States—Race relations.
Classification: LCC LC212.42 .G38 2021 (print) | LCC LC212.42 (ebook) | DDC 379.2/60973—dc23
LC record available at https://lccn.loc.gov/2021016303
LC ebook record available at https://lccn.loc.gov/2021016304

*To my wife, who has stood by me despite significant
loss and hardship and still makes me laugh.
To my daughter Isabelle, whose passion for dance and music
reminds me of Yeats's "Among School Children."
To my daughter Maya, whose compassion and
empathy is like a flower in the wind.
And to my youngest daughter Ava, you are a joy I never
saw coming but that I look forward to every day.*

Contents

Introduction

The Insurrection: The First Battle in a New War

A noose hung down from a gallows outside the United States Capitol. Insurgents carried flags emblazoned with Swastikas and the Confederate Stars and Bars. Battle cries aligning the crowd with white militias and white supremacist groups like the Three Percenters, Oath Keepers, and Camp Auschwittz echoed throughout the sunny Washington, DC day.

Banners and t-shirts glorifying Donald J. Trump's 2020 presidential campaign and announcing January 6, 2021, as the Make America Great Again Civil War paraded through the crowd. Once the Capitol Building's locked doors were breached, the insurgents poured in the marble hallways. They first desecrated the Rotunda, where American giants of democracy, John McCain and John Lewis, had recently lain in state. But the white supremacist mob and attempted coup did not stop there.

Tear gas plumed in the stairwells. One bomb exploded. A car full of Molotov cocktails was found in the area surrounding Capitol Hill. The first battle of the new white nationalism against American democracy was underway. This war, however, was not a surprise to many who had paid attention to a decades-long posturing of white domestic terrorists that warned of a forthcoming attack on American ideals.

As I write the new introduction to this book, one month after the new white nationalist insurrection, national media and the judicial system minimize the threat it presented and still presents. The severity and seriousness of that January day cannot be ignored. It was an overt attempt of domestic terrorism to overthrow the American government: Insurgents with red Make America Great Again hats carried zip-tie handcuffs, pistols, hockey sticks, and flag poles, chanting "hang Mike Pence," and "tell [Nancy] Pelosi we're coming after that bitch." The focus on Vice President Pence and House Speaker Nancy Pelosi during a riot where a noose and gallows, bombs, and

1

other weapons were present is proof enough of an attempt to assassinate some of the highest-ranking political officials in the American government. Those who gathered that infamous day were not just any other mob. Rather, they were seeking to overthrow the seat of democracy. Both Vice President Pence and House Speaker Pelosi were in the Capitol Building to oversee the congressional certification of the 2020 presidential election—a solemn ritual that ensures peaceful transfer of power.

In their attempt to overthrow the government, the insurgents, monolithically white, chased a single black police man, Eugene Goodman, up the stairs. Later hailed a hero, Goodman led these insurgents away from the Senate floor where many legislators were still conducting business. Without his quick diversion, January 6, 2021, would most likely be remembered as a day when insurgents massacred half of the American legislative branch.

In contrast, some white police men were seen taking selfies with the insurgents and offering the terrorists entrance into the Capitol. Their actions left Congress to later question whether or not there was inside support for the attempted coup. Five people, including one Capitol police officer, ultimately died.

The treasonous and terrorist act carried out by well over 10,000 American citizens, and catalyzed by leaders of what are considered to be different factions of white supremacy, operated, not for the first time, with a common intention and coordinated fashion. The insurgents' intent was singular: to derail the certification of the 2020 presidential election. Their collective action and singular purpose belied the myth that the many factions of white supremacy represent a fragmented movement. Rather, the insurgency on January 6, 2021, represented the most violent infiltration of white supremacy into the political sphere that America witnessed in the twenty-first century. However, white supremacy and white nationalism's infiltration into national politics and other American institutions had been pervasive and effective for well over four decades leading up to that day of treasonous rioting, and it was incrementally and predictably leading to this moment.

Indeed, disparate white supremacist groups have infiltrated political, social, and cultural spheres. They have common ideologies and a singular purpose that collectively form what I call the new white nationalism. The new white nationalism's most extreme elements consist of white supremacist groups like the Oath Keepers, the Proud Boys, QAnon, and Neo-Nazi militias. Over time, these groups have found affiliations with mainstream politicians and spread their ideologies pervasively through mainstream media. Their success in connecting with politics, other social institutions, and utilizing different media to spread their ideologies has equated to the mainstreaming of what, at one time, were considered extremist views.

I write this introduction as this book goes to press, and so argue that the events of January 6, 2021, are not surprising. Indeed, the insurrection of January 6, 2021, is irrefutable proof of this book's thesis, which was in publication process prior to the COVID-19 outbreak, George Floyd's lynching, the riots that followed, or the insurrection. January 6, 2021, however, solidified that the relationship between factions of our national political sphere and the new white nationalism is strong—so strong, that white supremacists traveled from as far away as Alaska and Hawaii to be part of the insurgence on January 6, 2021.

THE NEW WHITE NATIONALISM, TRUMP, AND THE INSURRECTION

Early that January morning, President Trump, his son Donald Jr., his lawyer, Rudolph Giuliani, press secretary, Kayleigh McEnany, and many congressional officials, gathered for a fomenting-named rally called "Save America." At the rally, Giuliani, who was the major strategist behind over sixty different and failed lawsuits attempting to overturn the 2020 presidential election results proclaimed that the crowd should engage in a "trial [to overturn the election] by combat."[1] Congressman Mo Brooks elated the crowd by saying, "today is the day American patriots start taking down names and kicking ass."[2]

Just days prior, Senator Ted Cruz aligned those citizens supportive of overturning the election with patriots at Bunker Hill and Valley Forge who fought for American independence during the Revolutionary War.[3] Senator Josh Hawley raised a fist in the air toward the gathered crowd demonstrating support. Trump proclaimed, "I will never concede" and told his supporters to march down to the Capitol building and give congressional Republicans the courage to steal an election:

> You'll never take back our country with weakness. You have to show strength, and you have to be strong. We have come to demand that Congress do the right thing and only count the electors who have been lawfully slated, lawfully slated . . . . Our country has been under siege for a long time, far longer than this four-year period. We've set it on a much straighter course.[4]

What followed at the Capitol hours later was predictable, incited, and one of the most horrific displays of white terrorism attempting to overthrow America that the country had ever witnessed.

Hours after the Capitol was cleared of the insurgent, treasonous actors, the resiliency of American democracy was also revealed as Congress returned to certify the election results. However, that certification occurred only after over two-thirds of house Republicans, 147 in total, voted to effectively overturn the election, aligning their goal with the insurgents'. All 147 votes were cast by Republicans. The insurgents and the Republicans who voted to overturn the election were nearly monolithically white. "The country" the insurgents and 147 politicians were trying to "save," therefore, was not one that was diverse.

Although many of the 147 representatives distinguished between the violence the insurgents engaged in and the process-oriented approach to overthrowing the election in the House, the intended outcome for a broad swath of Americans would have been the same: the disenfranchisement of voters' voices, especially those voters who were staunchly opposed to a new form of white nationalism. Each one of those 147 votes illustrated a member of Congress directly aligned with the new white nationalism's goals, which the next chapter illustrates, is to wrest civil liberties away from minorities. The alignment of politicians' voting and the new white nationalism's goals illustrates that what was once considered an extreme philosophy and movement had concretely infiltrated and been mainstreamed within American politics.

But the insurgency on January 6, 2021, should have come as no surprise to any institution in America. The 2020 presidential election was clearly about the new white nationalism and resisting it. During the first presidential debate of 2020, then-president Donald Trump was asked if he would commit to a smooth transfer of power by telling the white supremacist group, the Proud Boys, to stand down if he lost the election. His answer: "Proud Boys—stand back and stand by." Immediately after the debate, former deputy director of the Federal Bureau of Investigation, Andrew McCabe, asserted that the president's remarks were taken as signals by white supremacists to take up arms should Trump lose. On Parler, a digital application that became the home for white extremism, the Proud Boys leaders exclaimed, "THANK YOU PRESIDENT TRUMP! . . . Proud Boys Standing By."[5] During that same debate, Trump singled out Democratic governor Gretchen Whitmer for her restrictions on businesses during the global pandemic that, at the time, had claimed 150,000 American lives. Eight days later, thirteen white supremacists were arrested in a plot to kidnap her, take over the Michigan State House, and charge her, without authority to, with treason. Whitmer's address to the nation following this episode correctly linked Trump's rhetoric to the rise of white supremacy in the nation.

National media during that week suggested that Trump's comments revealed a new crescendo on the arc toward hatred and its proximity to political power.[6] Joe Scarborough exclaimed of Trump's alignment with the Proud Boys: "If that's not what fascists do, I would love for a professor or somebody who studies fascism to let us know."[7] Another outlet claimed that Trump's comments "caused shock waves across the nation and social media, provoking a flurry of tweets from NBA stars and rappers, civil right activists and political pundits, as well as actors and actresses."[8] While Trump's rhetoric was shocking for a sitting president, it was not new. Nor was the threat on Whitmer's life. The fall of 2020 and winter of 2021, rather, was marked by a national media waking up to a new white nationalism that was being mainstreamed more and more over a four-decade period.

However, the rhetoric and strategy of the new white nationalism is not limited to political spheres. For instance, in late September 2020, the Trump administration implemented an executive order on Combating Race and Sex Stereotyping. The executive order claimed to "combat offensive and anti-American race and sex stereotyping and scapegoating . . . [by rejecting] misrepresentations of our country's history." The executive order targeted "instructors and materials, teaching" what were labeled as "divisive concepts." The order performed acrobatic maneuvers to suggest that what amounted to critical race theory and intersectional approaches to historical knowledge were racist because they are "designed to divide us and to prevent us from uniting as one people in pursuit of one common destiny for our great country."[9] What the order represented, however, was an overt attack on higher education by the new white nationalism the likes of which had not been seen in over two decades.[10] In short, the infiltration of the new white nationalism into politics was violent. The infiltration into higher education represented an attempt to ensure that the knowledge produced by scholars and imparted to students would not continue the project of American equality.

The executive order's infiltration into higher education was not the first nor will it be the last attempt of politicians who seek to preserve the social, political, economic, and cultural power of whites through limiting the sort of knowledge produced in higher education. But each time the political sphere seeks to censor work done in the academic sphere, the power of that academic sphere is also highlighted. What academia does with that power is fundamentally important for what it means to be American in the future. The critical analysis of America, its history, and culture is necessary to achieve true social justice, and this is what many of those privileged by power fear the most: a well-educated citizenry capable of critically analyzing how power and privilege work. Indeed, Trump and his most avid partners in politics garner up to 72 percent of the noncollege-going white population of voters.[11]

A TRANSFER IN POWER IS NOT THE LACK OF POWER

There is a tendency to suggest that the new white nationalism was catalyzed by the Trump administration, and so that with his removal, such mainstreamed, racist, and nationally threatening views will dissolve. As the remainder of this book will show, however, the mainstreaming of the new white nationalism has been a decades-long project, and a transfer in power at the presidential level will not result in an end to this mainstreaming. Indeed, Trump may have lost, but he also garnered the second-highest vote count of all time (74,223,744), trailing only his contemporary opponent who gathered the highest vote count tally (81,283,485). CNN reported on December 28, 2020, that President Trump had the highest approval rating of any president to lose office. The same report showed that Trump had the highest rating of any Republican and therefore was a lock to win the Republican candidacy for the 2024 election should he desire it.[12] Whether or not Trump decides to run again is not the point. The point is, simply, that a broad swath of Americans believe that the policies, rhetoric, and isolationism characteristic of the Trump presidency was attractive. As a result, the traction of the new white nationalism and its capacity to permeate among those who see and saw value in Trump's politics and rhetoric that continuously marginalized non-whites, women, non-Christians, and non-Americans, is strong.[13] A transfer in power at the presidential level may give the illusory feeling that the systems, structures, policies, and cultural norms that underpin the Trump era have been eradicated. Concealment of the desire is not disruption or eradication.

What follows in this book will make some uncomfortable. Most of us Americans like to believe that the country is always progressing toward racial and social justice. We also like to believe that the status of racial and social justice can be measured in a quantifiable way, as if there is a thermometer for American racism. Believing that we are always progressing toward racial and social justice comforts us. It makes us feel that we are always working toward a common good, and that we are not complicit in oppression. But James Baldwin, one of America's greatest thinkers, wrote in disillusionment. "You always told me 'It takes time.' It's taken my father's time, my mother's time, my uncle's time, my brothers' and my sisters' time. How much time do you want for your progress?"[14] Being tricked into the notion that the country is always progressing allows a nexus of power that intentionally and urgently operates invisibly through political, educational, health, and cultural institutions to remain unchallenged. It allows, in short, for whites and the privileged to fall back on platitudes for solutions: "we need a national conversation on race"; "we need to meet people where they are"; "we need to ensure buy-in"; "it just takes time." However, the past six years in America have shown that such platitudes and mantras do little to change the conditions of the marginalized. They also leave the new white nationalism unchecked. These platitudes are the weapons of complacency, and complacency serves only the actively racist.

Many readers may find it inconceivable that scholars and critics would criticize with a country they love. But these scholars, who are my brothers and sisters, we love the idea that defines America so much that we are unwilling to let it be anything less than a beacon of justice. Well enough is not good enough, and an America that is regressing is far from what is well enough. Indeed, it is inarguable that there has been progress made with regard to the racism in America since the Civil Right Era. It is also inarguable that there have been regressions since that time. Many Americans find these statements to be contradictory and frustrating. But the reality is that racial and social justice is measured and felt in different ways depending on context. There is no thermometer. And knowing when we arrive at justice may also be impossible. But we certainly know when we are not there. Now is one of those times.

In my first book, *Sports in the Aftermath of Tragedy*, I argued that white supremacy was a network of individuals gaining power in 2010 and that it would only gain in power if ignored. In that book I saw the cultural moment as "rife with opportunity for intellectuals." I argued that white supremacy was gaining strength, but with intentional intervention in spaces that were not generally considered to be those where learning about social justice occurred, scholars of race theory could potentially disrupt the gathering inertia of white supremacy. Now, in 2021, the tactics, reach, and goals of that white supremacy have been so successful that America is facing the new white nationalism. It is a movement that has become so mainstreamed, scaled, intentional, and coordinated that the aggregate of its success has been characterized by its invisibility. This book is therefore an attempt to make those tactics and attacks visible to ensure that the new white nationalism's inertia can be slowed. Many may claim that America has always been a white supremacist and white nationalist country. This is true. However, the manner in which the new white nationalism is functioning is different. Today, in 2021, the new white nationalism is so strong and strategic that it is no longer a fringe movement. To ignore its power, its infiltration into political, educational, legal, and other spheres is to accept further threats to the nation. Complacency is a choice. It is a choice that threatens the very nation itself.

NOTES

1. Rudolph Giuliani, "Save America Rally Speech." *Rev.com.* January 6, 2021.
2. Mo Brooks, "Save America Rally Speech." *Rev.com.* January 6, 2021.
3. "CNN Newsroom." *CNN.* January 7, 2021.
4. Eli Stokolos, "Trump Vow to 'Never Concede' Incites Mob of Supporters." *LA Times.* January 7, 2021.

5. Adam Brown, "The App That the Proud Boys Used to Celebrate Donald Trump's Debate Performance." *Forbes*. September 30, 2020.

6. Variety Staff, "President Donald Trump Tells Hate Group Proud Boys to 'Stand Back and Stand By.'" *Variety*. October 1, 2020; Dana Milbank. "President Donald Trump Tells Hate Group Proud Boys to 'Stand Back and Stand By.'" *Washington Post*. October 1, 2020.

7. Joe Scarborough, Morning Joe. MSNBC. October 1, 2020.

8. Jenny Jarvie and Brittany Mejia, "'Are We Going to Choose White Supremacy?' Voters of Color React to Trump's Comments." *LA Times*. October 1, 2020.

9. Office of Management and Budget, "Executive Order on Combating Race and Sex Stereotyping." September 22, 2020.

10. Colleen Flaherty, "Diversity Work, Interrupted." *Inside HigherEd*. October 7, 2020.

11. William A. Galston and Clara Hendrickson, "The Educational Rift in the 2016 Election." *PEW Research*. December 2016.

12. Harry Enten, "Why Donald Trump Is Already the 2024 GOP Frontrunner." *CNN*. December 27, 2020.

13. Chris Kahn, "Majority of Americans Want Trump Removed Immediately after U.S. Capitol Violence—Reuters/Ipsos Poll." *Reuters*. January 8, 2021.

14. James Baldwin, *I Am Not Your Negro* (New York: Vintage Books, 2017).

Chapter 1

Nostalgia Matters: The Theoretical Framework

He drove a black Hyundai through the lazy streets of Charleston, South Carolina. Despite that he told his friends he would be carrying out the attack at the College of Charleston, he brought his car to a halt at the Emanuel African Methodist Episcopal Church.

Unassuming and calm, he sauntered through the sanctuary, and sat in a circle of twelve African Americans who were attending Bible Study. Their hospitality stuck him—so much so that he began to doubt his mission. After approximately ten minutes, however, he pulled out his glock and murdered nine of those twelve welcoming men and women. Three were allowed to escape so they could report what happened. He later stated that his motive was to start a race war in America.

National outrage ensued.

Artifacts like the Confederate flag and statues of Confederate generals became focal points in a national debate about racism's past and its place in the present. Some people claimed that the artifacts displayed historic pride in the South and others defined them as symbols of oppression, pain, and racism.

Only five days after the shooting, Nikki Haley, then-governor of South Carolina, argued that the Confederate flag hanging outside the South Carolina State House was "an integral part of [the state's] past, [but] it d[id] not represent [its] future."[1] Days later, the South Carolina legislature voted to remove the Confederate flag from State House grounds.

Later, in his eulogy to South Carolina State senator Clementa Pinckney, one of those slaughtered at Emanuel African Methodist Episcopal Church, President Barack Obama said: "By taking down that flag we express God's grace. But I don't think God wants us to stop there."[2] On the makeshift alter constructed in the College of Charleston's gym where the memorial was held,

President Obama then swung side to side and led the congregation in a slow-paced rendition of "Amazing Grace."

Over the next years, Americans of disparate mindsets looked at manifold nostalgic symbols of the Southern past scattered across the county in oppositional ways: To some, these symbols represented a time in America that was simpler and stable; to others, these same symbols represented a past full of racism and violence, and a complacency toward systemic racism in the present. The disputes over representations of the Southern past and their place in the present only strengthened as time went on.

For instance, in August 2017, two years after the Charleston shooting, torch light punctured the darkened University of Virginia's academic quad. An army of white nationalists banned together under the Unite the Right movement. Angered by the planned removal of a Robert E. Lee statue from Lee Park, they marched in unison on the campus designed by Thomas Jefferson. They threatened violence and projected their chants of anti-Semitism and racialized national unity into the summer night. Their language of "Jews will note replace us" and "blood and soil" were references to Nazi philosophies that linked a specific race, defined through blood, to a geographical location, the soil or land. The phrases, in short, were references to white nationalist beliefs and values.

The next morning, Unite the Right demonstrated on the streets of Charlottesville, Virginia. When one of the Unite the Right activists rammed his car into a crowd of protesters, thirty-two-year-old Heather Heyer fell limp and dead under his vehicle.

President Trump, when asked about his response to the escalating white nationalism in America, and the Unite the Right violence in Charlottesville specifically, responded: "You had some very bad people in that group, but you also had people that were very fine people, on both sides." When criticized for supporting white nationalism in this response, the president said, "I was talking about people that went because they felt very strongly about the monument to Robert E. Lee, a great general."[3] Given that many of the people who "felt strongly about the monument" were those from the Unite the Right movement, President Trump's response became a lightning rod for debate about American value systems and a general fear that diversity and inclusion were under attack in a more significant way than had been the case for decades previous.

Although the Charleston and Charlottesville events were horrifying, they were far from anomalous in nature and should not be viewed as isolated from one another. Nor are they isolated from other disturbing events regarding race and nationhood in the recent and distant past. These events are underpinned by manifold movements and structures with a common philosophy revealed in particular moments, policies, or political and mediated narratives. I call this philosophy the new white nationalism. The new white nationalism is not characterized as "new" because it has desired outcomes that are distinct from the traditional white nationalism. Rather, the new white nationalism has adopted new tactics for individuals within the movement to infiltrate spaces like higher education campuses not only for recruitment, but also for intimidation purposes. Also, the new white nationalism, this book contends, operates beyond individual people or events, and is becoming baked into major American institutions as a result of arcane policies and practices in institutions, and mediated stories that have been told over time. As these policies, practices, and mediated stories occur in one era, they necessarily snowball into the next. And at the aggregate, the new white nationalism is not only a racist movement that individuals support and enact. It is also a systemic problem that limits Americans' ability to see the way in which social justice, equality, and democracy are being impinged upon through the inertia that normalizes arcane policies, practices, and mindsets through the stories politicians and national media tell.

HIGHER EDUCATION AND THE POLITICS OF NOSTALGIA

In my previous book, I warned that a growing white nationalist movement was reaching beyond the "lone-wolf" terrorist acts that mainstream media generally focused on, and was already a "national network" of power. Since 2013, that network has expanded and deepened, redefining what white privilege and power looks like and its consequences.

The new white nationalism movement, moreover, views higher education as a threat to its goals and subsequently seeks to infiltrate it in ways that old forms of white supremacy did not. Examining the history of white nationalist and supremacist activities on higher education campuses over the past fifty years, it is clear that a remarkable shift in strategies, tactics, and behaviors has manifest since 2015. According to the Southern Poverty Law Center, white supremacists like David Duke and Wesley Swift visited college campuses from the 1960s through the turn of the century mainly for recruitment purposes. However, by 2015, white nationalists were targeting campuses in order "to inject their views into spaces they view as bastions of liberal thinking and left-wing indoctrination."[4] Likewise, according to the American Defense League, white nationalists have spent the past decade seeking to infiltrate higher education's walls in more aggressive ways than ever before. White nationalists have developed an intentional strategy to infiltrate higher education "because the schools are seen as liberal bastions that either need to be exposed to right-wing ideologies or called out for their political leanings."[5]

Hence, the new white nationalism is characterized as seeking a whole new population to invite into its racist, misogynistic, anti-Semitic, and general bigotry. The new white nationalism is focused on "influenc[ing] *mainstream* whites by exposing them to the concept of white identity and racial consciousness. . . . [and] reject[ing] multiculturalism or pluralism in any form (emphasis mine)."[6] As a result, the new white nationalism is focused on mainstream citizens. It sees college campuses, with their courses and majors that study the realities and histories of oppression through multicultural, sometimes anti-racist lenses, as posing significant threats. Ultimately, the new white nationalism seeks to reject and deter access to higher education whereas college campuses were generally thought of as recruiting grounds before.

Nowhere was this made more clear than in President Trump's "Executive Order on Combating Race and Sex Stereotyping" released in fall 2020. The executive order misrepresented the sort of knowledge produced in higher education and training circles regarding race, sex, gender, nationality, and other identities. The executive order claimed that such training embraced the notion that America has:

> hierarchies based on collective social and political identities rather than in the inherent and equal dignity of every person as an individual. This ideology is rooted in the pernicious and false belief that America is an irredeemably racist and sexist country; that some people, simply on account of their race or sex, are oppressors; and that racial and sexual identities are more important than our common status as human beings and American . . . this malign[ed] ideology is now migrating from the fringes of American society and threatens to infect core institutions of our country. Instructors and materials teaching that men and members of certain races, as well as our most venerable institutions.

Any scholar worth their salt in social justice, equity, diversity, inclusion, and anti-racism (heretofore referred to as anti-racism), however, sees the inequities that exist in American institutions as problematic, and is engaged in such training to make the nation less, or eradicated of, the hierarchies referenced in the executive order. The executive order, in short, was not intended to secure rigorous training and scholarship for anti-racism. Rather, its purpose was to limit such training and put those performing the training and scholarship under a scrutiny reminiscent of McArthyism, as many scholars have pointed out throughout Trump's presidency.[7]

The new white nationalism has thus taken to threatening those who promote anti-racist efforts on college campuses when before white supremacist tactics were limited to simply disparaging multiculturalism and those who espoused it.

However, seemingly benign American systems have become a product of and a means to produce the outcomes desired by the new white nationalism, and so should be considered part of that cause. Simultaneous to this new white nationalism's berth in the early twenty-first century, the American middle class began to shrink significantly and big data became the generally accepted mechanism to define direction for nearly all American political, economic, and cultural sectors. Under this big data paradigm, colleges face more scrutiny than ever before. Such scrutiny has led to intense questioning about higher education's very value and function in the new economy. This scrutiny is characterized by a return-on-investment lens taken toward higher education that:

- Questions tuition's cost;
- Criticizes completion rates and numbers without context;
- Suggests students do not learn the necessary knowledge, skills, and abilities for the market economy;
- Continuously delegitimizes the utility of humanities and social sciences disciplines—those disciplines where studies of anti-racism, white privilege, identity studies, multiculturalism, power of structures reside;
- Reduces higher education's purpose to prepare graduates to earn high salaries one year after matriculation rather than to be better citizens of the nation (which was the original purpose of higher education, and is found in many colleges' mission statements); and
- Ultimately works to limit broad access to higher education and the knowledge produced by it.

The contemporary scrutiny that higher education is currently experiencing threatens to have outcomes that align the new white nationalism's goals: to limit access to higher education and specifically anti-racism. In both the new white nationalism and the current discourse regarding higher education's value, students are potentially veered away from college altogether, or disciplines where social justice is taught. Indeed, there are those who understand this connection between the current discourses of higher education and the new white nationalism's goals and utilize both for their racist causes.

There are many who are privileged by race or class and operate in sinister ways from their positions of power. Their actions and comments reveal a desire to justify their privilege and power, which was tautologically offered to them as a result of the cyclical nature of systemic power and privilege. Alternatively, there are those who buy into the narratives regarding higher education's value and/or liberalism without being aware that those narratives can have sinister outcomes, despite intent. Although the motives and goals of those engaging in the discourses about higher education's value are not the same as those of the new white nationalist movement, the outcomes of their practices and narratives are the same. Hence, it is no surprise that the new white nationalism is all-too-happy to see the apparatus of educational, political, and media spheres engage in the discourse that is continuously scrutinizing higher education. Moreover, the histories of higher education, politics, and media have been plagued by white privilege.

WHITE PRIVILEGE AND WHITE NATIONALISM IN DIFFERENT SPHERES OF POWER

To understand the apparatuses that secure white privilege and the new white nationalism requires an analysis of racial theory in relation to power dynamics that manifest at the national and day-to-day individual levels. Since whiteness became a major field of study, the thinking regarding its power has shifted in many ways. Some of the earliest thinkers about whiteness as a construct and race focused mainly on structures of power and privilege and how they centralized whiteness as a norm against which all other structures, systems, and identities are defined. George Lipsitz, David Roediger, and Candice Chuh illustrate how structures of power and privilege exert influence over entire groups of people based on race, gender, sexuality, nationhood, or other constituents of identity. This group of thinkers tracked racial stratification resulting from policies and practices as early as colonial America to as recent as a global market economy of the twenty-first century. Throughout their collective work, they illustrate the common denominator over time periods was and is the support of white, elite, heterosexuals, and the marginalization of other identities through legalized policies or cultural constructions of race. Lipsitz, for instance, illustrates that beginning with slavery and through the 1990s, manifold policies at national, state, and local levels progressively permitted African Americans to live in geographical areas that were at one time reserved for whites. However, he illustrates, the passage of these policies did not lead to integration of neighborhoods. Minority access to white and/ or middle-class neighborhoods required education that would lead to well-paying jobs as well as realtors who would show African Americans places to live where whites resided. In short, this group of scholars illustrates that the structures, systems, and policies required cultural mindset changes in whites in such a way as to ensure de facto segregation and oppression over time.

This group of scholars also illustrates that in a globalized economy, American borders are not as rigidly defined as many would generally consider or prefer. Still, this globalized economy operates in ways that invisibly privilege whiteness. With regard to the current moment, Lipsitz uses the example of the Walt Disney Corporation's production of Pocahontas pajamas to claim that "members of different social groups have very different relation-ships to the common objects that seem to unite them."[8] Pocahontas pajamas, made in Asian countries for pennies on the dollar, are sold to American parents at prices exponentially beyond the production costs of those pajamas. The apparatus of economic and cultural spheres leads to the exploitation of brown bodies to serve the pleasures of middle-class families and the Disney Corporation executives. American white and middle-class privilege controls the lives of black and brown bodies beyond American borders in very invis-ible ways.

The other camp of whiteness scholars focuses on revealing to white indi-viduals the privilege their skin color offers them. These scholars argue that whites have a duty to renounce their privilege and to take up the mantle of anti-racism. One of the most astute and helpful thinkers in this camp of scholars is Robin DiAngelo. DiAngelo's books *What Does It Mean to Be White* and *White Fragility* have provided helpful toolkits for white people to understand their complicity with racism in their everyday experiences and interactions with people of color. Tim Wise, author of *White Lies Matter*, *Under the Influence*, *Dear White America*, and *Colorblind*, has brilliantly explained white privilege by deconstructing the manner in which mediated news stories, American history, or social constructions of identity continu-ously operate from and protect white complacency, comfort, and privilege. Wise, like DiAngelo, has a purpose of illustrating to whites that their privi-lege affects society and their interactions with people of color negatively. These two camps of scholars have very little they argue about, and are more alike than not.

However, in the scholarship of whiteness, there is a tendency to either emphasize the institutional form of white privilege as evidenced in the first camp, or the negative experiences that people of different backgrounds have with one another because whites may not understand their own privilege. Yet, there is very little scholarship that emphasizes the cyclical relationship between structures/systems and individuals that occurs in the context of white privilege. Likewise, there is a tendency among scholars of whiteness to use particular moments in time, such as the Charleston or Charlottesville tragedies, to unpack how white privilege and power is or was evident in them. However, in considering the new white nationalism as a construct, it is possible to see that specific incidents, policies, narratives, and modes of thinking are part of an always-accumulating story of white nationalism and power. And in the second decade of the twenty-first century, there is a mainstreaming of white nationalism, not only because mindsets of culture are normalizing extremism. The mainstreaming also occurs because the structures and systems that have been operating over time have accumulated, rolled over into the present, and resulted in a mainstream American context policies, systems, and narratives present themselves as benign but still serve that construct's goals.

Simultaneously, and because of the conditions that have been created by these systems and structures, there are people, as evidenced in the Unite the Right Rally and President Trump's rather lackadaisical response to it, who feel freer than ever to assert their racist ideologies, which are subsequently becoming mainstreamed. These individuals, who are operating in the mainstream and in new ways to assert white supremacist goals, are themselves those leading the charge of the new white nationalism.

Whiteness and its power is defined by a cyclical relationship between individuals and systems and is a flexible system of control that changes over time, always ensuring that institutions, policies, and practices benefit, at minimum, white elites. Ibram Kendi's revolutionary text, *Stamped from the Beginning*, built a foundation for understanding the relationship between systems and individuals. There is a tendency among scholars of race to consider structures like cultural, educational, political, or economic institutions as relatively rigid and static over time. Similarly, these institutions are often perceived and interrogated as if they are isolated from one another. However, the social systems of American society are tangled together so much so that a change in one often results in a change in another. The opposite, of course, is also true. For truly transformational change toward an anti-racist and democratic society to occur requires that multiple sectors of society operate in unison with one another. Seeing this, Kendi distinguishes between racist ideas and policies, arguing that:

> [H]ate and ignorance have not driven the history of racist ideas in America. Racist policies have driven the history of racist ideas in America . . . racially discriminatory policies have usually sprung from economic, political, and cultural self-interests that are constantly changing.[9]

Kendi's insight is fundamentally important for understanding the power relations at play when social institutions are examined in relation to racism and individual thought and behavior. Kendi inverts the traditionally held belief that individuals enact racist policies because they are racist people. He illustrates that policies exist prior to individuals being in positions of authority. And these policies form those peoples' ideas about race. Individuals thus reinforce or create racist ideas to justify those policies' existence and the condition of the world that privileges them and that they were born into. Those justifications supply a rationale for those who are privileged by racist policies to remain complacent toward oppression—and to create more racist policies to ensure their own and their children's place in the world remains privileged. This dynamic ensures that the racist institutions, practices, policies, and narratives remain relatively strong in their foundation and continue with a snowballing effect in the future.

In his thinking, however, Kendi yet maintains that a cause-and-effect dynamic exists between institutions, policies, practices on the one hand, and individuals on the other. I see the dynamic between institutional racism and individual prejudice as cyclical. I also extend on Kendi to argue that social institutions, policies, practices, and narratives span across generations and that each generation of humans interact with the history of those institutions, policies, practices, and narratives in the present. By offering a cyclical and generational element to the discussion about race, structures, and individuals' role in each, I hope to plug a significant gap that currently exists in whiteness studies. For institutions like higher education, capitalism, American politics, and the media do not end or begin again when a generation ends or begins. Institutions themselves are dynamic, long-lasting entities that operate upon the way in which people think over time and vice versa. As such, it is possible for complacent people to enter into systems characterized by white privilege, and continue such privilege because of the systems' inertia. That inertia builds when people remain unaware or uncaring of their own and institutional privilege in general.

Below is a representation of how the generational inertia of systems that privilege whiteness is maintained through simple complacency toward institutional racism. This is the cycle that has produced the conditions for the new white nationalism to reveal itself in the second decade of the twenty-first century.

It is clear to see in this cycle that there is interaction between individuals and systems. Moreover, it is also possible to see that individuals enter into the world with systems of privilege and power that will necessarily shape their experiences and general worldviews. These individuals will make decisions based on their own privilege. Those decisions will strengthen institutional racism, but not necessarily because they intend to. This point of intention not equating to outcome is very important to underscore as it is often missed in the current discourses of race and race privilege. There are a number of people (both white and of color), born into privilege, who have not had the opportunity to be exposed to the sort of thinking that would lead them to challenge their own privilege. For doing so requires significant understanding of the context and history of the context into which they were born.

In these cases, individuals' limited point of view may lead to decisions or thoughts that exacerbate institutional racism. This dynamic is a dangerous one in the context of a discourse and paradigm that scrutinizes higher education's cost, efficacy, and commitment to anti-racism. Scrutinizing education's efficacy and value risks creating a citizenry lacking faith in higher education so much so that it does not go to college, and thereby bolsters one of the goals

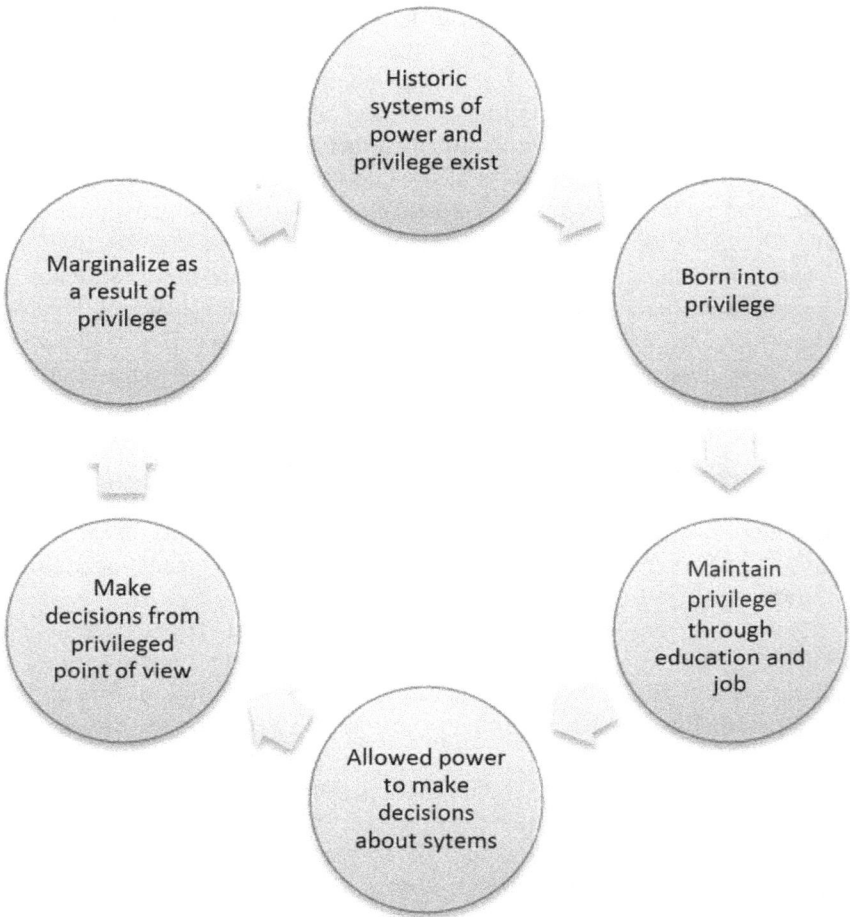

**Figure 1.1   The above image illustrates how the lifespan of an individual does not out-
last the social and political institutions that they operate in**. Rather, people are born into
systems and if they adopt a complacent approach to anti-racism, they do little if anything
to disrupt the cycle of privilege and power. As such, over time, the marginalized become
more and more marginalized from the privileges of whiteness in America. By the author.

of the new white nationalism. Because the manifold institutions that comprise
American society are so intertwined, a citizenry that avoids higher education
courses and programs that resist the new white nationalism—which have
only been pervasive in higher education for a generation—will potentially
unwittingly support white privilege and power. And slowly, the institutions,
policies, and practices of America will only maximize the power of whiteness. This cyclical inertia of systems and individuals in the context of a nation

scrutinizing higher education presents a perilous dynamic for the greater American experiment of democracy and equality.

WHITENESS AS A POWER CONSTRUCT RATHER THAN A SKIN COLOR

For this book the term "white" is defined in a similar fashion that I defined it in my first book, *Sports in the Aftermath of Tragedy*. To be sure, whiteness is a racial category that needs interrogation. However, it is also a flexible system of power that is better defined by what it does than skin color alone. In fact, interrogating whiteness as a race only is an impossibility. Black and Asian American feminist theorists have shown this to be true in their development of intersectional analysis. Patricia Hill Collins, for instance, reminds us that "oppression cannot be reduced to one fundamental type [race, class, gender, sexuality]. [O]ppressions work together in producing injustice."[10] She goes on to suggest that "oppression is always changing [and that] different aspects of an individual" become "more salient" depending on context.[11] Kandice Chuh suggests there are problems of homogenizing through labeling race under a single sign like "Asian-American."[12] In *Immigrant Acts*, Lisa Lowe extends on Chuh to write that race is a construct that is problematized not only by intersectional theory, but also by the historic normalization of whiteness. She illustrates that the "categorization of [people] as diverse, racialized ethnic groups, rather than a single racialized category, supports and obscures the powerful centrality of the white racial category."[13] I extend on these theories to illustrate that whiteness itself cannot be reduced to a single racialized category when it comes to people. However, this is not true of American institutions, policies, and practices. For American institutions, policies, practices, and narratives have continuously gone to great lengths to ensure that at the very minimum, wealthy whites are privileged. The circle of those privileged has indeed extended to a wider group of people since the inception of American independence. However, it has done so only with complicity from the whites who are in charge of drafting the institutional policies, practices, and narratives for different sectors of the country. Hence, I define whiteness as a national identity that limits and controls who is offered privilege, power, civic, and cultural citizenship. Whiteness has an origin story of being berthed to ensure white and elite privilege primarily, and appeasing other identities over time with legal or cultural citizenship based on particular conditions of the time. Whiteness therefore intentionally limits who is included or excluded in the notion of "American-ness," while allowing that power and privilege to define "American-ness" to only a small group of people, especially whites. Whiteness and American-ness can be interrogated by examining institutional inclusions and exclusions that occur in policies and practices of the nation.

RATIONALE FOR THE LABEL "NEW WHITE NATIONALISM"

The constructs of white power, privilege, and supremacy are already becoming tangled together as a result of the cyclical system of inertia. For example, the traditional white supremacy is said to have two major camps of thought related to white *nationalism*. One camp accepts that races other than whites will exist in the nation, but insists that in the future "white domination is complete and un-complicated by civil rights laws and voting rights for people of color." The other camp imagines "a whites-only republic carved out of the remains of a collapsed and dissected United States of America."[14]

These two camps of thought reveal an ugly but unavoidable truth facing America in the second decade of the twenty-first century: They are reflected in the policies, practices, and narratives that permeate American social, cultural, and political institutions. This permeating force in the mainstream is what characterizes the new white nationalism. The new white nationalism is disguised as benign, but that has become mainstreamed. And there is a general desire among the mainstream to deny this reality. Mainstream politicians, media, and modes of thinking may perform rhetorical acrobatics to avoid language that can draw lines between current national and institutional policies and practices and a desire for a "white nation." However, the current moment consists of many national policies, practices, decisions, and discourse that seek to:

- Reduce citizen's civil rights;
- Distance people of color, women, and LGBTQ people from a whitewashed, imagined future of America;
- Segregate people of color, women, Muslim, and LGBTQ people from mainstreamed amenities citizenship, higher education, or the good life that results from it;
- Limit black and brown immigrants' entry to America and higher education;
- and more.

Collectively, the above equate to policies, practices, and narratives that lead to a nation that draws sharp borders between people of color and whites in terms of rights, privilege and even neighborhoods. The fact that such segregation occurs through seemingly organic means is the trick of the new white nationalism that does its work at times covertly and at times overtly. The new white nationalism, moreover, is intersectional in how it oppresses, meaning it oppresses the manifold parts of people's identities in different ways and at different times. Races, ethnicities, religions, sexualities, classes, genders, nationalities, and even political beliefs that do not align with the rigid definitions of what the new white nationalists define as belonging in their ideal nation are seen as threats and subsequently marginalized and, as of 2020, often physically harmed or killed. Over and again, we will see, the policies, practices, narratives, and mindsets in politics, media, and higher education perform work with a singular result: They secure the privilege and power of white people and their children in the present moment. The people who are in positions of authority in the institutions that affect policies, mediated narratives, and higher education, however, are often in those positions as a result of the historic privileging of whiteness. As a result, history is present but also, without conscious resisting of that history, it is reinforced and made stronger through new policies, practices, and narratives that build off the past. Over time, then, the normalization of whiteness becomes stronger through invisible inertia. This invisible inertia of strengthening past oppressions is a major element of the new white nationalism.

Without conscious resistance, the present, always a product of the past, organizes a future that is more racially extreme in how it isolates and segregates minorities from whites both physically and in terms of citizenship rights. Non un-coincidentally, this truth serves the goals of the new white nationalism. The new white nationalism functions in new ways and can be understood by looking at outcomes rather than intent of policies, practices, individuals, and narratives. However, the new white nationalism functions with the same goals as white supremacists and white nationalists of old. A singular phrase commonly repeated among white supremacists and white nationalists known as "the fourteen words" has circulated for decades: "We must secure the existence of our people and a future for white children."[15] We will see, as a result, that the manifold policies, practices, and narratives that, at the aggregate, have led to the mainstreaming of what I call the new white nationalism are directly related to the mantras and philosophies of what has traditionally been understood as white supremacy and white nationalism.

I am hopeful that it is clear that I offer the label of the new white nationalism for tactical reasons and not to blame well-meaning and good people or institutions—for there are people and institutions who would, through recognizing the implications of history and their position in it, actively resist the inertia characterized by the new white nationalism. However, there are those who embrace the label of white nationalist, like those who marched with Unite the Right. And in between there are those who would deny the label of new white nationalists, but support and defend white nationalist movements.

The ex-president of the United States, Donald Trump, for instance, is in this camp.

The term "new white nationalists" is also meant to assist with definitions and terms. There is a tendency among those in politics and mediated spheres to tiptoe around labels even if certain individuals' actions clearly indicate that they deserve them. The label and definition of new white nationalist allows an understanding of what is occurring nationally with regard to racist policies and narratives that are happening right before our eyes in the mainstream. It situates clearly racist policies, narratives, and individuals with language, the new white nationalism. The new white nationalist individual, we will see, gains strength and power by enacting, supporting, or using policies, systems, and narratives while wearing suits rather than hoods, robes, or wearing tattoos celebrating Hitler. This distinction is important for understanding what is happening in the twenty-first century, not necessarily to define which sort of white nationalism is better or worse. It also underscores that those who desire a racially segregated country in terms of either geography or rights may look differently than what Americans have been accustomed to for the past decades, and they are gaining positions of power. In those positions, more and more, they are actively inciting and protecting the typical white nationalists groups like the Proud Boys, Oath Keepers, and those attending their rallies like Unite the Right or the January 6, 2021, insurrection.

Finally, as the new white nationalism is both a tactic of individuals and the context produced by the institutional histories of American sectors, it is also possible to view those privileged by race in a new way. Many of those privileged by race buy into the rhetoric and policies of leaders espousing philosophies, policies, and practices that align with the new white nationalism. Because of the contexts in which they were raised, many may unwittingly support a white nationalist agenda by advocating for a singular policy, practice, or narrative because they do not have the full historical context of that policy, practice, or narrative. The decontextualization of singular policies, practices, or events from histories that inform them is an intentional tactic of the new white nationalist leaders seeking to gain support from unwitting citizens. Indeed, presenting policies, practices, rhetoric, or events in an ahistoric fashion is part of how the new white nationalism gains power. The new white nationalism operates covertly by decontextualizing policies and practices and narratives from their historic context. In the process, what is presented to the mainstream may often seem benign when it is anything but. This decontextualization of history is a tactic to buy unwitting support for a white supremacist agenda. That is, many may support the new white nationalism because they are not aware of the histories associated with its policies, practices, and narratives. Yet, they would be horrified if they were to understand the racial implications of what they supported.

HIGHER EDUCATION AND THE
POLITICS OF NOSTALGIA

Higher education plays a significant role in how society has been, is, and will be structured with regard to race. As early as the seventeenth century, the template for the American higher education system was set. That template was developed with a very specific race, gender, and class in mind—the wealthy white male. Higher education, the site theorized to be a mechanism of social uplift, has been and is one rife with power relations; one that has historically acted upon individuals through exclusion. It is a site where the ideas regarding science, technology, business, arts, and humanities would be developed and necessarily affected by the very exclusions upon which the system was built. Hence, higher education has a history that cannot be divorced from the absences that have created it. Higher education, in short, shapes the power structures of the world outside of it. Thus, higher education and its exclusions are symbiotic with the other major institutions' power structures outside of it.

Although individuals may shift the course of history's inertia, that history has an origin that is rarely if ever totally disrupted. And this lack of disruption of any system's origin, especially higher education's, leaves the residue if not the burgeoning of white power and privilege that characterized its beginning. This lack of disruption of the central origins of whiteness in structures and systems in higher education writ large is the story of *New White Nationalism in Politics and Higher Education*. To truly resist racism requires contextualization of all things in an intentionally and comprehensive history so as to understand and disrupt the power relations at the origin of the philosophies, policies, practices, and narratives of the institutions that were created through exclusionary practices. In both its scholarship and the graduates it produces— (who go on to become leaders of many different institutions)higher education plays a significant role in how we all perceive of what counts as "American," and also race in general.

Hence, rather than seeing the events of Charleston and Charlottesville as anomalous events isolated to a particular time and place, it is more helpful to see them as points on a singular, centuries-long spectrum. That spectrum is characterized by a tension between two oppositional polls, each defined by how individuals imagine America and how racial history is situated therein. That tension manifests itself as having, on one extreme, those with a forward-looking, inclusive vision of America. This extreme sees the necessity of understanding the history of America's racist institutions in order to address them in the present. On the other extreme are those holding onto a nostalgic and clouded version of an idyllic American past that does not need contemplation or interrogation in the present.

For the former group, inserting historic context into the present allows for a broader understanding of the complexities of race in American history. For the latter group, inclusion of more minorities in the power dynamic is often perceived to equate to a loss of privilege and power. Introduction of more minorities to spaces and institutions that were once exclusionary in nature equates to a potential obliteration of the constructs of history, nation, race, and institutions of the idyllic past constructed by and to privilege whites. In other words, for the latter group, the desire is to ensure the past remains the present—nostalgia matters. To understand how these two extremes see the world, and specifically race and history's role in contemporary America, requires a tool that is multidimensional in nature. I call this tool the nostalgia spectrum.

The nostalgia spectrum allows examination of particular phenomena in American culture and is capable of delineating between and among various mindsets that exist within groups based on intention and perceptions. Specifically, this tool delineates among and between those with mindsets of (1) white nationalism versus white privilege versus anti-racism; and (2) intentional attempts to assert white nationalism versus complacency typical of white privilege versus measures taken to enact an anti-racist present and future. It also allows analysis of outcomes versus intent of initiatives. The nostalgia spectrum likewise reveals the latent and significant power that white complacency plays in allowing the inertia of oppression to continue when not actively resisted. Finally, the nostalgia spectrum explains that individuals and groups look at singular events, national initiatives, or paradigms in oppositional ways as a result of their view of history and how that specific history manifests itself in the current society. My claims about history here build off my earlier thinking in *Sports in the Aftermath of Tragedy*. They accept Marita Sturken's argument that history and cultural memory are tangled together in the stories Americans tell themselves in order to make meaning of their place in contemporary American society. These stories are fundamentally important to understand. For Sturken writes that:

> Debates about what counts as cultural memory are also debates about who gets to participate in creating national meaning. When people participate in the production of cultural memory. . . . they do so both in opposition to and in concert with a concept of the nation.[16]

I want to extend on my own and Sturken's thinking about cultural memory and history, however. Sturken's *Tangled Memories* and my own *Sports in the Aftermath of Tragedy* were very interested in the body as a repository of knowledge, memory, and place in particular moments of national importance, such as 9/11 or Hurricane Katrina. I am now arguing something quite different about history and its relationship to the body. The construct of history comprises of social institutions, people, ideas, practices, and procedures that act upon people long before they are born, while they live, and long after they die. The story of American race, oppression, and marginalization must indeed focus on the body and how it is written upon through power relations. However, focusing on the body often makes the construct of history seem as a distant one that is not actively operating through institutions that outlasts individuals. History and cultural memory have a life of their own and cannot be considered foreign to the discussion of race and its meaning for nationhood. History and cultural memory are concretely present and shape how the body and race is perceived, contextualized, and operated upon. In this way, it is important to consider history and nation as just as dynamic as the body, and subsequently, discussing them both as we do the corporeal. The nostalgia spectrum allows for history's dynamic realities across generations to thus be tracked and considered when interrogating present or past issues about race and nation. It also allows the construct of history to be considered much like Foucaultians consider the body—as written upon and continuously a locus of power.

Moreover, because history plays such a significant role in how race is defined in contemporary America, higher education's role in developing knowledge about race, history, social institutions, and oppression is fundamentally political and part of the greater American experiment of democracy and equality. This latter statement should not be misunderstood. When discussing race, culture, education, economics, literature, and more, all people enter into adulthood with implicit and powerful assumptions about oppressions (or lack thereof) and subsequently develop their viewpoints accordingly. People see oppression as related to the dynamic nature of history or as wholly ahistorical in nature. Whether or not one subscribes to the notion that history plays a significant role in defining social institutions, policies, practices, and individual ideas about the present moment does not matter. For subscribing to an ahistorical view is often telling of the conditions that allow one to subscribe to such a view.

Native American author Sherman Alexie confirms the way in which history, the present, and future are intertwined with one another. He writes:

> I think a lot of people want to deny that something that happened 100 years ago or 300 years ago still has long-lasting effects, and still changes, alters and mutates the way that we relate to each other . . . . You hear people say, "I didn't do anything. I'm not responsible for something 100 years ago" . . . . But the fact is, we are all responsible for it and we all deal with the legacy of it . . . . The way that the country deals with its African American and Native American populations remains basically the same—we are still oppressed, we're still subjected to racism, we're still living in poverty, living in threat of violence from institutions, and still dealing with a white power structure that diminishes us on a daily basis.[17]

History is present, is racialized, and continues to racialize the nation itself. Even those who have very little care or knowledge of history live in a nation haunted or privileged by that history. And all citizens have opinions about history's role in the present. As such, we all fall on different points of the nostalgia spectrum. Hence, I offer the nostalgia spectrum as a tool to analyze how diverging viewpoints of singular events, national initiatives, or paradigms emerge and reveal how the past informs the present disagreements.

There are four major categories of people when considering white power, privilege, and anti-racism and they fall on the nostalgia spectrum in different places and may move among and between those places depending on the issue or moment under consideration.

First are the white terrorists. This group of people is committed to white supremacy but uses physical violence to reinforce their ideology. This group of people does not need much elaboration.

Second are the new white nationalists. This group of people consists of those with power and privilege. They may not act as terrorists, but they are aware of how privilege works, and actively seek to ensure white power and privilege remain as the dominant organizing force of social, political, and cultural institutions in America. This group of people should be considered as ill-intended and also seeking oppressive outcomes. These people may not cause physical violence, but do cause oppression intentionally. As a result, these people are white nationalists and are the leaders of the new white nationalism, even if they many not label themselves as such. As seen in the January 6, 2021, insurrection, however, this group of people are more and more closely aligning themselves with white terrorists.

The third group of people are those who are innocently unaware of how privilege works as a result of not having been exposed to how it functions and its history. These people rarely have any ill intentions. Some are rife for recruitment toward white nationalism or terrorism. However, most are happily complacent about oppression and believe their understanding of how history and social systems operate is benign and correct. These people operate from a position of privilege that is based on either their skin color, class, sexuality, religion, nationality, or more. Privilege, for the purposes of this book, is thus defined as having certain systematic advantages as a result of the historic and oppressive ways in which American society was built. Privilege, then, is a fact. It is created and perpetuated by systems, institutions, and their histories. People are born into the world with privilege without any fault of their own. Systems operate upon those with privilege just as they operate on those without it, but in extremely different ways. Because of the historic nature of institutional systems, policies, and narratives moreover, those with privilege may be completely blind to the privilege they have and may resent being told they have privilege or deny that oppression has an origin that is historic in nature. Although some of my counterpart scholars in whiteness studies do not believe that intent matters in how or why whites react regarding racial issues, I disagree. Within this group of people, those innocently unaware of how privilege works, intention matters greatly. To be sure, it is possible for well-meaning people, unaware of how privilege works and its history, to operate with intentions that are genuinely good, but have racist effects because of their being unaware of their privileged lens. Hence, the nostalgia spectrum also accounts for the fact that intentions and outcomes may not necessarily align. The nostalgia spectrum, therefore, functions to show this group of people that their thinking and actions/inactions may indeed reinforce the new white nationalism's goals simply if they remain complacent. However, to blame this group of people for knowledge they may not have is counter-intuitive to the overall goal of anti-racism, which is "to make coalitions with people who are different from you . . . [in order to dismantle the oppressions of] race and sexual and class and sexual identity all at one time."[18] To blame people for impact they *unwittingly* have exerted only alienates them from the cause of anti-racism. And it blames them for not having the understanding and knowledge of oppression and how it works—which in itself is a result of the white power and privilege cycle illustrated above. Of the four categories, the one that has the highest potential to disrupt the inertia of history's oppression is this group. This group of people are powerful because they can be persuaded to become anti-racist. But their complacency is also powerful. The work for the anti-racists seeking to transform the complacent is difficult as it requires changing the entire world view of a people who may not be interested in having their worldview changed. In contrast, the new white nationalism needs only to ensure the complacent group of people remain complacent toward their own privilege in order for systems of white nationalism and privilege to continue to assert their power. As a result, alienation of this group of people by blaming them for impact of their ideas and decisions of which they were not aware only serves the new white nationalism's ability to recruit them toward complacency or worse, activism on their end.

The final group of people outlined in the nostalgia spectrum are the anti-racists. Anti-racists understand and seek to reveal how the history of institutions, policies, narratives, and practices carry over into the present and so future unless there is disruption of the systems that oppress.

All of these groups fall at different points on the nostalgia spectrum. Institutions, policies, practices, and narratives situate people in these categories early on in life, and they can be positioned elsewhere based on their experiences. Moreover, it is important to use the nostalgia spectrum and these categories in examining different institutions, policies, practices, and narratives so that full understanding of intent and outcome can be delineated for strategic approaches to anti-racism in the immediate and long-term future.

The diagram below makes an attempt at illustrating the multidimensional nature of racist versus anti-racist views, intentions versus outcomes and how they are wrapped up in historic power and privilege.

For the purposes of this book, I will refer to the left side of the nostalgia spectrum to be those who adhere to a mythological version of the past or ahistoric versions of the present. This side intends to maintain white power and privilege through policies, practices, and narratives that benefit whites and exclude others. The right side will be the opposite. Note, too, that the top half of the spectrum delineates the oppositional intentions with regard to anti-racism. I choose left and right intentionally so as not to mix up the argument I am making about anti-racism with stereotypical political ideologies of liberal and conservative.

The ultimate goal of the nostalgia spectrum is to provide insight into how, over four centuries, American institutions, policies, and practices have been built by and to privilege whiteness, defined intersectionally and aggregately. That history is still relevant today as the structures and systems that were built long ago have only been reinforced, and perhaps changed. But they certainly

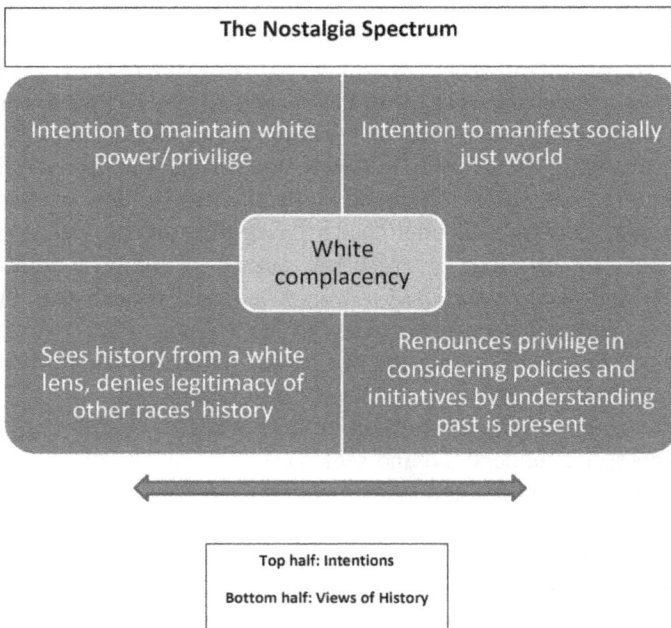

The Nostalgia Spectrum

Intention to maintain white power/privilige

Intention to manifest socially just world

White complacency

Sees history from a white lens, denies legitimacy of other races' history

Renounces privilige in considering policies and initiatives by understanding past is present

Top half: Intentions

Bottom half: Views of History

Figure 1.2   The nostalgia spectrum allows a multidimensional understanding of race, intentions, outcomes, and view of history for strategic purposes. It also centers white complacency as that group of people are the ones who can do the most harm or good in social transformation. By the author.

have not been infiltrated at their origin. Hence, the nostalgia spectrum does not look at isolated events or paradigms to unpack meaning from them, as the bulk of whiteness studies does. Rather, it provides a tool with which to illustrate that history is dynamic and the aggregate of single events, policies, or narratives over time, arrives in the present to guide, and often limit contemporary thought.

METHODOLOGY FOR REMAINDER OF THE BOOK

The conclusion this book arrives at is that higher education has a potentially significant role in disrupting the social stratification of America. However, for higher education to play such a role requires that it become positioned in the visions for the future as one of many institutions that will catalyze an anti-racist agenda. Higher education, though, must confront its own racial past while negotiating the racial pasts of other social institutions to resist the new white nationalism's goals. In the interim, the new white nationalism benefits from the inertia of white power and privilege so much so that it is becoming more difficult to separate systems that privilege whites from those that are overtly tied to the new white nationalism's goals.

Each chapter of this book thus examines policies affecting, narratives about, and requirements for higher education in conjunction with larger but related political and cultural paradigms in which they have taken place. This approach to offering context contemporary with higher education's changes over time illustrates that higher education is one of many social institutions that has a history—one that is operated upon by and operates symbiotically with changes in American institutions. Ultimately, by contextualizing major policies, narratives about, and requirements for higher education within a history and contemporary moment, the way in which historic oppressions reach into the present to form current ideas becomes revealed.

Because race is constructed by a variety of sectors and has a history, those sectors require analysis to understand new thoughts about higher education and its roles and responsibilities in delivering on the national promise of equality and democracy. The chapters that follow illustrate how different policies, practices, institutions, and discourses currently scrutinizing higher education fit in with the five white nationalist agendas of:

- Creating separate geographical spaces in the nation based on race—from elite colleges to white neighborhoods, to prisons, to the nation itself;
- Ensuring that America works to minimize entry of black and brown people into the nation and elite colleges;

- Securing the existence and future of white people;
- Impinging on the civil rights of minority people to support white supremacy;
- Actively infiltrating spaces that seek to enhance democracy from the January 6, 2021, insurgence at the Capitol building to higher education itself.

Each chapter illustrates how history is a construct made active through institutions, policies, practices, and narratives that last generations. Each chapter illustrates that what have often been described as systems and structures that operate to support privilege, in this era of a shrinking middle class and big data, conflate with the goals of the new white nationalism.

Further, because institutions, policies, practices, and narratives of American institutions have a strong history, each with their own inertia, the ability for white privilege as a construct to continue only because of inertia is real. It is with this inertia that the new white nationalism's goals are slowly being baked into the institutions that guide America and its citizens' ways of thinking. The result is that the new white nationalism and white privilege are tangled significantly, and the delineation between the two is difficult to assign. The result is an America that is becoming more like the past version of national race relations with each new policy, practice, or narrative that is tinged with white privilege or the new white nationalism's tenants. These are indeed perilous times.

WHAT DOES HIGHER EDUCATION HAVE TO DO WITH NATIONALISM?

Most of the information about the apparatus of white privilege comes from a sector of that very apparatus: mainstream media. Media, however, does not cause, but rather reveals, a dominant culture's tastes and desires in a specific moment. Douglass Kellner writes that studying specific texts, especially those that make it into the mainstream, allows for "critique which analyzes the social interests and ideologies served" if the conditions that surround the texts themselves are interrogated.[19] Peter Berger and Arthur Luckman's *The Social Construction of Reality* illustrates that "society is a human product. Society is an objective reality. Man is a social product."[20] Hence, unlike many of my counterpart thinkers focusing specifically on higher education, I focus on how a matrix of texts about higher education collectively construct the discourse of colleges from a point of view that reinforces or deconstructs white nationalism. I do so because the dominant discourse substantially affects how colleges are situated in mainstream America. It also plays a role in how legislators and politicians react to that discourse through policy, accountability measures, or funding. Moreover, studying this discursive frame allows an understanding of how the national identity has been, is, and will be defined with relation to higher education.

Two of the most helpful thinkers about how a collective group perceives itself to be part of a single community and create what is perceived to be a national identity are Benedict Anderson and Ernest Gellner. Both agree that one of the major elements involved in allowing disparate peoples to imagine themselves part of a similar community and hence providing "a people" was the proliferation of commonly viewed print media culture. In *Imagined Communities*, Anderson claims that the increase in intensity of print culture from the mid- to late 1800s allowed "people to think about themselves, and to relate to others in profoundly new ways" through the imagination.[21] This leads him to define nations not as lands with borders and policies and politicians, but as "imagined communities." Herein, Anderson illustrates the importance of media culture in how people consider themselves as part of a nation. He also underscores the importance of human imagination in establishing nations. Hence, as people produce and consume media culture about the value of higher education in America, an American value system is both constructed for and by them.

Similarly, Gellner believes that a division of labor allows print and media to be owned by a privileged elite, who then create that same material in their own image and from their own perspective; they thereby manifest a national identity in limited and privileged fashion. The division of labor, that is, establishes a specific people, usually in racially homogenous terms, as the elite representatives of the nation-state. Gellner believes that nationalism is the inevitable outcome of industrialization, where specific requirements are placed on individuals in order to be considered part of the national community: when "fully human men can only be made by educational systems, not by families and villages, [there] underlies an amusing fact—the inverse relationship between the ideology and the reality of the nation."[22] Herein, Gellner argues that educational systems are part of a process by which the concept of what a nation is manifest and an individual's place in it is created. Moreover, he shows that the manner in which educational systems and nations operate necessarily marginalize those without the capacity to go to the best schools and have influence over how media defines nations. Hence, higher education is indeed part of the matrix that creates and is created by the national identity that is manifest; that reinforces or deconstructs white supremacy and privilege depending on the tact it takes toward social justice.

In sum, there is no political sphere that is separate from the educational sphere—there are actors attempting to shape meaning and using their different powers of thought, finance, and media to do so; and in so doing they construct an imagined nation, one that will reflect contemporary versions of what an elite identity is. Often this reflection of an elite identity is not sinister in motive, but does have sinister outcomes. Hence, this elite identity plays a role in creating and being created by the left poll of the nostalgia spectrum. For "the basic deception and self-deception practiced by nationalism is this: nationalism is, essentially, the general imposition of a high culture on society."[23]

Moreover, it is becoming clearer over time that the current battleground is not only higher education, but the minds of those privileged, for it is with their help that anti-racists can intervene within systems in order to disrupt the privilege and supremacy at their center. Ultimately, this book is not all dire and gloom. For it utilizes the nostalgia spectrum as a tool to show how simple mindset shifts can revolutionize the manner in which the world is perceived, and in the cases shown throughout this book, in changing the way higher education is situated in the greater American experiment.

The role the imagination plays should not be minimized. Major scholars on nationhood, race, and geography illustrate that the imagination plays profound effects how policies are often developed. Edward Said's major point in *Orientalism* is that the Western world imagined the East in a way that was totally divorced from reality, but that dictated policy for over two centuries. Likewise, from "The Declaration of Independence's" first line that America is "dedicated to a *proposition*," to "The Gettysburg Address'" proclamation that the nation was *conceived* in liberty to Martin Luther King's "I Have a Dream," those at the forefront of political movements have inspired cultural *imagination* to manifest new realities.

Today, in 2021, there is not such an inspirational call so much as a cultural malaise and assumed futility when the future of social justice in America is considered. However, that malaise does not have to remain. There are visions for a more socially just future. Those visions need only a toolbox with which to unpack how politics, funding, cultural mindset, and higher education work to maintain the status quo or disrupt it. The nostalgia spectrum is part of that toolbox.

NOTES

1. Mark Niquette, "South Carolina Governor Backs Removal of Confederate Flag." *Bloomberg News.* Retrieved June 22, 2015, https://www.bloomberg.com/news/articles/2015-06-22/south-carolina-officials-call-for-confederate-flag-to-come-down.

2. Mark Niquette, "South Carolina Governor Backs Removal of Confederate Flag." *Bloomberg News.* Retrieved June 22, 2015, https://www.bloomberg.com/news/articles/2015-06-22/south-carolina-officials-call-for-confederate-flag-to-come-down.

3. Jordyn Phelps, "Trump Defends 2017 'Very Fine People' Comments, Calls Robert E. Lee a Great General." *ABC News,* https://abcnews.go.com/Politics/trump-defends-2017-fine-people-comments-calls-robert/story?id=62653478.

4. American Defense League, "White Supremacists Continue to Spread Hate on American Campuses." June 27, 2019, https://www.adl.org/blog/white-supremacists-continue-to-spread-hate-on-american-campuses.

5. Brett Barrouquere, "Richard Spencer Took Universities, Protesters by Storm; They Adjusted and Brought His Speaking Tour to an End." *The Intelligence Report,* Southern Poverty Law Center, August 5, 2018, https://www.splcenter.org/fighting-hate/intelligence-report/2018/schools-out.

6. Anti-Defamation League, "Alt Right: A Primer about The New White Nationalism." https://www.adl.org/resources/backgrounders/alt-right-a-primer-about-the-new-white-supremacy.

7. Peter Bienhart, "Trumpism Is the New McCarthyism." *The Atlantic.* June 16, 2020.

8. George Lipsitz, *American Studies in a Moment of Danger* (Minneapolis: University of Minnesota Press, 2001), 5.

9. Ibram Kendi, *Stamped from the Beginning* (New York: Bold Type Books, 2016), 9.

10. Patricia Hill Collins, *Black Feminist Thought* (New York: Routledge, 2000), 18.

11. Ibid., 274.

12. Kandice Chuh, *Imagine Otherwise: On Asian Americanist Critique* (Durham: Duke University Press, 2003).

13. Lisa Lowe, *Immigrant Acts* (North Carolina: Duke University Press, 2003).

14. Devin Burghart and Leonard Zeskind, *Tea Parties—Racism, Anti-Semitism and the Militia Impulse* (Institute for Research & Education, 2010), 59.

15. Anti-Defamation League, "Alt Right: A Primer about The New White Nationalism." https://www.adl.org/resources/backgrounders/alt-right-a-primer-about-the-new-white-supremacy.

16. Marita Sturken, *Tangled Memories: The Vietnam War, the AIDS Epidemic, and the Politics of Remembering* (Los Angeles: University of California Press, 1997), 13.

17. Mythili Rao, "Sherman Alexie: How Storytelling Can Create Social Change." *The Takeaway.* September 23, 2015.

18. Barbara Smith, Gloria Anzaldua, and Cherrie Morage, eds., *This Bridge Called My Back* (San Francisco: Persephone Press), 126.

19. Douglass Kellner, *Media Culture* (New York: Routledge, 1995), 23.

20. Peter Berger and Thomas Luckman, *The Social Construction of Reality* (New York: Doubleday, 1972), 50.

21. Benedict Anderson, "Imagined Communities." In *Nationalism*, edited by John Hutchinson and Anthony D. Smith (New York: Oxford University Press, 1994), 90–91.

22. Ernest Gellner, "Nationalism and Modernization." In *Nationalism*, edited by John Hutchinson and Anthony D. Smith (New York: Oxford University Press, 1994), 90–91.

23. Ernest Gellner, "Nationalism and Modernization." In *Nationalism*, edited by John Hutchinson and Anthony D. Smith (New York: Oxford University Press, 1994), 90–91.

Chapter 2

The Cartography of the New White Nation

On April 27, 2011, Donald J. Trump appeared on Fox News and animated an already-bizarre discourse concerning the birthplace of U.S. presidential candidate, Barack Obama. Of Obama, Trump said, "he doesn't have a birth certificate. He may have one, but there is something on that birth certificate—maybe religion, maybe it says he's a Muslim; I don't know. I have people that have been studying it and they cannot believe what they're finding."[1] Later in that same campaign, the Republican candidate for president, Mitt Romney, explained how it was clear that he was an American citizen, and therefore "no one's ever asked to see my birth certificate; they know that this is the place that we were born and raised."[2] The issue of Barack Obama's birthplace became a lightning rod for debate and conspiracy theories during the 2011 election cycle, culminating in Obama's revealing his long-form birth certificate as proof of his citizenship. Although often decried as a conspiracy theory or a campaign tactic revealing of a racist view of Obama, the questioning of Obama's birth place revealed something greater that had been developing in American mainstream politics for centuries. The imagined nation and citizenship of that imagined nation is clearly white. While the borders of that nation may be imagined, they are drawn with firm consequences in reality.

For instance, Donald Trump announced his candidacy in the very next presidential election. He glided down a golden escalator at Trump Towers. In announcing his candidacy, Trump referred to the need to reduce the quantity of brown people entering American borders by vilifying Mexican immigrants:

It's true, and these are the best and the finest. When Mexico sends its people, they're not sending their best. They're not sending you. They're not sending you. They're sending people that have lots of problems, and they're bringing those problems with us. They're bringing drugs. They're bringing crime. They're rapists. And some, I assume, are good people.[3]

So began the Trump candidacy for and eventual administration of the American presidency. The common theme underpinning both the candidacy and the presidency was use of calculated and sinister rhetorical strategies that invoked a nostalgia for a better time. That better time included an America isolated from the rest of the world's bodies of color and that also shifted the blame for economic conditions negatively affecting a broad swath of middle-class Americans onto brown bodies.

Through an odd amnesia, the truth that black and brown people have, over centuries, experienced violence and economic tragedy is omitted from this nostalgic invocation of a better past.

HIGHER EDUCATION AND ITS RELATIONSHIP TO THE DISCOURSE OF NOSTALGIA

Trumpian political rhetoric and mediated narratives about America, race, and nation were taking place during a time wherein big data proliferated and dictated much of the decision-making processes at national and state levels. Through that data-based analysis, white privilege and power was certainly baked into certain systems but easily overlooked. In *Weapons of Math Destruction*, Cathy O'Neil argues that in the early 2000s big data became the major emphasis of the American business and educational worlds. O'Neil, one of the major thinkers behind the big data movement, argues that the metrics used to define whether or not institutions are working or cost-friendly are formed by humans, who themselves often have benefited and continue to operate from privileged points of view. According to her, the data in the twenty-first century, even when it is disaggregated, often lacks necessary nuance and is quite dangerous:

> The math-powered applications powering the data economy were based on choices made by fallible human beings . . . . Nevertheless, many of these models encoded human prejudice, misunderstanding, and bias into the software systems that increasing managed our lives . . . . And they tended to punish the poor and the oppressed in our society . . . [and contain] many poisonous assumptions [that] are catalogued by math and go largely untested and unquestioned.[4]

To this end, the relationship among historic minority attendance in higher education and state and federal policy and funding can be directly related to racial biases, but couched in terms like "tuition costs" or "return on investment." Those setting the metrics and data use regarding tuition costs as well as success, that is, often benefit from privilege and power, and in the process, knowingly or unknowingly can create of college campuses the same sort of imagined nation projected in the racist nostalgia the Trump agenda typifies. Politicians and national media do this by oversimplifying the issue of tuition costs and access in their policies and stories. The result is an apparatus that is the very definition of the new white nationalism. It secures white privilege through a closed system that funds higher education in inverse proportion to minority attendance and in the process represses knowledge of past oppression from current discourse—despite that the present is still haunted by the very past that is being repressed from memory. The overall result is a social system that is working in opposition to diversity and toward the development of racialized geographical spaces throughout the nation, thereby supporting the white nationalist needs of segregationist society. These racialized spaces are manifest both in the college campuses as well as the racially and socially stratified landscapes of urban and suburban blight. Moreover, these racialized spaces are developed and reified over time.

Hence, there is, this chapter argues, the residue of privilege and segregationist attitudes underpinning the national outcry of escalating tuition that ignores community colleges as a potential solution to this problem. For that outcry is predicated on making the oppression of minority and impoverished citizens' concerns invisible by:

1) Raising the concern of escalating tuition *only* when middle class and white families cannot afford it;
2) Making invisible the history of higher education's access problems in the current debate about cost and access;
3) Minimizing the fact that there is an inverse trajectory of minority attendance and state and federal funding over the past four decades;
4) Ensuring that community colleges, with their cheaper tuition, are socially constructed to be inferior and the domain of minority and lower-class families; and
5) Negating the benefits of multiculturalist approaches to education while Otherizing community colleges to such an extent that they do not appear in the discourse about higher education's cost.

POLITICAL SPHERE AND ITS IMPACT ON A RACIALIZED ACADEMIC WORLD

Who holds the power to frame the debate and its parameters also dictates, whether intentionally or not, how it will unfold. And the current moment seems to lean toward more, not less, white and class privilege in policiy and discourse about higher education. Likewise, the circular nature of privilege explained by O'Neil is evident in how the federal, political sphere has become comprised by even further privilege: Currently, "[m]ore than half of the [the members of Congress] earned an undergraduate or graduate degree from one of the nation's most esteemed colleges."[5] Less than 1 percent of Congress does not have a bachelor's degree.[6] In contrast, thirty-five years ago in the 97th Congress (1981–1982), 84 percent of house members and 88 percent of senators held a bachelor's degrees. In short, the more expensive tuition for college has become, the less likely it has become for a citizen to become a member of Congress. And it is in Congress that many decisions about federal funding for higher education are made.

In "The Intellectuals," Antonio Gramsci identifies the way in which the educational complex, supported through politics, media, and economics, defines what legitimate knowledge is and who can obtain it in class-based and racial fashion. Gramsci notes that education, traditionally acquired by elites, becomes a very real manner in which power manifests itself. And over time, the elites reify their own power by ensuring that they control education and who can and cannot have it. As a result, elites ensure their bloodlines remain elite through the matrices of power and how education fits in those matrices. And ultimately, according to Gramsci, this dynamic is what underpins all oppression. It is with this in mind that the nostalgic understandings of America have to be considered as having political, racial, economic, and cultural implications.

USING THE NOSTALGIA SPECTRUM TO UNDERSTAND "MAKE AMERICA GREAT AGAIN"

The bright lights of Joe Louis Arena in Detroit, Michigan, pierced through the multicolored balloons. They rested in a pregnant net hanging from the ceiling. Ronald Reagan grasped the podium and accepted the Republican nomination for president of the United States. In a softened yet assuring tone, he addressed a sector of the American population whose middle-class jobs were either dissolved or under threat of being taken oversees as a result of changes in the auto and steel industries. He said to an American audience full of anxiety about the future of the American economy:

> It's time to put America back to work, to make our cities and towns—make our cities and towns resound with the confident voices of men and women of all races, nationalities, and faiths, bringing home to their families a paycheck they can cash for honest money. For those without skills, we'll find a way to help them get new skills. For those without job opportunities we'll stimulate new opportunities, particularly in the inner cities where they live. [F]or those

who've abandoned hope. We'll restore hope, and we'll welcome them into a great national crusade to *make America great again.* [emphasis mine][7]

The changes in auto and steel narrowed the pathway to middle-class jobs for noncollege degree workers. American outsourcing of steel and auto manufacturing during the 1970s and 1980s impacted African American and Latinx populations in the long-term more significantly than any other group. In "The Causes of Inner-City Poverty: Eight Hypotheses in Search of Reality," Michael Tietz and Karen Chapple show that African Americans were the demographic most geographically bound and educationally limited since the 1970s as a result of this disruption.[8]

However, since that economic disruption, a matrix of institutional policies and practices ensured the middle class was still achievable for whites, and less so for minorities. The result of these policies was to relegate the inner cities—like Detroit, Pittsburgh, Baltimore, and Philadelphia—to the domain of impoverished African American and Latinx populations. Ultimately, African American and Latinx populations were isolated financially and geographically from whites, achieving a tenant of white nationalism.

The new white nationalism, in which sinister leaders and the inertia of institutions' policies and practices collaboratively work to secure the future of whites and their children, can be seen in the pessimistic conclusion Chappel and Teitz arrive at regarding the social and economic segregation of races since that was exacerbated since the 1980s:

> The industrial transformation that destroyed the employment bases of inner cities is effectively irreversible . . . . However, it must be stressed that, the fact that inner-city poverty is demonstrably complex and resistant to change does not imply that equally complex policy responses are the only way to proceed. Given that poverty is remarkably complex suggests that it requires a sophisticated response strategy that takes into account its complexity but relies on multiple and simple elements for implementation. If the War on Poverty was not won, perhaps that is because, like all wars, victory requires a strategy that combines a deep understanding of the environment within which the war is waged and the willpower, resources, and weapons to do the job.[9]

Chappel and Teitz thereby illustrate that to change the trajectory of racialized poverty, especially in those very cities to which Reagan referred to forty years ago, requires complex and systematic overhaul of policy responses. Despite the fact that up until 1970, integration of neighborhoods was progressing throughout the nation, Douglass Massey illustrates that racialized isolation of Latinx and African American populations from whites since that time has only increased. Of African American residential segregation, Massey writes that:

> Twenty years after the Fair Housing Act, Blacks were still unlikely to come into residential contact with members of other groups. The large ghettos of the North have remained substantially intact and were largely unaffected by Civil Rights legislation of the 1960s . . . [I]solation [for both Latinx and African Americans from whites was] high and rose somewhat from 1970 to 1990.[10]

Although often remembered as a Republican giant, Reagan was complicit in the slow squeeze of minorities out of the middle class while supporting the burgeoning of a new tier of economic elite that exploited people of color both at home and abroad. He did this by "presid[ing] over an economic restructuring that caused extreme pain to many Americans, eliminating millions of jobs and forcing the shutdown of thousands of companies."[11] Although seemingly unrelated, this economic strategy was directly connected to a desire to destabilize the already-hurting African and Latinx populations of America.

Paradoxically, then, the past yearned for in Reagan's Make American Great Again phrase did refer to a time that was more integrated than ever before, the 1970s. However, the policies enacted by the Reagan administration, coupled with the racial discourse he invoked in his political career were in polar opposition to integration and social justice. Indeed, Reagan's Make America Great Again phraseology was part of a moment that catalyzed what Republicans have called the Southern Strategy. That strategy actively exacerbates prejudice through mediated narratives about race in order to garner votes and the power to enact policy: "The Republican Party, in the wake of the civil rights movement, decided to court Southern white voters by capitalizing on their racial fears."[12] Herein is a concrete example of how systems work with individuals in a dynamic that the new white nationalism as a construct provides.

Specifically, Reagan fully adopted this Southern Strategy, often vilifying black America through unfounded stereotypes, while simultaneously blaming minorities for injecting race into the politics of the day.

> [Reagan] encouraged Americans to move past race, but also invoked the image of the "welfare queen," a black woman whom Reagan described as having "80 names, 30 addresses, [and] 12 Social Security cards," resulting in a tax-free income of $150,000. In doing so, he portrayed racial minorities as undeserving "takers," while erasing the institutional racism at the heart of economic inequity. The message to Southern white voters was both that African Americans were to blame for their own standing in society and that government programs aimed at alleviating racial inequities would disadvantage white Americans.

This Southern Strategy led to Reagan's being elected twice as president, an eight-year period in which the government reduced spending on welfare, higher education, training for employment, food stamps, child nutrition, and more. "[A]t the same time that income tax reductions [we]re cutting tax rates for the rest of the population and thereby increasing their prosperity . . . the elimination of programs [aimed at the poor] . . . made [their] economic advancement" less likely.[13] Collectively, Reagan cut a matrix of programs that could have served as a social, cultural, educational, and economic lattice to alleviate the poverty and that ultimately isolated whites and minorities from one another.

THE SLOW ACCEPTANCE OF THE
NEW WHITE NATIONALISM

The notion that minorities have gained the same advantages that whites have is untrue. Yet, the Southern Strategy positioned its rhetoric and then its policies to suggest that programs focused on minorities gave resources to minorities that whites did not receive. The Southern Strategy leveraged the construction of *black and minority* privilege to inspire a collective, white backlash against alleviation of poverty and institutional racism. This strategy also called on a nostalgic time period, which through an odd amnesia, erased the memories of violence and oppression against minorities. This backlash is underpinned by a victim mentality pervasive in the left side of the nostalgia spectrum. It also glosses over the Reagan era's use of the term "family values" to justify the marginalization of all identities that did not fit into a construction of a white, middle-class, heterosexual families.

For instance, Reagan's encouragement of segregation and the institutional racism was rather overt in his early career. Opposed to both the Civil Rights Act and the Fair Housing Act, Reagan famously said, "if an individual wants to discriminate against Negroes or others in selling or renting his house, it is his right to do so."[14] As I wrote of in *Sports in the Aftermath of Tragedy*, he actively ignored the HIV/AIDS epidemic facing the nation in the early 1980s because it was considered to be a gay disease—even as over 10,000 Americans died and hundreds of thousands more were infected.[15] Reagan, in short, was fully engaged in an agenda that marginalized multiple different kinds of minorities while ensuring that privileges traditionally the domain of whites would remain so. In Reagan, we see the origin of what, over time and with much more intensity, would become the new white nationalism of the twenty-first century. For the political, economic, educational, and social policies that reduced programming for minorities coupled with rhetoric that demonized African American and gay people specifically. Together, these were successful strategies to gain political prowess. Reaganism, therefore, became the foundation for what would become the new white nationalism as one can see beginning with him a resistance of the Civil Rights Movement's agenda, and policies and narratives that his successors adopted and built on in further extremes, until the present moment in 2021.

Specifically, Reagan's vice president and successor as president, George H.W. Bush, ran a presidential campaign that can be encapsulated in a single advertisement that is today remembered as the essence of race-baiting in order to energize a base: the Willie Horton ad. The ad showed the mug shot of Willie Horton, a convicted killer, who on a weekend furlough from prison, raped and killed a white couple. The intention of the ad was to drive whites to the polls out of fear of African American crime. Implicit in this ad was a message that African American males belonged in prison, and letting them out would only lead to more crime. Couple this with a war on drugs that today is viewed as having a racist agenda to imprison African Americans, and it is clear that the Reagan and George H.W. Bush presidencies were characterized by spatially, criminally, and economically segregating African Americans through the prison complex. Those policies, moreover, fed the fears of whites and have resulted in a general acceptance that African Americans be geographically segregated from whites either through the prison complex or the inertia of policies, practices, and narratives that relegate inner cities to African Americans and other people of color. Indeed, illustrating the manner in which the new white nationalism is defined by aggregated policies and practices arriving to affect the present "normal," the Reagan administration marked a 78 percent rise in the number of people put in prison. Adopting his policies and practices, Bush marked a 39 percent rise on top of Reagan as he adopted the War on Drugs. These policies reached forward through Clinton and George W. Bush's presidencies, which saw 56 percent and 32 percent increases, respectively. In that twenty-four-year period, then, America witnessed a 700 percent increase in federal prison sentences. By 2017, the number of African Americans in federal prisons was 500 times higher than that of whites.[16]

Collectively, the policies and rhetoric of Reagan, Clinton, the Bushes, and their political counterparts created systems of power that operated to oppress minorities and support whites. To be clear, the new white nationalism, with the outcome of racial segregation, is typified by the aggregation of policies over time and the general acceptance that these policies and systems are acceptable and "normal." Progress toward equality and democracy is actively resisted albeit in invisible ways, through inertia. The invisibility occurs when policies, practices, and even narratives like the Southern Strategy are viewed as connected to, for instance, a single presidential term, rather than having an origin and/or history that spans decades. The intersectionality of the new white nationalism is important to understand. The new white nationalism functions by ensuring the prosperity of white, heterosexual, middle- to upper-class identities at the expense of others.

The center that the new white nationalism consistently protects is important to understand in terms of how power consistently is exerted in the mainstream. For instance, President George H.W. Bush's son, President George W. Bush, ran his presidential race on a platform to limit the rights of LGBTQ people and ensure that marriage was defined as a union between a man and a woman. Conservative Christians and the Evangelical right flocked to the polls. During this time, the Southern Strategy pivoted to create a movement in the Tea Party. The Tea Party began its work of narrowing its imagined nation to be one that has a purpose of supporting white, heterosexual males and vilifying all others. According to the Institute for Research and Education on Human Rights' 800-page report on the Tea Party, the members of this new political movement believed themselves to be hyper-patriotic and part of an American nationalism new to the country. "It is a nationalism that excludes those deemed not to be 'real Americans;' including the native-born children of undocumented immigrants (often despised as 'anchor babies'), socialists, Moslems, and those not deemed to fit within a 'Christian nation.' "[17] The same report illustrates that rejecting immigrant pathways to citizenship, conspiracy theories regarding Obama and birther-ism, and overt distinction between who is considered an American and who is not based on race is where the explicit racism of the Tea Party Movement is obvious and leans toward white nationalism. In this vein, although there are different tiers and strains within the Tea Party Movement, there are connections to make between the Tea Party Movement and the defining of "American" as white, heterosexual, and of a particular religion. Hence, the imagined nation projected through the Tea Party, an offshoot of the Southern Strategy, excludes minorities from its imagined borders. What has been confusing for much of American culture is the overt marginalization of non-whites and LGBTQ people from the Southern Strategists and Tea Party enthusiasts. For these philosophies are clearly antithetical to the notions of democracy and equality and more aligned with white nationalism. Yet, the people often espousing these philosophies wear well-tailored suits and work in the government. Hence, a tactic of the new white nationalism is to present itself as anything but what we have been trained to think a white nationalist to look or speak like. And yet, in the Tea Party, an outgrowth of Reagan and George W. Bush's policies, was a mainstream movement that had direct connections to the tenants of white nationalism, and that became mainstreamed through racist and homophobic policy cloaked in rhetoric about Making American Great, or American value systems. This approach to racism and homophobia, however, came from politicians who slowly but surely moved closer and closer to agendas that resembled white nationalism, but did so in covert ways while also infiltrating the major political institutions of the country and wearing suit and ties. In short, a new form of white nationalism not mainstreamed since the Civil Rights Movement was manifesting in American political systems, and this is why I call it the new white nationalism.

Over time, and certainly by 2015, the new white nationalism was tolerated and perhaps even celebrated in the mainstream. It was no coincidence that manifold Tea Party events were attended by white nationalists, and that, by 2019, a variety of Tea Party originalists signed on to an America First philosophy that defended the notion and label of 'nationalism.' For instance, Republican senator Steve King asked the *New York Times*: "White nationalist, white supremacist, Western civilization—how did that language become offensive . . . . Why did I sit in classes teaching me about the merits of our history and our civilization?"[18] Months later, President Trump defended nationalism in a speech to the United Nations, warning leaders of the world not to send their immigrants to America. These manifestations of nationalism were the result of the inertial of policies, practices, and rhetoric over time, and the subsequent acceptance of such mindsets as legitimate in politics and the voters.

Indeed, according to Republican strategist Liam Donovan, "a lot of people also see the roots of the racial resentment that has animated Donald Trump supporters in the Tea Party. There have been studies that showed that many in the Tea Party were more likely to hold racist beliefs."[19] Likewise, the Tea Party Movement, gaining in its extremism to overtly vilify minority races also has a "tendency to view opponents as illegitimate and un-American, and compromise as treason."[20] Overt attempts to marginalize and gatekeep immigrants of color, and to set up boundaries among and between races through housing laws, voting practices, educational policies, and imprisonment, all seen in the Southern Strategy adopted by presidents since Reagan, illustrate the slow but sure movement of a new white nationalism to the mainstream political world. And in the general labeling of those who disagree with them as un-American, there is a clear border being drawn of what sort of people and thinkers the new white nationalism sees as part of its future country. The harbingers of the new white nationalism and the movement itself see that the battle for what it means to be "American" is being waged on an imagined border that has very real implications for the country. And so the struggle to define what "American" means is one about identity, one that those of the new white nationalism have been waging for decades. In the second decade of the twenty-first century, with the increasing white terrorism and the discourse and policies that are working to limit minority access to the amenities of being "American," it is clear that the battle for who is imagined to be "American" is real and potentially perilous.

HIGHER EDUCATION'S CURRICULUM
AS A BORDER WAR

Higher education's role in both supporting and resisting the knowledge underpinning the Southern Strategy and later the new white nationalism is significant. Since the Civil Rights Movement, as the values of multiculturalism and diversity became more and more complex and pervasive in academia, so too has the resistance of it. The subsequent cultural war can be crudely reduced to being between a nostalgia for the past where white males determined what counted as legitimate knowledge, and a more inclusive curriculum that interrogates, challenges, and works to be more inclusive than that nostalgic curriculum. This culture war has thus become a mainstay in higher education.

Through the 1960s, for instance, minorities had limited access to higher education. However, as more women and minority students attended colleges in the 1960s and began to become professionals in academia in the late 1970s, serious feminist and African American studies permeated college curricula. By the 1980s, such disciplinary lenses and fields were mainstays of many campuses. Much like the pattern seen in the inner cities of which Reagan spoke, once minorities were welcomed into a space that had been reserved as white, a white backlash occurred, and an attempt to relegate minorities back into their isolated spaces began. For instance, in reaction to the cultural turn in academia, as well as the demographics in higher education, Allen Bloom, a literary scholar who taught at top American universities like Cornell and University of Chicago, published *The Closing of the American Mind*. The book became a totem of resisting multiculturalism throughout the 1980s and 1990s. The 1987 publication reverberated across America, and was touted by conservative scholars as well as critics from the *New York Times* and *The New Yorker*. In fact, Bloom's texts are still referred to on conservative outlets like Fox News to suggest that multiculturalism is akin to political correctness, and lead American culture in the wrong direction.

Bloom's central arguments regarding multiculturalism originated from his horror at seeing the academic curriculum shift away from a focus on the likes of John Locke and William Shakespeare and toward inclusion of feminist and black scholars and artists like Alice Walker and Richard Wright. Prior to the 1980s, literary and artistic studies were predicated on the notion that there were single, universal truths that only the canonized artists had access to and that others simply did not. Similarly, scholars believed they alone had special abilities to decode the hidden meaning of the texts produced by these artists. These belief systems served as self-fulfilling prophecies as to whom would be included for study in college curricula as well as who could be deemed a scholar in those disciplines.

However, as more feminist and minority readings of canonized texts produced unique but legitimate meanings, and as feminist and minority scholars unearthed heretofore ignored texts that were indeed worthy of canonization, the very idea that artists and scholars were of a secret club with secret powers seemed mislead. *The Closing of the American Mind* was an attempt to resist the new kinds of knowledge that were eroding the foundation of an academic curriculum built on white privilege and power. The challenging of what was studied as high art, as "American literature," was a deconstruction of whiteness: Up until that point in higher education, the definitions of "Americanness," or "high artist" equated to "white" in the literature and texts chosen for study. Likewise, generally speaking, those studying and teaching the texts were "white." Therefore, higher education consisted of and created knowledge of an America that was white.

Bloom coined a term in opposition to multiculturalism, value relativism—a term with the same ring as political correctness, which the Southern Strategy utilized to excuse its own racist comments. Value relativism worked to dismiss any sort of thought that challenged white and patriarchal knowledge systems in higher education. His strategy, then, was not to engage with the merits of multiculturalism in considering the way knowledge was constructed. Rather, it was to minimize, vilify, and set up obstacles for the legitimization of multiculturalism in general, much like the Southern Strategy did with minorities by creating policies that reduced funding germane to social uplift and utilizing narratives about their inferiority.

Multiculturalist approaches to the curriculum, however, explained that the dearth of minority scholars and artists in academia resulted from a structure of oppression. That structure made higher education an impossibility for minorities for most of American history. This view was oppositional to the mythological manner in which many scholars looked at the canon prior to 1980. Up until that point, the assumption made was that minority and woman artists and thinkers were not part of academia because they were inferior. However, anti-racist scholars began to show that the social, economic, and political realities minorities and women faced made it impossible to find the time and space to create literature and theory, let alone earn a degree in higher education. As more minority identities attended college and became faculty in higher education, new ways of thinking about how the curriculum had been constructed were introduced.

THE BORDERS OF HIGHER EDUCATION
CAMPUSES AS A WAR

To understand the full context of Bloom's reaction to multiculturalism, however, requires seeing the decades preceding the diversification of academia leading to the 1980s.

For instance, one of the most significant national policies that provided increased access to higher education for minorities was the implementation of the G.I. Bill in 1947. The policy itself was created to allow funds for housing and college tuition to millions of World War II veterans, many of whom were

Latinx, Indigenous, and African American. The G.I. Bill met its challenges with implementation, however. Those making decisions about housing often limited minorities' access to neighborhoods that had been traditionally white. The same was true of tuition uses as well. African American, Latinx, Asian, and Indigenous American veterans eligible for G.I. benefits ultimately coined their experiences as the "double-v," having to be victors against one oppressor in Hitler abroad, and then come home to another oppressor at home. At home, their fight was for access to the funds and experiences they were eligible for per the G.I. Bill.

The G.I. Bill itself had its own racialized problems, however. For instance, the Bill encouraged vocational rather than academic pursuits for minorities. Even in those cases where minorities attended vocational training programs, the skilled trades programs that led to the highest paying jobs, like plumbing and HVAC, were reserved for whites.[21] Likewise, although the G.I. Bill provided for mortgage and tuition relief, the Civil Rights Act had not yet been ratified. As a result, minorities may have applied to colleges or sought to purchase homes, but racism and individual prejudice within those very industries ensured minorities would not gain access to the new experiences the G.I. Bill intended to provide. Of the nearly 1.5 million minorities eligible for the G.I. Bill, estimates are that well below 100,000 minorities were able to register for college using G.I. Bill benefits.

In the following decade, however, as community colleges proliferated, so too did the number of minorities receiving access to higher education:

> In the 1960s, an enrollment surge occurred and the community colleges grew more rapidly than any other segment in higher education. The World War II baby-boom generation became of age and sparked this surge. Community colleges expanded during this time at the rate of one new college per week.[22]

During the 1970s, community colleges continued rapid enrollments going from 1.6 million students to more than 4.5 million in 1980.[23] While it was indeed encouraging to see the access to higher education for minorities expand, the increased number of minorities receiving access to college education was not a result of four-year institutions opening their doors widely. Rather, for minorities to gain increased access to higher education required that spaces that had been reserved for the elite and whites remained so and that an entirely new sector of education that would not disrupt the privilege of white and middle class would be created. In other words, while it is true that many four-year colleges increased their diversity since the 1970s, the major way in which higher education became diversified was through community college, and this was by design.

One of the major advocates of increasing the number of community colleges in the nation was James Bryant Conant, former president of Harvard. In the early 1950s, he became a vocal proponent of the community college, not necessarily to ensure minority access to higher education, but in order to ensure that national pressures to enhance educational access would *not* result in integration of elite colleges.

> Conant's compassion was not for the two-year colleges as much as it was to protect the elitist approach, which viewed the research university as properly available only to a select few. Equal opportunity did not exist at the university level, except for the select few. Education of the masses would be through two-year institutions. And these institutions should be viewed as terminal colleges, according to Conant.[24]

Community colleges were a mechanism to ensure that elite colleges remained the domain of the elite. Hence, community colleges were created, in part, to protect the sanctity of elitism, which equated, at the time, to whites. In this way, the community college system being separated from four-year, elite colleges, both in terms of what they provided for in education, and their basic place in American society, was a microcosm of the white nationalist goal of ensuring the populations of whites be secured in their privilege and power, and minorities be separate. This fact bares out in how community colleges are funded over time.

Simultaneous to the construction of community colleges and subsequent increased minority access to higher education, federal and state funding of colleges decreased. As a result of these significant funding cuts, the cost of college tuition was transferred to families and students, making minority access of such academic spaces difficult again.

> The cost shift from states to students has happened over a period when many families have had trouble absorbing additional expenses due to stagnant or declining incomes. In the 1970s and early to mid-1980s, tuition and incomes both grew modestly faster than inflation; by the late 1980s, tuition began to rise much faster than incomes.[25]

And the tuition escalation exponentially increased since that time: The average cost of tuition and fees in current dollars at a private, non-profit, four-year university in 2019 is $31,231 annually. This cost is up sharply from $1,832 in 1971–1972 in current dollars. And at public, four-year schools, tuition and fees cost about $9,139 annually in 2019. In the 1971 school year, they added up to less than $500 in current dollars, according to the College Board.[26] According to the Center on Budget Funding and Priorities, tuition has increased 281 percent while median household income has increased 13 percent since 1973. It is not a coincidence that the early 1970s was the time when tuition began to escalate and was also the time that the first, major cohorts of minority college-going intellectuals would be entering academia as a result of the Civil Rights Movement and later generations of World War II veterans coming of age.[27] Further, it is difficult to divorce the fact that federal and state funding for colleges reduced while tuition for colleges increased in the same years that African American and Latinx enrollment in colleges significantly increased: By the 1990s, when tuition was nearly double what it had been in 1973, adjusted for inflation, the African American student population had nearly doubled and the Latinx quadrupled. By 2008, the Latinx enrollment increased seven-fold.[28] In short, since the late 1970s, when minority attendance of higher education began to significantly increase, federal and state government funding of higher education began a significant downward trajectory. Although it is clear that minority enrollment in higher education is increasing, it is also clear that federal and state funding for such enrollment has been inversely proportional to that increase. The outcomes of policies and practices of the political realm have been to reduce support of minority attendance. The complexity of policy and resources that Chapple and Teitz advocate for to enact equality were not offered since the 1980s, when the industrial economy stifled; and since then, a concerted culture war about multiculturalism manifest in higher education.

FEDERAL AND STATE SUPPORT OF A WHITE COLLEGE CULTURE

There is a direct connection between the funding of higher education, the escalation of tuition, the cyclical nature of poverty, and the subsequent assurance that impoverished African American and Latinx populations remain separate from middle-class, white America. A massive cross-generational study by the Pew Research Center indicates that the higher education complex plays a significant role in potential uplift of particular demographics, but that race is the fundamental indicator in whether or not one will succeed in brining one's family to middle-class status through traditional, educational means. After comparing across generations and races, Richard V. Reeves and Christopher Pulliam found that African American intergenerational wealth, despite the class one was born into, deteriorates exponentially as time goes on. Race, not class, determines intergenerational upward mobility, and subsequently neighborhood residence.[29] It is with this truth in mind that the current discourse and concern about higher education's cost must be situated. For cost of tuition is indeed a concern. However, college tuition has escalated only when minorities gained more access to higher education, and the curriculum supporting white males began to be challenged. And so while access to higher education became somewhat more possible for minorities, there is evidence that federal and state governments actively played roles in making it harder than it should have been for minorities to attend college.

As indicated in chapter 1, the early 2000s have been marked by discourse that suggests college's value is not worth the tuition. However, that discourse should be informed by the nostalgia spectrum and include information of race and federal and state policies and actors who have, in no uncertain terms, been using covert rhetoric to ensure the agenda of white nationalism through higher education access over time.

For when federal and state funding decreases, the only lever that higher education institutions have to remedy budget shortfalls is tuition and fees. Rather than looking at the cost of tuition in 2019 as a concern isolated to the twenty-first century, it is more helpful to view the current value of higher education discourse as being dominated by those on the left-hand side of the the nostalgia spectrum. The metaphor of health is relevant here: If a doctor uses one's temperature as the only mechanism to diagnose a disease, the patient would potentially be misdiagnosed. Through intervention, the fever may be reduced. But without understanding patient and family history, it is easy to miss underlying problems. Arguments that focus on the cost of tuition generally benefit those assuming already that their family members would attend four-year schools. Stakeholders of higher education, from families to presidents of colleges, are looking at a fever, not the systemic disease as they focus on tuition. To see the disease fully requires an examination of higher education as part of a greater ecosystem. And who decides what metrics are prioritized for action are part of that ecosystem. The problem to be addressed is not higher education's tuition.

The twenty-first century discourse about higher education's value, and also the general fact that higher education's tuition is rising is not reflective of a problem originating in colleges themselves. It is rather a problem of how colleges are situated in the narratives about the nation, and the subsequent ways in which federal and state governments have consistently reduced funding of higher education in ways that make tuition escalate. Moreover, the reduction of federal and state funding matches a similar national and political movement in which it is clear the new white nationalism has gained traction. Another question that must therefore be asked is how the new white nationalism is acting upon the policies and practices that are being implemented and considered in the current moment. Herein is again where the nostalgia spectrum is an important tool.

The barrier of tuition and the current discussions about tuition permeating media in 2020 is taking place as if access to higher education does not have a history. Much like the Make America Great Again nostalgia, the manner in which this discourse is conducted is as if the cost of higher education has been prohibitive only in the past few years. But the cost of higher education has been a barrier for a broad swath of Americans for centuries. It was only in the past decade that the value of higher education began to be questioned in a return on investment capacity. Moreover, the focus on four-year schools' tuition in the twenty-first century is developed from a mindset that aligns with the Southern Strategy and white nationalist agenda of building spaces and identities for whites and excluding minorities. Given the histories of four-year versus community colleges, and their racial pasts as well, it is impossible for newer concerns about cost of tuition to be divorced from the racist paradigms of access that have plagued America since the mid-1600s. In other words, the spheres of influence have taken note of higher education's inaccessibility as a result of cost in the 2010s. However, despite significant improvements over time, higher education has been inaccessible for minorities as a result of racist laws and economic hardship for over three centuries.

As I wrote of in *Sports in the Aftermath of Tragedy*, issues that are germane to minority populations become national foci only when middle-class, white identities are affected by those issues. There is a paradox confronting and created by American policy makers in the current thoughts and discourses about higher education, then: There are stated values about diversity in the Constitution, state and federal laws, and in much of the rhetoric politicians utilize. But white privilege and power are baked into American mindsets and systems, including higher education, so well that it is often difficult to see when decisions or policies or discourses are characterized by that privilege and power.

More clearly, the problem is not that higher education is cost-prohibitive, for community colleges are relatively cost-friendly. The problem is that more middle-class white families are now having to consider sending their children to community college. The historic policies and practices that had generally made four-year higher educational institutions the domain of white and middle-class identities in the second half of the twentieth century are becoming the domain of the white elite only.

This shift in who may attend which colleges has caused great disruption in America during the twenty-first century. The new white nationalism, hence, yearns for a past when tuition for a four-year college, full of mainly white bodies and white knowledge, was affordable to whites. Now that such an educational experience is out of reach for many families, there is a reaction to higher education itself—its very value being called into question. This value discourse, therefore, is not limited only to college's cost and return on investment, it is also a result of the racial formation of the twenty-first century.

Michael Omi and Harold Winant illustrate that race as a social construction is shaped not through stereotypes and people's implicit biases, but through historic, social, and political forces, what they call racial formations. "We define racial formation as the sociohistorical process by which racial categories are created, inhabited, transformed, and destroyed."[30] That is, "race" as a formation is created by and shifts within political, social, and structural power systems. Race, according to Omi and Winant, is a shifting construct and has meaning in different eras as a result of institutional and discursive practices regarding race. There is no doubt that in the funding practices and the discourse about tuition, race is being defined through the higher education system in ways that will have ramifications for decades to come: For in this debate and the funding decisions therein are policies that make access to college possible for some, impossible for others, and so the social stratification of tomorrow is being organized contemporaneously.

Much like the fever in the cancer patient, tuition, not funding for or the kinds of knowledge created in higher education institutions, is the focus of stakeholders. But by limiting the discourse to higher education's cost and value, the new white nationalist goal of turning as many people away from exposure to knowledge about anti-racism is being served without having to discuss race or racism. The discourse serves to vilify higher education and the knowledge it imparts because of cost and curriculum. Yet, there is a cost-friendly sector of higher education in community colleges. As a result, the systemic and stakeholder issues with regard to higher education are rarely the focus of policy or even narratives. Rather, discourse and narratives limit themselves simply to tuition cost.

Hence, the political realm is generally protected within this discourse, as media coverage of tuition costs rarely delves into the general decrease in funding from federal and state levels, which themselves are racially formed. Through the nostalgia spectrum, however, one is able to interrogate the history of tuition and knowledge that is yearned for in the Make America Great Again philosophy. The nostalgia spectrum makes clear that a major issue confronting higher education in the current moment is the same issue that faced it 300 years ago: higher education and the state and federal support of it have an origin of white power and privilege, and the political, cultural, and social landscapes affect and are affected by it. In this way, the same power dynamic is continuously controlling the direction of American institutions, albeit in new ways.

DEMOGRAPHIC DATA AT COLLEGES AND WHAT IT MEANS FOR THE FUTURE OF AMERICAN EQUALITY

There is no doubt that the closed systems of how data is viewed, and which data is prioritized in contemporary discussions about higher education's value and efficacy not only reinscribe but derive from the powerful and privileged dynamics that have permeated American social structures since the country's inception. This reinscription of racialized power dynamics is clear by looking at the social stratification and resultant intergenerational wealth that occurs based on colleges attended. Whereas 36 percent of community college enrollment comprises of Hispanic and African American students, only 20 percent of private four-year colleges comprise of the same. Furthermore, the average income of families whose students attend Ivy League colleges or their caliber is $723,000. Compare that with the average income of $73,000 of families whose children go to nonselective colleges like community colleges:

> Much as they do in elementary and secondary education, low-income students who pursue a higher education tend to go the colleges with the least resources, be they community colleges, regional state schools, or non-selective or barely-selective private colleges. No wonder that the odds of moving up the economic ladder are so stacked against them.[31]

These discrepancies show that much like housing and public schools, our higher education system is racially and economically stratified. Moreover, they show that higher education is part of a matrix that "secure[s] the existence of white people and a future for white children."

Ultimately, the ecosystem that higher education functions in ensures community colleges are *reserved* for the already-marginalized; but they are not funded in a way to fully *serve* the already-marginalized. That is, they serve the white and privileged by ensuring that there is a space for the marginalized to attend—that not too many of the marginalized will attend the institutions where middle class and white students attend. Whether or not stakeholders realize it, the tendency to view community colleges as separate and apart from four-year schools in terms of solutions for enhancing the cost of tuition and moving America toward democracy and equality is undergirded by a nostalgic and privileged view of higher education.

VARSITY BLUES AS A SYMPTOM

A concrete example of how higher education is a vehicle for privileged individuals to make what they perceive as benign decisions that contribute to the perpetuation the new white nationalism was on display in national media in 2019. In spring 2019, Rick Singer, an admission fixer, was charged with bribing college officials and manipulating admission procedures to ensure that children of elite parents would gain admission to elite colleges. Records showed the operation, labeled Varsity Blues, to have been at least a $25 million enterprise.

Because some of the families involved in the scandal were celebrities, news of the scandal reached national headlines. National outrage was sparked. Responses ranged from disbelief that families literally bought admission slots that otherwise deserving children should have earned to a metaphoric shrug of the shoulders as it was already assumed that such underhanded practices were happening across the country anyway. However, there was a general dearth of discussion about why these families would rather bribe their children's way into elite colleges than send their children to colleges with more open admissions practices. This dearth is revealing of the geographical spaces public and community colleges hold in the imagined nations of Americans in general. Ben Miller, vice president of postsecondary education at the Center for American Progress, touched on this concept when he said:

> To zoom out a little bit, when you see critiques about how we have structured an economy that has different rules for different people, [the Varsity Blues scandal] is Exhibit A. A low-income family would never think to claim they falsely compete on a crew team.[32]

To be sure, there was outrage that wealthy families bribed their children's way into colleges. However, there was very little questioning of the assumptions made by those families—mainstream mindsets generally assumed that children of the privileged elite would attend elite colleges. But given the social structures within which higher education operates, these families were not just buying four years of education through bribery. With the earning potential of elite college graduates being literally seven-fold those of other colleges' graduates, it is clear that elite families were buying their children access to a wealthy lifestyle in the future. Clearly, many of these parents believed that their intention to secure both happiness and a successful life for their children was part of their responsibility. However, the outcome of an enterprise like Varsity Blues is to perpetuate economic and racial inequities that have underpinned American social systems for centuries, but in rather covert ways. Herein again is why it is important to distinguish between systems and people when examining how the new white nationalism operates. The parents involved in the Varsity Blues scandal most likely would be horrified to understand that their actions supported a form of white nationalism. Yet, they perpetuated a powerful new white nationalism by acting unethically, and in the process reinforced that very system's inertia. *U.S. News'* education editor Lauren Camera also notes that the Varsity Blues scandal revealed privilege that had always been existent in higher education:

[Elite] families who can also afford coaching for the SAT and ACT, additional counselors who go over college essays with a fine-tooth comb and costs for recreational sports, music lessons and other extracurricular, and admission to the most elite colleges is assumed by many lower-income families to be out of reach.[33]

In short, entire enterprises like coaching for ACT and SAT are set up for the privileged to buy into. They feed into and also cause social stratification. And the elite colleges with their ways of measuring admissions applications ultimately create the same social stratification that exists outside the walls of those institutions, as chapter 3 will illustrate. Moreover, these institutions hold racialized and classed meanings in American minds of being largely affluent. From admission to tuition, to the life that a diploma from each of these institutions buys, privilege and oppression is baked into American social, educational, and political matrices of power. Individuals are born into and operate within these systems, often in ways that give them more power, even if they may not intend to.

HIGHER EDUCATION AND THE NOSTALGIA SPECTRUM'S IMPORTANCE

James Baldwin famously taught us: "History is not the past, it is the present. We carry our history with us. We are our history."[34] In a twenty-first century so focused on data and the efficient use of the dollar, the notion of what higher education can and should do for the greater good escapes the grand narratives about value. Individuals continuously find themselves presented with un-nuanced data that glosses over implications for accepting current and past paradigms. Those same individuals, even with good intentions, often make decisions they consider as benign but that actually perpetuate oppressions. For instance, the discourse about higher education's value has an origin and continuous return to the data regarding cost and, we shall see, graduation outcomes. In a cyclical fashion, then, cost and graduation outcomes are presented as both *the* problem and *the* solution. But how these data came to be the point of emphasis for higher education in the first place must be interrogated.

Higher education, in short, is in a crisis. But the crisis does not originate from the effectiveness of the institutions themselves. The crisis is one that has been manufactured by paying attention to and emphasizing the wrong narratives and metrics.

A more visionary and socially just approach to higher education could reach back in memory to find the philosophical underpinnings of higher education in America. American higher education was originally founded on fending against a potential tyranny of the state and was summed up well in a letter that Ben Franklin wrote to Samuel Johnson:

> Nothing is of more importance to the public weal, than to form and train up youth in wisdom and virtue. Wise and good men are, in my opinion the strength of a state: much more so than riches or arms, which, under the management of Ignorance and Wickedness, often draw on destruction, instead of providing for the safety of a people.[35]

Franklin's summary of the purpose of higher education is a relevant piece of higher education's value. This is true especially in a time when the new white nationalism and the shrinking middle class operate together to create further marginalization and oppression of black, brown, and lower-income people.

Indeed, the very discourse of return on investment for higher education could be read as a product of a society that has lost its way. It is no coincidence that higher education's value is being questioned at the same moment that there is a scaled, decreased focus on global citizenship and social justice throughout the states of the nation. Nor is it a coincidence that the twenty-first century's political discourse has become quite comfortable with overtly racist comments and policies. In short, the American focus on numbers and return on investment is not a disease of higher education. Rather, the value discussion regarding higher education reveals, rather than is separate from, the psychic structures of mainstream American society. The crisis is one of American values of equality being minimized under the shadow of profit and comfort. It is in this vein that the next chapter illustrates how the new white nationalism is actively working to minimize the role higher education plays in Americans' lives and through that project, the notion of citizenship.

NOTES

1. Adam Serwer, "Birthirism of a Nation." *The Atlantic.* May 13, 2020.
2. Ibid.
3. Donald Trump, "Here's Donald Trump's Presidential Announcement Speech." *Time.* June 16, 2015, https://time.com/3923128/donald-trump-announcement-speech/.
4. Cathy O'Niel, *Weapons of Math Destruction* (New York: Penguin Books, 2017), 3–7.

5. Michael Nietzle, "The College Profile of the 116th Congress' First Class." *Forbes*, December 10, 2018, https://www.forbes.com/sites/michaeltnietzel/2018/12/10/the-college-profile-of-the-116th-congresss-first-year-class/#446afe7d3bcc.

6. Congressional Research Service, "Membership of the 115th Congress: A Profile." Accessed June 1, 2019, https://fas.org/sgp/crs/misc/R44762.pdf.

7. Ronald Reagan, *1980 Republican Convention Address* (Detroit, MI: July 17, 1980). https://www.americanrhetoric.com/speeches/ronaldreagan1980rnc.htm. Emphasis mine.

8. Karen Chappel and Michael Tietz, "The Causes of Inner-City Poverty: Eight Hypotheses in Search of Reality." *Cityscape* 3, no. 3 (1999).

9. Karen Chappel and Michael Tietz. "The Causes of Inner-City Poverty: Eight Hypotheses in Search of Reality." *Cityscape* 3, no. 3 (1999): 27.

10. Douglass Massey, "Residential Segregation and Neighborhood Conditions in U.S. Metropolitan Areas." In *America Becoming: Racial Trends and Their Consequences*, Vol. 1 Smelser, Neil J., William Julius Wilson, and Faith Mitchell, Editors. (Washington, DC: The National Academies Press, 2001).

11. Michael Aho and Mark Levinson, "The Economy After Reagan." *Foregin Affairs*. Winter, 1998.

12. Angie Maxell, "What We Get Wrong about the Southern Strategy." *The Washington Post* (Washington, DC), July 26, 2019.

13. Sheldon Danziger and Robert Haveman, "The Reagan Budget: A Sharp Break with the Past." *Challenge 24*. May–June 1981.

14. Angie Maxell, "What We Get Wrong about the Southern Strategy." *The Washington Post* (Washington, DC), July 26, 2019.

15. Lauren Berlant, *The Queen of America Goes to Washington City* (Durham: Duke University Press, 1997).

16. John Gramlich, "Federal Prison Population Fell during Obama's Term, Reversing Recent Trend." *Pew Reseach Center* (Washington, DC), January 5, 2017. Devin Burghart and Leonard Zeskind, *Tea Parties—Racism, Anti-Semitism and the Militia Impulse* (Institute for Research & Education, 2010), 59.

17. Institution for Education and Human Rights, *Tea Party Nationalism* (Kansas City: MO: IPRHR Press, December, 2010), 11.

18. Justin Wise, "Steve King Asks How Terms 'White Nationalist' and 'White Supremacist' Became Offensive." *The Hill* (Washington, DC), January 10, 2019.

19. Lulu Garcia-Navarro, "From the Tea Party to Trump: The GOP in the 2010s." *National Public Radio* (Washington, DC), December 29, 2019.

20. Geoffrey Kabaservice, "The Old Tea Party May Be Over, but the New One Is at Its Peak." *The Washington Post* (Washington, DC), March 16, 2018.

21. Erin Blakemore, "How the GI Bill Promise Was Denied to a Million WWII Veterans." *History*, https://www.history.com/news/gi-bill-black-wwii-veterans-benefits.

22. Richard Dury L., *Community Colleges in America: A Historical Perspective. Inquiry*, 8, no. 1, (Spring 2003). Accessed July 2019, Virginia Community College System.

23. Richard Dury, L. *Community Colleges in America: A Historical Perspective. Inquiry*, 8, no. 1, (Spring 2003). Accessed July 2019, Virginia Community College System.

24. Richard Dury, L. *Community Colleges in America: A Historical Perspective. Inquiry*, 8, no. 1, (Spring 2003). Accessed July 2019, Virginia Community College System.

25. Michael Mitchell et al., "A Lost Decade in Higher Education Funding." *Center on Budget Funding and Priorities* (Washington, DC), 2019. Accessed August 10, 2019, https://www.cbpp.org/research/state-budget-and-tax/a-lost-decade-in-higher-education-funding.

26. John Schoen, "Why Does College Cost So Much?" In *CBS News* (New York, December 8, 2016). Accessed August 1, 2019. https://www.cnbc.com/2015/06/16/why-college-costs-are-so-high-and-rising.html.

27. Michael Mitchell et al., "A Lost Decade in Higher Education Funding." *Center on Budget Funding and Priorities* (Washington, DC), 2019. Accessed August 10, 2019, https://www.cbpp.org/research/state-budget-and-tax/a-lost-decade-in-higher-education-funding.

28. Status and Trends in Racial and Ethnic Minorities, National Center for Education Statistics, 2019, https://nces.ed.gov/pubs2010/2010015/tables/table_24_1.asp.

29. Richard Reeves and Christopher Pulliam, "No Room at the Top: The Stark Divide in Black and White Economic Mobility." *PEW Research Center*. February 14, 2019.

30. Michael Omi and Howard Winant, *Racial Formation in the U.S.* (New York: Routledge, 1994), 57.

31. Steven Burd, "Even at Private Colleges, Low-Income Students Tend to Go to the Poorest Schools." *New America*. May 18, 2017, https://www.newamerica.org/education-policy/edcentral/private-colleges/.

32. Lauren Camera, "White Privilege and the College Admissions Scandal." *US News and World Report*. March 13, 2019.

33. Lauren Camera, "White Privilege and the College Admissions Scandal." *US News and World Report*. March 13, 2019.

34. *I Am Not Your Negro*, directed by Samuel L Jackson, James Baldwin, and Raoul Peck (Los Angeles: Magnolia Home Entertainment, 2017), DVD.

35. Benjamin Franklin, "Letter to Samuel Johnson." *Founders Online*. Accessed November 5, 2019, https://founders.archives.gov/documents/Franklin/01-04-02-0009.

Chapter 3

Close the Borders

Constructing Higher Education as a Foreign Threat

December 12, 2015, was a bright day in San Bernardino, California. Employees at the Inland Regional Center gathered in a conference room to celebrate the upcoming holidays. They laughed. They talked about their families. Music played in the background.

Shortly before 11 a.m., two masked and armed individuals burst through the doors reigning bullets down on the unsuspecting employees. Most of the employees sprinted to the nearest exits or fell to the ground. Three sprinted toward the terrorists. These three were killed immediately. The attackers lurked through the hallways hunting for more victims.

One of the shooter's bullets pierced a sprinkler spigot, triggering the system to go off, building-wide. The deluge of water clouded the attackers' visibility. Without this happening, the number of causalities, it is theorized, would have extended beyond the fourteen murdered and twenty-two injured.

The two shooters escaped the building unscathed. A national manhunt ensued.

Republicans vying to be the party's candidate for president of the United States uniformly claimed that this attack was an act of war that radical Islam ignited against the United States.

Just one year later, utilizing memory of this horrific attack, newly elected president Trump, in his first major policy initiative, signed executive order 13769, titled "Protecting the Nation from Foreign Terrorist Entry into the United States." In alignment with the white nationalist goal of manifesting a country that eliminates black and brown bodies, this Executive Order sought to ban immigrants from countries with high Muslim populations from coming to the United States. Some immigrants were literally in-flight to the United States when the ban was implemented, and therefore turned away upon their arrival at United States terminals. Legal intervention of the Executive Order ensued. Courts ruled that the ban was, both in intention and outcome, racist and unconstitutional. Three years later, however, a similar order was upheld by the Supreme Court in a five-to-four decision. The Court found that the president does have constitutional authority to define who is permitted within the nation's borders if the premise is protecting citizens. The dissenting view, however, argued that a travel ban singling out specific countries with high Muslim populations furthered American legacies of exclusion seen in *Korematsu v. United States*, the 1944 decision that permitted detention of Japanese-Americans during World War II, known as internment camps.

Two years after the original executive order was lifted, and at nearly the same time the Supreme Court permitted the second order to be implemented, President Trump hosted a White House meeting with Republican senators on the topic of immigration. In discussing the immigration of Hattian, African, and El Salvadoran nationals, he asked, "why are we having all these people from shithole countries come here?" A media frenzy of outrage and empty gestures took root. He later complained that Nigerian immigrants should "go back to their huts" and Haitians "all have AIDs." He doubled down at an Oval Office meeting discussing immigration policies for Haiti: "Why do we need more Haitians?" Trump asked. "Take them out."[1]

Trump's attacks of black and brown people were not limited to immigrants, however. He later called Baltimore "rat infested," asking why anyone would ever visit there. Politicians and news outlets proclaimed this assertion to be racist as it Otherized an entire city that was experiencing violence, corruption, and racial strife over the previous decade. Moreover, given President Trump's overtly racist comments in the past, it was unclear if he was using the trope of "rat" to define the people of Baltimore, a majority of whom were black.

On November 7, 2018, midway through Trump's first term, Americans went to the polls to elect a new Congress. The election was hailed as a referendum on President Trump's tenure in the White House. By the time the polls closed, democrats netted forty-one seats in the House of Representatives. Among the newly elected House members were Alexandria Ocasio-Cortez of New York, Ilhan Omar of Minnesota, Ayanna Pressley of Massachusetts, and Rashida Tlaib of Michigan, who collectively comprised a group of left-leaning and diverse individuals, affectionately labeled "The Squad."

Nine months into these Congresswomen's tenure, President Trump launched verbal attacks against them. He claimed Congresswomen to be "very racist" and "not very smart." Later, he argued that they should "go back" to the "totally broken and crime infested places from which they came."[2] At a rally with supporters, he referenced the Squad and rambled about the problems of Mexican immigrants crossing the border. A member of the crowd shouted, "How do you stop these people?"

"Shoot them," the president replied.[3]

Two weeks later, a gunman walked through the parking lot of an El Paso, Texas, Walmart. He fired one shot, then another, and then entered the store. He ultimately killed twenty-two innocent people. In investigating the crime, El Paso police found a manifesto written by the terrorist that articulated his rationale for the attack. It amounted to a desire to stop Mexicans from coming to America. Days later, President Trump condemned "white supremacy, whether it's any other kind of supremacy, whether it's antifa."[4] No policy action or executive order followed this white terrorist attack, however. The lack of an order evidenced a double-standard in which terrorism is viewed by the new white nationalism. If a black or brown body carries out a terrorist attack, the nation itself is threatened. If, however, a white body carries out that attack with the intent to protect the nation from more black and brown bodies entering it, then that act does not rise to a level of political urgency.

Attributing cause and effect between political rhetoric and subsequent physical violence is not helpful. Instead, understanding that political rhetoric focused on defining America as white and terrorism that does the same both stem from the same problematic philosophy. The connection between what I call the new white nationalism and mainstream politicians is not just theoretical. For instance, the Southern Poverty Law Center released a slew of White House advisor, Stephen Miller's, emails in late November 2019. The emails revealed Miller's white supremacist views that Western civilization would fall as a result of immigrants infiltrating American borders; and that the races, simply, are not equal. Analyzing these emails, NPR correspondent Joel Rose wrote:

> To Miller's critics, the leaked emails—and the muted reaction on the right—suggest that the political dynamic around race and immigration has shifted to include ideas that were once beyond the pale . . . . [I]n a White House where turnover is high, Miller is one of the staffers who have been there from the beginning. And he continues to be a key architect of the president's hardline immigration policies.[5]

Clearly, throughout his presidency, President Trump imposed a racial hierarchy of countries, American cities, and people in general that derived from and reinforced a white nationalist philosophy. That such policies and rhetoric were supported by a broad swath of Americans and leading politicians illustrates that the new white nationalism has slowly been normalized not only by those supporting it, but also to those who are complacent toward it.

THE PROBLEM OF LABELS

In the twenty-first century, alarming policies and rhetoric regarding immigration and black and brown people are being utilized with such frequency that they are being baked into the psychic structures of Americans. Racist attacks and policies are slowly becoming normalized in American consciousness, and solicit a shrug of the shoulders reaction rather than any vitriol. The desensitization toward white terrorism and white nationalism has deleterious effects on how the American citizenry imagines and defines "American-ness."

Disturbingly, until the end of his tenure as president, many news outlets and national politicians were weary of calling the president's remarks and, more importantly, policies racist. Instead, pundits and news outlets asked questions like: "Is President Trump's rhetoric racist?"[6] Such questions actively supported the new white nationalism in two ways. First, they focused on the president, a single individual, rather than the network of support that lifted him to the White House and which supported him through his tenure. An individual with problematic views towards race is better characterized as *prejudiced*, not racist. Still, such focus does very little to engage with the systemic oppression and violence underpinning white nationalism, privilege, or power, what I define as *racism*. My first book, *Sports in the Aftermath of Tragedy*, made the case that focusing on individual prejudice rather than institutional racism and the network of white power and terror that is expanding across the nation serves only to ensure that white nationalism and white terror continue. Such foci are, even if well-intended, part of how the new white nationalism is perpetuated by media narratives and white complacency.

The second way in which mediated questions about an individual's prejudice contributes to the new white nationalism is that they pretend that classifying people as prejudice or white nationalists is difficult. With a senior advisor in Stephen Miller, and rhetoric and policies that clearly lead to support of white nationalism, it was not difficult to label Trump or his administration racist and supporting white nationalism. In fact, when labels are not accordingly affixed, the result is a suggestion that white nationalist behavior of elected officials is somewhat acceptable, and the subsequent acceptance of prejudice, racism, and bigotry as "normal." The effect is and will be that this "normalcy" will become part of the structures, polices, practices, and ways of thinking for tomorrow's structures, policies, practices, and ways of thinking. Indeed, the final chapter of this book focuses on the white nationalist and terrorist insurrection at Capitol Hill on January 6, 2021, the goal of which was to overthrow an election and government in favor of Trump and his administration. Tens of thousands of white nationalists did not find their will and courage on that day spontaneously. They found their will and courage as a result of the slow inertia of the new white nationalism, and the general normalization of it through the policies, systems, structures, and mediated narratives that supported rather than actively resisted it.

In short, in Trump and Miller, the tactic of dressing in a suit while using rhetoric and developing policies that intentionally oppress minorities is clearly visible. The skin-headed, black-booted, Confederate flag-waiving stereotype of white nationalism no longer is the reality or future of white nationalism. Indeed, members of the many white nationalist groups throughout the nation have been "instructed to blend in at political rallies with polo shirts, khakis and military-style haircuts."[7] And although President Trump may not identify with a white nationalist group, it is difficult to look at his policies and rhetoric and not associate him and his administration with white nationalist goals. Hence, his lack of desire to be labeled as a white nationalist, yet enacting policies and ideas that actively and overtly support such an agenda while in dress that is more mainstreamed than marginalized is an example of the new white nationalism.

Trump and his administration is part of a network of the new white nationalism, it is not the cause of it. To that end, since 2015, a clear escalation in white supremacist violence, propaganda, and political power has visited the country, not the least of which was the January 6, 2021, insurrection. During the Trump presidency, white domestic terror rose 35 percent, and the FBI in September 2019 classified white nationalism as a domestic terror group for the first time in American history.[8]

CULTURE WARS ARE CIVIL WARS
OF THE IMAGINATION

The new white nationalism is not limited to stereotyping, racist comments, violence, and problematic policy creation, however.[9] The new white nationalism understands that there is significant power exerted through the imagined nations constructed in everyday citizens' minds. As a result, what higher education guides young minds to imagine as the America of today and tomorrow is of utmost importance. The battleground is therefore being waged in the minds of the American public. That battle is characterized by a fight for where the *imagined* borders of America are drawn—for those imagined borders have implications for the material and real borders of tomorrow.

As established in chapter 2, with the introduction of a significant number of minorities into higher education, there was an understanding that American higher education' had marginalized and repressed the experiences and standpoints of the marginalized from study for a majority of its history. Hence, in disciplines that proclaimed to study the actual happenings of America, social thought, or even civilizations' art and literature, there was a significant portion of history, experiences, and creative spirit that was amputated from study through the 1970s (if not still today). To suggest that disciplines like history told the full story of the past was simply untrue—for those disciplines had repressed minority experiences and points of view from their studies altogether.

The history of knowledge development has a direct connection to white nationalism in America. Through slavery and for many years after its abolition, many states adhered to anti-literacy laws. Further, through the early 1900s, education required social and cultural privilege: A family would have to have enough money to sacrifice the labor time a child would otherwise spend in a field or factory for that child to go to school; to do any sort of homework required money to afford electricity or a candle by which to read. Schools were not integrated until 1957, and even then, integration and equality was not a reality. It was only as racial minorities and women explored the material realities of their own and ancestors' experiences in the context of higher education that the very foundations upon which the traditional disciplines of the liberal arts had been built were beginning to be interrogated.

Much like the Trump administration's approach to immigration, there is a current desire among many in academia to marginalize those schools of thought that challenge whiteness as the central force of American identity in academia. Chapter 2 already made reference to the protectionism to the backlash of whites against multiculturalism in scholars like Bloom. But such protectionism exists yet today. For instance, in *The Assault on American Excellence*, Anthony Kronman claims that America is an overly sensitive culture, and argues that rigorous academic debate in 2019 is weaning away in American college classrooms. He claims that accounting for raced, classed, gendered, sexed, and other points of view in constructing arguments limits the capacity to arrive at *the* truth. *The* truth, he claims, is actually accessible if debate sticks to its truest forms, espoused by John Adams and Alexander de Tocqueville. Kronman, clearly a descendant of Bloom's thinking, claims a multicultural approach to truth and argumentation is dissolving the democratic sphere. Yet, many of his counterparts would see that same phenomena as indicative of American democracy becoming strengthened over the centuries since De Tocqueville and Adams.[10]

Although arguments scholars like Kronman are right to situate higher education in the greater narrative about democracy and equality, they suggest they are the canary in the coal mine warning of crisis, when they are actually the carbon monoxide. Just like Make America Great Again, scholarship claiming that multiculturalism obfuscates truth performs a diversionary tactic by relying on foundations of *the* truth that were arrived at in eras where white privilege and power remained unchallenged in the academy. They implicitly invoke a nostalgia for a past characterized by oppression. Kronman recently wrote, "The Downside of Diversity" for the *Wall Street Journal* in which he called for a return to a time that was predicated on white and normative points of view. There is privilege of being able to label new ways of thinking that are uncomfortable in pejorative fashion:

> Motivated by politics but forced to disguise itself as an academic value, the demand for diversity has steadily weakened the norms of objectivity and truth and substituted for them a culture of grievance and group loyalty. Rather than bringing faculty and students together on the common ground of reason, it has pushed them farther apart into separate silos of guilt and complaint.[11]

When the discourse about higher education yearns for an objective past, it is necessarily focused on concerns of people who have been privileged in the past and an objectivity that is predicated on the exclusion of experiences and points of view that are not-white. These discourses do more to affirm rather than deconstruct the social stratification that education and the very country was meant to resist.

INVISIBLE STATE INTERVENTION IN HIGHER EDUCATION

These arguments have intersections with the economic and political. They are not simply esoteric musings of a privileged elite. What is and has been projected as *the* truth reflected in *the* curriculum has been funded from *the* state and federal governments in ways that are also aligned with privilege and power. For instance, during the 1950s and 1960s, liberal arts and social sciences were funded heavily through grants from government and corporations as long as they "tended to reinforce the dominant culture rather than critically analyzing it."[12] These grants funded *The American Adam*, *Virgin Land*, *The Jacksonian Persuasion*, and *The Machine in the Garden* to name only a few. All of these texts were underpinned by an adherence to American exceptionalism and promoted the study of canonical texts written by white males to articulate what *the* American identity was. The group of scholars who collectively produced work that was considered authoritative on American identity formed a "fraternity where basic assumptions about *the* culture and ways of studying it were shared and reinforced, and where powerful institutions of American society nurtured their work."[13] A decade later, in the 1970s, scholarship began to challenge the notion of a single American identity and included women and minorities in the curriculum.

Alice Walker's "In Search of Our Mother's Gardens" was a pivotal text explaining the necessity of such interrogation of the curriculum. Walker makes the point eloquently that it was not a dearth of creative spirits or talents that led to a minimal amount of literary and artistic texts by African

American women being studied through the 1970s. Rather, because African American women had to work for white families during the day and then their own families at night, the time they had to devote to artistry as defined by the academy—painting, poetry, and novels—was limited at best. However, their art was clearly visible in the quilts and gardens they created as part of their everyday work. As the sociological explanations for a dearth of literature and art by African American women was offered, academics reassessed what "literature" or "text" meant. This reassessment revealed the very assumptions upon which fields of study like art and literature were built. Resistance in academia ensued. And the resistance took root in the same way that challenges white power and privilege does: Many scholars and their counterpart thinkers in the culture at large saw the interrogation of the foundational disciplinary assumptions resulting from a multicultural and sociological lens on those disciplines as political in nature. Viewing identity studies as "political" ignores the point that that the curriculum prior to the development of identity studies was also political.

Hence, scholars like Stuart Hall and Douglass Kellner, recognizing the need to interrogate the power upon which academic disciplines were constructed, developed a way of seeing how knowledge needed to be reconsidered. In "Cultural Studies and Its Theoretical Legacies," Hall claims that "power, not disciplines, needs to be interrogated in academic learning" in order for equality and democracy to manifest.[14] To be sure, new ways of seeing the academy from disruptive points of view threatened to change the whiteness, patriarchy, heteronormativity, and more that underpinned the very structures upon which higher education was built.

It is no coincidence that federal funding for the humanities, arts, and social sciences, with the inception of these kinds of arguments, has been cut significantly. In "Popular Culture, Theory, and American Studies," Lipsitz chronicles the consistent cuts in funding that minority studies experienced beginning in the 1970s. He writes that:

> Scholars in cultural fields not only confront a power structure hostile to their ideological interests, they face as well a political and economic apparatus determined to undermine public education, cultural diversity, and mechanisms for equal opportunity–in short the entire social base necessary for their survival.[15]

There are manifold examples of the political maneuvers that individual politicians have made in order to secure whiteness as the central construct of American higher educational curricula. For instance, at the height of the Civil Rights Movement, 1967, Ronald Reagan took on the governorship of California. Immediately upon taking office, he defunded many of the liberal arts disciplines in California's state higher education system. Moreover, the

University of California system as too liberal and "a hotbed of subversion," Reagan removed Clark Kerr from his position as president.

The University of California was indeed in a moment of subversion. Not only were more minorities attending higher education in greater numbers than ever before, but the colleges that comprised the California system included scholars who performed teach-ins in order to espouse activism against the Vietnam War and general oppressions across the nation. The strategy to squelch that subversion was to remove those educators who believed in social justice and multiculturalism from the system. It was later found out, too, that the FBI played a significant role in portraying Kerr as a danger as a result of his liberalism, and this portrayal was based on information known to be false.[16] Hence, the federal and state governments played a significant role in policing how higher education was situated in California and extracting leadership that supported a different view of America than had been constructed in the centuries leading up to the 1960s and 1970s. It was with this background of repressing subversive mindsets, mindsets that supported Civil Rights and anti-racism, that Reagan ran on a platform of Making American Great.

The protectionism that has characterized white privilege in academia in the 1960s is reflected in today's scholarship. As an example, in *The Case Against Higher Education*, Bryan Caplan argues that student loans cost the federal and state governments copious amounts of money with graduation rates remaining problematic over the past decade. His ultimate conclusion is that higher education should be limited in terms of access. "Government heavily subsidizes education. In 2011, U.S. federal, state, and local governments spent almost a trillion dollars on it. The simplest way to get less education, then, is to cut the subsidies."[17] Fiscal and educational efficiencies could be accomplished, according to Caplan, by increasing the enrollments at elite universities, and shutting down a significant number of lower-performing colleges across the nation. Those not accepted to elite universities would be relegated to apprenticeships in the skilled trades, some of which lead to high-earning jobs.

Missing from his argument, however, is a thoughtful solution for those students who may desire but cannot attend elite institutions because of life circumstances, such as having children, living a distance from those elite universities, emotional readiness, or the fact that they were raised in a public school setting that was not conducive to submitting the most robust college application. In short, he minimizes education's role as a great equalizer and glosses over the fact that a majority of Americans are born without the privilege necessary to apply for and then ultimately attend one of the very few institutions that would remain open in his plan. Moreover, his book is predicated on a nostalgia equal to a curmudgeon complaining about the next generation's musical tastes. *The kids today are just not ready to learn*, he says while teaching at a somewhat elite university. He nostalgically yearns for a generation of students from the past (also mythological in nature), and in the process, invokes a social stratification that existed literally over a century ago, when no public, open admissions colleges existed at all.

When examined more closely, arguments like Caplan's equate to a desire to return higher education to a system that, like the Trump administration's approach to immigration, keeps minorities from the spaces reserved for whites—in this case, elite four-year schools. Hence, the debate about the value of higher education can be viewed as code for a desire to return to an exclusionary past where access to four-year schools was nearly compulsory for white, middle-class families, but out of reach for minority families.

Resistance from scholars should not be a surprise, however. Antonio Gramsci identifies that the political state has always played a role in defining who was considered a legitimate intellectual: intellectuals are the "dominant group's 'deputies' exercising the subaltern functions of social hegemony and political government."[18] Defining who is considered to be a legitimate intellectual is indeed political, for it represents how a nation will define itself. The cultural war being waged regarding what is legitimate for study and worthwhile to fund has been prevalent in the American academy for decades and is often reflective of a desire to maintain white power and privilege through the dynamic Gramsci identifies.

NEW TACTICS IN THE CULTURE WAR

Much like the manner in which the national immigration discourse and philosophy has shifted under the Trump presidency, the tactics used by the new white nationalism to engage whites' mindsets toward privilege and power instead of anti-racism are new in the early twenty-first century. The new tactics that exemplify the new white nationalism are touching higher education in the twenty-first century in new and intensified ways. From the mid-twentieth century until the very early twenty-first century, white nationalists mainly criticized ideas, played with funding models, and threatened through symbolic gestures such as racist graffiti on campuses. Indeed, in 2001, George Takaki argued that "what distinguishes the university from other battlegrounds such as the media, politics, is that the university has a special commitment to the search for knowledge."[19] He went on to argue that "the escalating war against multiculturalism is fueled by a fear of loss" (which is a central component of left hand side of The nostalgia spectrum).[20] Through the early 2000s, the major sentiments and the major resistances to multiculturalism and social justice that were felt in the academy were those that could be characterized as white privilege, with some anomalous incidents of white nationalism occurring through graffiti and flyers on campuses.

However, the battleground, by 2015, was characterized by a struggle to altogether intimidate people in the academy from producing, disseminating, or consuming work that would challenge white power's status quo.

Whereas in earlier eras, defunding multicultural epistemologies served as a sufficient weapon, today the new white nationalism seeks to silence individual professors by threatening them. Just as the white terrorism is escalating so are the threats against those who challenge whiteness as the central construct in academia. Many professors have been named on an online WatchList hosted by TPUSA, which claims to "to fight for free speech and the right for professors to say whatever they wish; however students, parents, and alumni deserve to know the specific incidents and names of professors that advance a radical agenda in lecture halls."[21] Reminiscent of McCarthyism, the intent of organizations like WatchList and Campus Reform is not just to ensure that students of a certain mindset avoid exposing themselves to thought that may challenge white privilege and nationalism. It is also to threaten academics who step out of the epistemological normativity that whiteness is the construct against which all identities should be measured.

Hence, a major battle of this cultural war for the imagined borders of the nation is an intellectual one, and the new white nationalism has developed new tactics to infiltrate American colleges' curriculum as a result. In both look and strategy, the new white nationalism is engaging the American higher education system in new ways, seeing it as a locus of power in defining how America is perceived, imagined, looks, and feels. Indeed, the America Defense League noted that "after the [Trump] election, the alt right moved from online activism into the real world, forming real-world groups and organizations and engaging in tactics such as targeting college campuses."[22]

Further, in "Academic Freedom in the Classroom: Students and the Trouble with Labels," Patricia A. Matthews explains the effect current struggles against multiculturalism have on the students' mindsets and view of knowledge. Matthews argues sympathetically of students who are caught in culture wars as they are exposed to rhetoric from news media, internet sites, and friends and family members about what they should believe prior to coming into her class. She writes most students who identify as conservatives seem to have a great deal of empathy for lessons about gender performativity and other theories that could be considered multicultural.[23] Yet organizations like Campus Reform, which target scholars with the goal of "polic[ing] the academy [and] seeking out faculty members and administrators who work to make it more inclusive" change the mindset of *students* prior to their even entering the class. From this she writes of a concern that:

Students of all political stripes are growing up in a cultural moment when the point is to pick a side and defend it uncritically. Questions that were provocative fifteen years ago when I started teaching are now seen as a demand for political fealty that must be performed in class discussions and written work. Campus Reform seems to hover over us all.[24]

Matthews' narrative is especially important as she articulates the trajectory of the new white nationalism and how it affects critical thought. Despite that she and authors like Kroman are both writing about critical thought and it being under threat, they are in direct opposition to one another. Fifteen years ago, Matthews notes, it was possible to have discussions about identity, social justice, and more in her classroom. However, slowly, over time, through calculated policies, procedures, narratives, and mindset changes, the new white nationalism has arrived as a true and rigid entity that casts a pall over the ability to engage in debates in the classroom about how people are situated in the landscape of America. Further, by funneling students away from courses and even discussion where white privilege is challenged, white privilege continues, and may even morph into white nationalism. The significant shift in tactics must be read as a backlash against an anti-racist approach to learning that aligns with the democratic promises of the nation. That backlash seeks to ensure that the present and the future of American is more like the racist past. It seeks to manifest the nostalgic America that was, according to those supporting this vein of thought, "great" when the studies were about white males who defined a singular American identity. It also seeks to Otherize and keep from the imagined American identity other minorities, women, and 'foreign' nationalities.[25] Evidence of the success of the new white nationalism is seen not only in the hostility academics and students experience in higher education environments, but also in the somewhat complacent reaction to aggressive immigration policies and racist rhetoric the Trump administration has taken against people of color since 2011. In all cases, the struggle is to draw rigid, racial borders around the imagined nation and to attack any people or knowledge that challenges whiteness as the central construct defining the imagined nation.

HIGHER EDUCATION AS A FOREIGN ENTITY

The new white nationalism also engages in rhetoric about higher education that is meant to indoctrinate those with white privilege into further complacency. Indeed, the new white nationalism delegitimizes higher education in general by suggesting that it comprises not of intellectuals or experts in fields, but liberals with agendas. Much like the discourse about the value of higher education, the discourse that argues higher education is liberal has the potential outcome of leading students and families away from attending college at all. Yet, the notion that higher education is liberal is both misleading and created by those that meet the definition of the new white nationalist.

Fox News, with its 94 percent white viewership—a mediated nation of whites—runs a daily segment that makes different claims about the reasons that higher education presents a problem for the country. "Jonathan Zimmerman, a professor at the University of Pennsylvania's Graduate School of Education, says of Fox News's coverage, 'every story about [a] university is essentially the same: Somebody on the left did or said a censorious thing that in some way victimizes a conservative.' "[26] In short, these stories about the victimization of whites are projected on screens to whites. The intention, in no uncertain terms, is to support the new white nationalism by leading consumers to believe that higher education, with its escalation in minority population, higher costs, and liberal agendas, is a threat. Again, though, the nostalgia spectrum illustrates that this narrative is just another point on the historic trajectory of white power and privilege: For the notion that higher education is liberal is closely aligned with Reagan's rhetoric that was used to de-fund and change the direction of higher education in California because it was "subversive." Hence, this argument is tinged by a desire to return to an academia and way of thinking from the 1960s, when whiteness was considered the normal condition of thought. But the construction of higher education as liberal and in opposition to "American-ness" is a strategy of the new white nationalism that has been built over time.

Since 2019, that construction has been overwhelmingly visible. Federal and state politicians who align with the new white nationalism are seeking to manage the imagined borders of the nation by infiltrating higher education in ways it never has before. For instance, "[a] state senator in Iowa has introduced a bill to require that no professor or instructor be hired by a public university if his or her most recent party affiliation would cause the percentage of the faculty belonging to one political party to exceed by 10 percent."[27] This legislation, in no uncertain terms, is an attempt to ensure that the nostalgia for the past can drive curricular decisions in higher education. But there is also confusion between the facts that are taught in higher education and the knowledge that the new white nationalism would like to project in order to maintain its power. Often times, the knowledge the new white nationalism would like to become normalized is not based on fact, and so runs counter to academia. A single example of how the new white nationalism supports untrue knowledge to further its agenda is available in Stephen Miller's approach to immigration and national policy.

Miller [is] pushing a supposed link between immigrants and rising crime, an idea that has been debunked . . . [he and his counterparts also] promote . . . ideas that are widely considered racist and cloaks them in the language of science. For example, he talks about black people having higher levels of testosterone and therefore being predisposed to commit more violent crimes—an idea that simply has no scientific support.[28]

Hence, academia, which Takaki claims focuses on the pursuit of truth, does not align with the new white nationalism's goals or narratives. There is therefore a strategy in diverting whites who are complacent away from higher education altogether: for exposing more whites to truth would also lead them to understand the baseless narratives of much of the new white nationalism. Hence, the new white nationalism characterizes academia as a place where liberals, with their esoteric ideas that do not match the real world, abound. And yet, typical of the new white nationalism's strategy to mislead for its cause, this narrative that higher education is liberal is not true at all:

[M]uch of the research says conservative students and faculty members are not only surviving but thriving in academe—free of indoctrination if not the periodic frustrations. Further, the research casts doubt on the idea that the ideological tilt of faculty members is because of discrimination. Notably, some of this research has been produced by conservative scholars . . . . Faculty members were more likely to categorize themselves as moderate (46.1 percent) than liberal (44.1 percent) . . . . At community colleges, 19 percent of faculty members called themselves conservatives, and only 37.1 percent said they were liberals.[29]

Whether through watch lists or delegitimizing higher education, the desired outcome is to slow or halt the expansion imagined nation's borders to be more inclusive while simultaneously limiting whites' attendance of college. The new white nationalism is using these tactics to implicitly argue that higher education is out of alignment with the rest of America's thinking, and suggest that it is not worth attending because of its multicultural approach. Edna Acosta Belen calls the desire to minimize the importance of multiculturalism as "xenophobic, homophobic, sexist, and racist." She claims that "the most threatening phenomenon at the beginning of the twenty-first century is found in the renewed life that right-wing demagoguery has gained" through its focus on curriculum and its work to suppress any attempts to widen its thinking beyond whiteness.[30] This right-wing demagoguery manifests itself in overt attacks of higher education using anti-racism as the rationale.

I agree with Belen, but suggest the tactics of the new white nationalism are new, not the philosophy. Indeed, the political machine that arguably is the face of the new white nationalism has been strong and clear in its resistance to multicultural points of view for decades. Trump spokesman Rick Santorum claimed that the city of Boston is a threat because it is the liberal center of academia, where feminist scholars abound.[31] Republican Robert Ehrlich in the early 2000s in a WBAL interview said, "Once you get into this multicultural crap, this bunk, that some folks are teaching in our college campuses and other places, you run into a problem . . . There is no such thing as a multicultural society that can sustain itself, in my view, and I think history teaches us this lesson."[32] Steve King, senator from Iowa, in 2019, stated:

> This whole business does get a little tired. I would ask you to go back through history and figure out where are these contributions that have been made by these other categories of people you are talking about. Where did any other subgroup of people contribute more to civilization?[33]

To the *Washington Post*, Mr. King said: "The idea of multiculturalism, which every culture is equal—that's not objectively true . . . . We've been fed that information for the past 25 years, and we're not going to become a greater nation if we continue to do that."[34] Jeb Bush once said:

> We should not have a multicultural society . . . . America is so much better than every other country because of the values that people share—it defines our national identity. Not race or ethnicity, not where you come from . . . . When you create pockets of isolation—and in some cases the assimilation process is retarded because it's slowed down—it's wrong. It limits people's aspirations.

In each of these cases, white males assert the need for assimilation into a white version of America, using terms like "our" country and "our" identity. The privilege of being able to universalize an identity to all Americans, many of whom have been oppressed if not terrorized is profoundly overlooked in these men's comments and resistance to multiculturalism.

Hence, these politicians are quite involved with attempting to police college curriculum so that it upholds a single American identity like that which was constructed in the 1950s. They are standing guard at the imagined borders of the nation seeking to ensure it remains the domain of whites.

WHAT DISCIPLINES MATTER MATTERS

But the new white nationalism works also by supporting specific disciplines in higher education while delegitimizing others. The typical narrative touting STEM and business disciplines and demonizing the liberal arts and social sciences performs the work, and at times is the work, of the new white nationalism. For instance, look around your home. That glass in your windows, the pants in your dresser drawer, the paper or the device you're reading this book on, they most likely all have a common origin: Some of the material these products consist of come from companies owned by the Koch Brothers. Careful not to make their family name well known, Charles and David Koch built a literal empire from oil refinery wealth and that wealth transcended into other products. With this wealth, they began a thoughtful and effective infiltration into political circles through long-term funding strategies. To this end, the Koch Brothers have long contributed their wealth to Fox News.[35] Their strategy was and is more pervasive than just politics and media, however. By the second decade of the twenty-first century, they understood that securing power and privilege depended on developing a hold over the matrix of educational and mediated spheres along with the political.

By 2014, the Koch funding agenda "consider[ed] the higher educational programs they funded a 'fully integrated' part of a massive organizational network fighting to enact deregulatory government policies and elect conservative political candidates."[36] The funding of specific centers on college campuses was strategic and part of a "dark money manipulation of our nation's colleges and universities [which] has been proven to harm communities of color, dismantle protections for workers, and obstruct environmental protections."[37] The Koch Brothers' funding supports texts, professorships, and curriculum that defend eugenics, anti-democratic phi-losophies, and focuses on debunking climate change science—some of the very philosophies to which Stephen Miller and his white nationalist counter-parts adhere. By infiltrating college campuses with propaganda that works to further marginalize and oppress communities of color, the Koch Brothers and the new white nationalism ensures that the same spaces, ways of think-ing, and policies of yesterday's racism are both reinforced and extended for tomorrow. The Koch Brothers, although often looked at as sinister billion-aires, could just as easily be characterized as funding sources for the new white nationalists of the twenty-first century. According to George Mason University scholar, Samantha Parsons, the Koch Brothers' threat is that they understand that:

> The production of knowledge [can be] controlled only by those who can pay for it. If the wealthy 1 percent is able to use that wealth to define the priorities of our K-12 education and our higher education agendas, that's essentially giving very few people control over our country's production of knowledge—at least in the formalized institutions.[38]

In short, the Koch Brothers are very well aware that the battleground for America is literally in the mind of Americans, and have thus infiltrated American higher education systems with funding attached to problematic agendas. A review of the Koch Brothers' tax information and emails with public higher education institutions they fund reveals that another strategy of theirs is to support disciplines like economics and shift resources away from the humanities.[39]

Although the Koch Brothers represent an extreme example, there is pervasive rhetoric and thought that business and STEM majors are more reasonable choices for students than the liberal arts because they facilitate entry into job markets that are robust with need and are well paying. Again, this rhetoric and the resulting approach to academia funnels students away from disciplines that traditionally have criticized racist power dynamics. Likewise, much like many of the other arguments developed by the new white nationalism, the notion that STEM and business majors lead to better paying jobs is a myth, one that indeed permeates much of mainstream media and American culture.

Touting of STEM fields because of the salaries they lead to does not necessarily hold water when aligned with job market needs, trends in the workforce demand, and salaries over time. In fact, an American Association of Colleges and Universities recently reported that:

> Liberal arts majors may start off slower than others when it comes to the postgraduate career path, but they close much of the salary and unemployment gap over time, a new report shows. By their mid-50s, liberal arts majors with an advanced or undergraduate degree are on average making more money those who studied in professional and pre-professional fields, and are employed at similar rates.[40]

The myth of liberal arts majors not leading to jobs or well-paying salaries serves the new white nationalism by working to ensure those with white privilege remain complacent—for they are not exposed to disciplines that would challenge the existence of that privilege. The disciplines funded by the federal government also reveals a privileging of those disciplines less likely to challenge the social stratification. Although it is difficult to quantify a single number because STEM versus humanities disciplines are categorized differently by different federal agencies, it is clear the federal government funds STEM disciplines much more heavily than humanities. It is generally reported that STEM education garners $2.8 to $3.4 billion a year, where humanities fields are funded at around $1 billion a year.

And yet, in "Whither the Humanities," Michael Nietzle, a former university president despairs at the decreased emphasis of humanities majors, arguing that while STEM fields are said to lead to high-paying jobs, "they are failing to graduate 'job ready' adults . . . Students in these majors may not be learning communication and critical thinking skills, which means they may lack the writing and reasoning abilities that employers want in new hires."[41] Further, students who have majored in business are 31 percent underemployed upon graduation.[42] Ironically, then, one of the very arguments that underpins the delegitimization of both higher education and the humanities—that they do not lead to jobs—could be used for STEM majors. Further:

> Not all occupational degrees are practical, which may explain why some popular majors don't always guarantee a good labor force outcome. These majors include business, legal studies, public administration and social services professions and parks, recreation and fitness studies. These degrees comprise 4 in 10 bachelor's degrees handed out by U.S. colleges, which the researchers called "troubling."[43]

And yet, the manifold ways in which liberal arts is delegitimatized while STEM is lionized has a real effect on the number of students enrolling in them.

> [Since 1986] English saw a decline of 22% or 12,301 graduates; Philosophy and religious studies declined 15%; Foreign language graduates were off 5%; Liberal arts and general studies had a dip of 3%; and identify studies decreased .5%" Recognize, though, that to decrease in number and the percent while there is a 29% increase in all graduates is a major loss.[44]

The shifting economy of the twenty-first century presents other evidence that touting STEM and delegitimizing the humanities serves the role of privileging whites over and again. For instance, Heather McGowan writes that the decades-long emphasis of STEM fields rather than skills of writing, thinking, and working on teams, has left a workforce with over 120 million workers who need retraining. McGowan notes a fundamental shift in the market economy has occurred with the advent of technology where focus on content has been the means to create a better workforce to the detriment of behavioral expectations. And the workforce would prefer that higher education focus on the behavioral.[45] Many of the "soft" skills that pundits gloss over in touting STEM and business are actually desired by the workforce. The foundation of these soft skills resides in the liberal arts curriculum. The minimization of liberal arts, whether through funding or discourse actually harms the long-term earning potential of graduates, McGowan writes:

> And given the speed of change, by some reports, much of the value of the content of an undergraduate degree expires at or before graduation. A survey by Career Builder found that half of graduates do not go into the field of their university major and one third of graduates never work in the field of their major. Over the span of a lifetime, the industries change and shift so much that the emphasis of a major makes little sense. What makes sense is the emphasis

on the desire to learn and capacity to work with others to adapt in majors. [L]
earning agility and adaptability are now paramount considerations in hiring.
Recent neuroscience research suggests that humans may be built for lifelong
learning. Business leaders report that social or behavioral skills are now the
most in-demand skills with 80% of CEOs reporting talent is their number one
concern.[46]

The alignment between job titles and majors, hence, is misleading. A computer programmer, for instance, must know the content of computer programming, but also must be able to work on teams. Likewise, a computer
programmer who is twenty-two may have a very different job at forty. The
emphasis of STEM and training over humanities and cultural competency not
only funnels students away from learning about power and privilege, but it
has also created a workforce that is not trained in the ways employers need.
The result is a workforce that continues to be held at a certain earning and
promotional level under the institutional leadership that already exists—one
that is overwhelmingly white and male.

HIGHER EDUCATION AND ITS
VALUE TO THE COUNTRY

In the discourse about higher education's value, there is an assumption that
students should select majors only to make as much money as possible.
However, students select majors for other reasons than economic. The fabric
of society depends on good people taking jobs that align not with economic
return on investment, but return on their own value systems being fulfilled.
Limited by the discourse in higher education's value, then, is an emphasis
that higher education can provide not just the "soft" skills needed in the job
market, but also the skills in fields that have a goal of the common good.
Many who major in areas like the humanities may be quite satisfied making
less money in the beginning of their careers because they are happy at what
they do. In fact, many studies have shown that "humanities majors are more
content with their financial situation than, say, business majors."[47]

Understanding the power of the imagination in constructing the current and
future conditions of America, the new white nationalism focuses its efforts on
manipulating those with privilege into not seeing the truth of higher education
and its role in constructing a new America. The new white nationalism lulls
those with privilege into complacency by:

1) Falsely defining higher education as a site that is overly liberal,
2) Threatening educators who interrogate power, and

3) Funneling students away from liberal arts curriculum with false narratives about its efficacy.

These strategies, coupled together, are a potent and dangerous elixir for social justice in general and higher education's role in supporting the direction of democracy. Given the rhetoric indicative of the new white nationalism, and the support its rhetoric seems to garner, it is clear that there is a broad swath of white America resistant to a nation that includes black and brown bodies in its physical and imagined borders. It is also clear that the new white nationalism is on the offensive in very aggressive ways. The current moment is far from benign, and complacent American citizens are no enemy of the new white nationalism.

Robin DiAngelo and George Lipsitz rightly argue that when the status quo privileges those in power, generally whites, they will not relinquish it. Martin Luther King noted the same in his Letter from Birmingham Jail, stating "lamentably, it is an historical fact that privileged groups seldom give up their privileges voluntarily."[48]

Those who are interested in advancing social justice must consider that there is collective power in addressing white moderates who work in fields outside academia, or even in academia. Those interested in social justice cannot rely only on themselves to enact the thinking and society they desire. They must create allies out of those who are well-meaning but not yet awakened to the oppressions that are currently manifest as a result of history. They must, in short, reach out to the complacent white. Martin Luther King wrote the same:

> I have almost reached the regrettable conclusion that the Negro's great stumbling block in the stride toward freedom is not the White Citizen's Council-er or the Ku Klux Klanner, but the white moderate who is more devoted to "order" than to justice; who prefers a negative peace which is the absence of tension to a positive peace which is the presence of justice; who constantly says "I agree with you in the goal you seek, but I can't agree with your methods of direct action;" who paternalistically feels he can set the timetable for another man's freedom; who lives by the myth of time and who constantly advises the Negro to wait until a "more convenient season."[49]

The white moderate is complacent because of the discomfort that would occur as a result of having to shift her mindset.. The one American institution with the capacity to shift minds about American identity, race, and politics is higher education. Understadning how new white nationalism diverts new thinkers away from higher education as part of a war for the imagined nation is of utmost importance. For these power dynamics can only be disrupted through deep examination—and such examination is the duty of a higher education system charged with educating a well-informed citizenry. It is with this in mind that the next chapter examines the national completion paradigm and its approach to social justice.

NOTES

1. Ibram Kendi, "The Day 'Shithole' Entered the Presidential Lexicon." *The Atlantic.* January 13, 2019.

2. John Wagner and Seung Min Kim, "Trump Accuses Four Minority Congresswomen of Being 'Very Racist' and 'Not Very Smart.'" *New York Times,* July 22, 2019.

3. Jeremy Diamond, "Trump Jokes After Rally Attendee's Suggestion to 'Shoot' Migrants at the Border." *CNN.* May 19, 2019.

4. Ibid.

5. Joel Rose, "Leaked Emails Fuel Calls for Stephen Miller to Leave White House." *National Public Radio.* November 26, 2019, https://www.npr.org/2019/11/26/783047584/leaked-emails-fuel-calls-for-stephen-miller-to-leave-white-house.

6. "Is President Trump's Rhetoric Racist?" *The Washington Post* (Washington, DC), August 12, 2019.

7. Alene Tchekmedyian and Brittny Mejia, "California White Supremacists Vowed to 'Reimagine' Racist Movements with New Look and Secretive Tactics." *L.A. Times* (Los Angeles, CA), October 25, 2018.

8. Elisha Fieldstadt and Ken Dilanian, "White Nationalism-Fueled Violence Is on the Rise, but FBI Is Slow to Call It Domestic Terrorism." *NBC News* (New York), August 5, 2019.

9. However, President Trump cannot be identified as the origin of white supremacism or sympathy or complacency toward it. To be sure, white supremacy has not left the country despite desires to suggest it has. In *Sports in the Aftermath of Tragedy,* I made clear the need for academics to separate white supremacists from those who benefit from white privilege. However, it is clear, more and more, that the white supremacist mindset is vying for power by contesting for the support of those who benefit from privilege.

10. Arthur Kronman, *The Assault on American Excellence* (New Haven: Yale University Press, 2019).

11. Arthur Kronman, "The Downside of Diversity." *The Wall Street Journal.* August 2, 2019, https://www.wsj.com/articles/the-downside-of-diversity-11564758009

12. Gene Wise, "'Paradigm Dramas' in American Studies: A Cultural and Institutional History of the Movement." In *Locating American Studies. The Evolution of a Discipline,* edited by Lucy Maddox (Baltimore: Johns Hopkins University Press, 1999), 185.

13. Gene Wise, "'Paradigm Dramas' in American Studies: A Cultural and Institutional History of the Movement." In *Locating American Studies. The Evolution of a Discipline,* edited by Lucy Maddox (Baltimore: Johns Hopkins University Press, 1999), 180.

14. Stuart Hall, "Gramsci's Relevance for the Study of Race and Ethnicity." In *Stuart Hall: Critical Dialogues in Cultural Studies*, edited by David Morley and Kuan-Hsing Chen (London: Routledge, 1996), 411–440.

15. Georg Lipsitz, *American Studies in a Moment of Danger* (Minneapolis: University of Minnesota Press, 2001), 327.

16. Michelle Goldberg, "This Is What Happens When You Slash Funding for Public Universities," *The Nation*, June 8, 2108.

17. Bryan Caplan, *The Case Against Higher Education: Why the Education System Is a Waste of Time and Money* (Princeton: Princeton University Press, 2018).

18. Antonio Gramsci, "Hegemony, Relations of Force, Historical Block." In *The Antonio Gramsci Reader*, edited by David Forgacs (New York: Schocken books, 2002).

19. Ronald Takaki, "Multiculturalism: Battleground or Meeting Ground." In *Color-Line to Borderlands*, edited by Johanna Butler (Washington: University of Washington Press), 10.

20. Ronald Takaki, "Multiculturalism: Battleground or Meeting Ground." In *Color-Line to Borderlands*, edited by Johanna Butler (Washington: University of Washington Press), 12.

21. "Professor WatchList." Accessed June 1, 2019, https://www.professorwatchlist.org/.

22. American Defense League, "New Hate and Old: The Changing Face of American White Supremacy." Accessed November 6, 2019, https://www.adl.org/new-hate-and-old.

23. Patricia Matthews, "Academic Freedom in the Classroom: Students and the Trouble with Labels." Last modified December 2019, https://profession.mla.org/academic-freedom-in-the-classroom-students-and-the-trouble-with-labels/.

24. Patricia Matthews, "Academic Freedom in the Classroom: Students and the Trouble with Labels." Last modified December 2019, https://profession.mla.org/academic-freedom-in-the-classroom-students-and-the-trouble-with-labels/.

25. Similarly, David Horowitz's book *The Professors: The 101 Most Dangerous Academics in America* makes no pretense about the fact that he wants parents to forbid students to enter the classes where scholars teach antiracism. In his book, he chronicles the work of Angela Davis, bell hooks, Gayatri Spivak, Fredric Jameson, and many others in short summaries to allow parents "information" on which professors and so knowledges they should keep their children from. This tactic, however, is not one that is really meant to "protect" students from "scary" knowledge.

26. Joe Pinsker, "Republicans Changed Their Mind About Higher Education Really Quickly." *The Atlantic*. August 21, 2019.

27. Joe Pinsker, "Republicans Changed Their Mind About Higher Education Really Quickly." *The Atlantic*. August 21, 2019.

28. Joel Rose, "Leaked Emails Fuel Calls for Stephen Miller to Leave White House." *National Public Radio*. November 26, 2019, https://www.npr.org/2019/11/26/783047584/leaked-emails-fuel-calls-for-stephen-miller-to-leave-white-house.

29. Scott Jaschick, "Professors and Politics: What the Research Says." *Inside Highered*. February 7, 2017, https://www.insidehighered.com/news/2017/02/27/research-confirms-professors-lean-left-questions-assumptions-about-what-means.

30. Edna Acosta Belen, "Reimagining Borders." In *Color-Line to Borderlands*, edited by Johanna Butler (Washington: University of Washington Press), 251.

31. Rick Santorum, *This Week*, August 20, 2005.

32. David Nitkin, "Ehrlich Calls Multiculturalism 'Bunk.'" *Baltimore Sun.* May 9, 2004.

33. Daniel Victor, "What, Congressman Steve King Asks, Have Nonwhites Done for Civilization?" *New York Times*, August 16, 2017.

34. Amber Phillips, "The Idea That Every Culture Is Equal Is Not Objectively True." *Washington Post.* June 20, 2017.

35. Common Dreams, "Report Shows How Koch Brothers Bankroll 'Fox News of the Regulatory Policy World' to Help Push Polluter-Friendly Agenda." June 3, 2019. Accessed June 10, 2019, https://www.commondreams.org/news/2019/06/03/report -shows-how-koch-brothers-bankroll-fox-news-regulatory-policy-world-help-push.

36. Dave Levinthal, "How the Koch Brothers Are Influencing U.S. Colleges." *Time.* December 15, 2015.

37. Common Dreams, "Report Shows How Koch Brothers Bankroll 'Fox News of the Regulatory Policy World' to Help Push Polluter-Friendly Agenda." June 3, 2019.

48. Rebeka Barbara, "Organizing Against Koch Influence on College Campuses." *Facing South.* March 15, 2019.

39. Dave Levinthal, "Spreading the Free-Market Gospel." *The Atlantic.* October 30, 2015.

40. Allie Grasgreen, "Liberal Arts Grads Win Long-Term." *Inside HigherEd.* December 14, 2014.

41. Aimee Picci, "English Majors, Rejoice: Employers Want You More Than Business Majors." *CBS News.* October 28, 2019.

42. Aimee Picci, "English Majors, Rejoice: Employers Want You More Than Business Majors." *CBS News.* October 28, 2019.

43. Aimee Picci, "English Majors, Rejoice: Employers Want You More Than Business Majors." *CBS News.* October 28, 2019.

44. Michael Neitzel, "Whither the Humanities: The Ten-Year Trend in College Majors." *Forbes.* January 7, 2019.

45. Heather McGowan, "The Workforce Is Calling, Higher Education, Will You Answer?" *Forbes.* September 10, 2019.

46. Michael Neitzel, "Whither the Humanities: The Ten-Year Trend in College Majors." *Forbes.* January 7, 2019.

47. Ben Felder, "How Colleges Are Adapting to the Decline in Liberal Arts Majors." *PBS News Hour.* November 30, 2018.

48. Martin Luter King, "Letter from Birmingham." *African Studies Center, University of Pennsylvania.* Accessed August 1, 2019, https://www.africa.upenn.edu /Articles_Gen/Letter_Birmingham.html.

49. Martin Luter King, "Letter from Birmingham." *African Studies Center, University of Pennsylvania.* Accessed August 1, 2019, https://www.africa.upenn.edu /Articles_Gen/Letter_Birmingham.html.

Chapter 4

Rationalizing Innovation

On a bright September day in 1962, President John F. Kennedy stood before a Houston, Texas, crowd at Rice University, and spoke of the capacity of human imagination and innovation. Without showing the way in which to accomplish his goal, Kennedy would reveal an initiative to put an American on the moon within a decade.

> We meet at a college noted for knowledge, in a city noted for progress, in a State noted for strength, and we stand in need of all three, for we meet in an hour of change and challenge, in a decade of hope and fear, in an age of both knowledge and ignorance. The greater our knowledge increases, the greater our ignorance unfolds . . . . Despite the striking fact that most of the scientists that the world has ever known are alive and working today, despite the fact that this Nation's own scientific manpower is doubling every 12 years in a rate of growth more than three times that of our population as a whole, despite that, the vast stretches of the unknown and the unanswered and the unfinished still far outstrip our collective comprehension.[1]

Here, Kennedy underscored that there was much he, along with the nation's scientists, did not know about the physics that would propel a rocket to the moon. Still, he continued:

> But why, some say, the moon? Why choose this as our goal? And they may well ask why the highest mountain climb? Why, 35 years ago, fly the Atlantic? Why does Rice play Texas? We choose to go to the moon. We choose to go to the moon in this decade and do the other things, not because they are easy, but because they are hard, because that goal will serve to organize and measure the best of our energies and skills, because that challenge is one that we are willing

to accept, one we are unwilling to postpone, and one which we intend to win, and the others, too . . . . To be sure, all this costs us all a good deal of money. This year's space budget is three times what it was in January 1961, and it is greater than the space budget of the previous eight years combined. That budget now stands at $540 million a year—a staggering sum, though somewhat less than we pay for cigarettes and cigars every year. Space expenditures will soon rise some more, from 40 cents per person per week to more than 50 cents a week for every man, woman and child in the United States, for we have given this program a high national priority—even though I realize that this is in some measure an act of faith and vision, for we do not now know what benefits await us.[2]

Kennedy's speech and vision was undergirded by a faith in American innovation. The goal was big, and the details were not necessary. But the commitment was made clear, and the resources earmarked. That very same decade, Apollo 11 set its engines down on the moon's white-dusted sphere, and Americans took their first steps on that gravitational body, a feat that seemed like an impossibility when Kennedy gave his speech in Texas only years prior.

Fifty years later, President Barack Obama stood resolute in front of an enthralled Texas crowd. Much like his innovative predecessor John F. Kennedy, he spoke about what he perceived to be the next frontier for American thought leadership. This time, however, Obama spoke of increasing the efficacy of higher education by doubling the number of graduates in America by 2020. In his inspirational call, the president stated:

In a single generation, we've fallen from first place to 12th place in college graduation rates for young adults. Think about that. Now, that's unacceptable, but it's not irreversible. We can retake the lead. Over a third of America's college students and over half of our minority students don't earn a degree, even after six years. So we don't just need to open the doors of college to more Americans; we need to make sure they stick with it through graduation. That is critical.

From Kennedy to Obama, a trajectory is evident where once imagination and innovation inspired action, now data and outcomes do.

But since Obama's speech, state and federal funding for higher education has been significantly reduced, according to National Clearinghouse data. Indeed, at aggregate level, state and federal funding for higher education has been on a sharp decline, ironically, since the call for more completions resounded.[3] The Center on Budget and Policy Priorities, moreover, using National Clearinghouse data, reveals that since 2006, state funding for higher education has decreased by as much as 53.8 percent, with only four states increasing funding over that time, and in those cases, minimally. The same report illustrates extreme variance in how higher education is funded state to state. In 2014, for instance, there was a variance of 3 percent to 80 percent of institutions' operational dollars being supported by state budgets.[4]

Reduced funding for colleges, coupled with discrepancies in how they are funded state-by-state presents challenges for national reform movements like the completion agenda, especially in community colleges.[5] Likewise, the fact that fiscal support for public colleges is decreasing while the calls for higher completion rates is increasing should give many pause.

There is a significant tension in how higher education reform is envisioned versus how interventions are implemented, and this tension can be unpacked through the framework provided in the nostalgia spectrum.

At the core of the completion work that transpired since President Obama's call to action is an assumption that what are considered to be low completion rates and high tuition costs are the basic problems confronting higher education. This assumption derives from data being examined by people external to academia and identifying two data points—completion rates and tuition costs—as the disease rather than the symptoms of a disease plaguing higher education. The metaphor of medicine is a good one to bring home the point.

Rather than looking higher education as having isolated problems as a result of its completion rates and tuition costs, it is more helpful to consider higher education as part of the body, and the nation itself—with all the political, mediated, financial, and cultural institutions of which it comprises—as the actual body. Completion rates and tuition costs, then, are best read as data points like a temperature, rather than a disease itself. In short, there is every reason to believe that there is greater disease that plagues American society leading to lower completion rates and higher tuition costs, especially when it comes to community colleges. One symptom of that disease is *how* we look at data as revealing of a truth without getting underneath the reasons that such data exists. As Catherine O'Neil eloquently states in *Weapons of Math Destruction*, today's world of big data produces "ill-conceived mathematical models [that] now micromanage the economy, from advertising to prisons."[6]

Carol Dweck's scholarship on "the deficit lens" is quite helpful to understand the frames and data used to set the agenda for the completion paradigm. According to Dweck, a deficit mindset always starts from a place of privilege and power. It views minority communities and students by perceiving what they cannot do as defining of their ability.[7] The completion agenda began with a similar mindset with regard to community colleges. Current discourses about value, likewise, stem from observations like the following: only 22 percent of community college students completed a degree in three years. Rather than perceiving that 22 percent of community college students complete in three years as indicative of a problem, there is also a way to see that 22 percent as a strength through the nostalgia spectrum: Despite that

70 percent of the students coming to community colleges are part time, and despite the many hardships—from working full time to requiring child care to having full-time jobs—that many of these students face are a result of the systematic oppressions they were born into in the first place, and despite that funding for these colleges is a fraction that many four-year colleges receive 22 percent gradate in three years![8]

The completion agenda did not seek first to understand then disrupt the mindset and processes that continue to marginalize and often lead to low completion numbers. Marginalization is all but guaranteed to continue in the future as a result. Further, the deficit lens stems from a tendency of humans to focus on the negative rather than the positive. This tendency is a result of what psychologist Paul Rozen call and Edward Royzan negativity bias.[9] However, the negativity bias is more telling of the position that individuals and institutions view from, rather than the qualities of that which is viewed.

The deficit lens and negativity bias assume urgent action is needed to remedy higher education but define current problems with higher education in an historic vacuum: The problems to solve are ones of completion and cost. Yet, the stakeholders and the discourse surrounding higher education do not delve into the historic privilege and power that underpins the entire enterprise of higher education. The result is a national deficit in the ability to identify what the problems are that lead to graduation rates that many feel are unacceptable. The problems identified in mainstream and reform movements are from a narrow and privileged position and do not challenge the already-existent and long-standing paradigms of social stratification. This lack of disruption, not the cost of college and low completion rates, is the core problem facing higher education.

Unfortunately, stakeholders have focused on scrutiny rather than support of higher education in the recent past. The scrutiny has been coupled with mandates that are imagined to deliver solutions to higher education's problems. But the problems being addressed are ones that avoid the most central truth that confronts and has confronted higher education for centuries: they build off positions of white privilege and power that has characterized America's major institutions for centuries, and as such are working to perpetuate systemic inequities even if unintentionally so.

THE COMPLETION AGENDA AND
THE PROBLEM OF HISTORY

The nation's call for increasing completion numbers and reducing costs for higher education has created interventions based on an ahistorical look at higher education. To create interventions on a national level, the completion agenda accepted using the same structures that existed in higher education for the past number of decades, if not centuries, rather than understanding the results of completion and cost were underpinned by centuries-old structures leading to the very data that needed to be addressed. To think that a better result would be catalyzed by implementing more interventions, rather than examining why the interventions were necessary, was a missed opportunity. Similarly, the end goal of creating more credentialed adults has been articulated in a faulty way, while lacking inspiration. Suggesting the American higher education systems need to focus on completing more students simply to ensure that the country remains first in the world with credentialed adults does very little to explain why education is necessary in the first place. The distinction between situating higher education as serving a workforce and national reputation as "number one" versus a vehicle to leverage the greater American promise is a significant one. The latter potentially requires a paradigmatic shift and adherence to citizenship as the fundamental reason that higher education exists; the former makes no such requirement and potentially reifies the same social structure albeit with more credentialed adults. Another way to put it: more credentialed adults does not equate to a more just society, social uplift, or a furthering of the ideals that are supposed to underpin the nation and higher education itself. The implicit message is that the completion agenda has an economic goal, not one connected to national ideals

While it is clear that most professionals working in higher education and committing to the completion agenda's goals do so with righteous intent, if the origin of systems and thoughts are not fully interrogated, and if privilege of people and systems are not checked, there is no reason to believe that the American higher education system will accomplish completing more students in equitable fashion. Likewise, there is every reason to believe that focus on acceleration toward completion will result in quick exacerbation of inequitable outcomes and reification of the social stratification by which the new white nationalism is characterized.

One of the greatest American thinkers about systems and oppression, James Baldwin, wrote, in "Sonny's Blues," how the imagination and creative spirit are essential to humanity's survival and progress. He wrote of the danger of not looking at systemic oppressions and their likelihood of being reinforced through simple inertia of systems and thought. One of the most poignant scenes of this story is when his narrator is traveling through Harlem noticing the housing projects he grew up in and escaped from, but which many of his peers did not:

> But houses exactly like the houses of our past yet dominated the landscape, boys exactly like the boys we once had been found themselves smothering in these houses, came down into the streets for light and air and found themselves encircled by disaster.[10]

Baldwin sheds light on how the past is always present if there is not intentional focus on disrupting the systemic oppressions that have haunted systems.

Underpinning the "traditional systems of higher education" is a symbiotic relationship between states, the federal government, and higher education that results in exclusivity. The original higher education institutions were developed within the thirteen original colonies. Craig Steven Wilder's *Ebony and Ivy: Race, Slavery, and the Troubled History of America's Universities* chronicles how the original thirteen colonies worked symbiotically with higher education institutions to ensure that power would continue through education and exclusionary practices.[11] And as time went on, new higher education institutions reproduced the same ways of thinking and structures by replicating the successful policies and practices those original colleges developed. As time went on, even if new institutions did not have intentions to bolster white nationalism and privilege, they did so through the curriculum, admissions practices, and funding models Even if the thinking embraced by those within newer colleges was overtly focused on anti-racism, many of the admissions practices, pedagogies, assumptions about what matters most in terms of student success and, we have shown, curriculum, were replicated based on the past experiences of those institutions that were part of an oppressive system from the beginning: Those working in these newer institutions graduated from the old ones. The replication of these policies and practices and ways of thought may have, over time, been quite benign in intention. But their outcomes of exclusion were not. We know this because there are excellent initiatives focused on equitable completion nationally. No doubt, these initiatives stemmed from the results of higher education's completion rates, disaggregated by race, gender, Pell status, veteran status, and more, which showed a need for improvement. But many of these initiatives comprise of new projects being built on old systems that privileged whiteness in the first place. Replicating policies, practices, and ways of thought without challenging underpinning structures reinforces white power and privilege. The completion agenda not only has begun from an ahistorical approach, but it has also gained significant momentum that could be infused with power, power that, with small tweaks from leaders at institutions across the nation, could re-direct toward social justice. To be clear, the completion agenda's greatest leaders have done excellent work with insisting on equity and use of data to account for institutional accountability. However, there have been no national calls for considering the historic way in which institutions themselves have been built in order to manifest the outcomes desired.

Further, with an ahistorical beginning, the completion paradigm has not yet revealed the actual obstacles to completion. Stakeholders of higher education have applied a manner of measuring effectiveness focused on metrics of efficiency, graduation, and return on investment. As such, the current paradigm in higher focuses:

- Metrics of success based on numbers and rates of graduates, rather than mission or quality;
- Being fast and flexible rather than fast, flexible, and socially just;
- Showcasing projects and interventions as the means for enhancing student success, rather than challenging the institutional policies, practices, and narratives that led to there being a need to create interventions in the first place.

A PARADIGM BUILT ON WHITE ASSUMPTIONS

When President Obama set the direction for the completion agenda, America was already ensconced in a paradigm of using data and technology to make consumer choice and experience simple and quick. Think Amazon. Think Netflix. Think Spotify.

It was no coincidence, then, that the interventions generally posited to lead to increased completion were those that hastened students through the process of college. This approach is a bit like suggesting that to make the good restaurant better, all that needs to be done is to implement a strategy to make the food faster and the customers eat quicker.

While the completion agenda has indeed manifest in more credentialed citizens, at its foundation is a philosophical issue that may be misaligned with the purpose of higher education in a democratic society. In short, the principles of a commodity-based industry have been applied to higher education. Those principles are to streamline customer experience to achieve the end product. There is the potential, as a result, to see mission creep away from learning and citizenship toward efficiency. In the process, the grander notion of what higher education is and can be are limited in our imaginations. The completion agenda has been heavily influenced by the customer-driven industry and social, economic, and technological paradigms surrounding higher education. Customer service and quick and convenient exchanges for goods are the most prevalent qualities of the day.

There are major distinctions between higher education and a customer-driven industry. And while those distinctions may seem obvious, I find it necessary to explain some of them in economic and return-on-investment terms. In higher education there is indeed an exchange of money for something in return. However, unlike the purchase of a product learning is also cumulative in nature. Unlike products that one purchases through the commodity-exchange market, higher education allows for appreciation of value, not depreciation, over time. Because higher education's benefits appreciate over time, it is potentially a bad fit for the commodity-based paradigm that has dominated the early 2000s. Likewise, although the purchase of a major commodity like a car or a house can take quite a long while to complete, there is a time when the purchase of such a product results in ownership. Knowledge is not owned, however. It is gained by individuals, and the epistemology of a discipline is never complete. One's knowledge of any discipline, therefore, is never fully obtained. The product-driven market economy paradigm, then, runs counter to some of the essential tenants of higher education. And yet, the completion and data-heavy paradigm of the twenty-first century has characterized how higher education operates and is measured by external stakeholders.

Of paradigms, American Studies scholar Gene Wise argues that what has been defined in specific "cultural and institutional context[s]," is a paradigm drama, and that a paradigm drama is an act "which spotlights changing boundaries of what is possible for a person or a group at a particular time and in a particular place and in a particular milieu."[12] Wise's description of a paradigm drama is helpful in understanding that American higher education reform may be limited both by the racial origins of higher education and the general market economy of the twenty-first century. We have already touched on the racial origins of the higher education enterprise in America. Additionally, higher education has been subsumed as one of those social institutions using and being held accountable by the paradigm that sees big data and technology as panaceas for achieving the goals of the completion agenda.

Higher education utilized the notions of the Amazons of the world to streamline processes and focus on customer service. This approach should not be seen as a surprise or misguided. Yet, upon looking back, it is clear that the completion agenda was limited by the paradigm of the twenty-first century where streamlined, quick, efficient, and individualized experiences and gratification for the purchaser of products was of highest importance.

As higher education utilized the tools of the current American market economy paradigm to enhance completion numbers, the new white nationalism was served in two ways through data. First, the data used to arrive at conclusions about the efficacy of community colleges came from a privileged point of view. Second, that data became such an emphasis that one of the the primary tenants of higher education, creating well-rounded citizens, may have been de-emphasized if not overlooked at times. In both, people and students have often been reduced to products. Students are not customers.

The first manner in which the paradigm of the new market economy of the twentieth century utilized data in potentially problematic ways was through the definitional terms agreed upon for measuring what counts as a "completion." These definitions of completion marginalize a majority of students attending community college, despite that nearly 50 percent of college-going students are attending these institutions. Given that community college demographics are heavily minority, it is simple to see that the definition of completion by which institutions of higher education are measured privileges a white, middle-class identity. For the federal government defines completion as "completers within 150% of normal time. Students who completed their program within 150% of the normal (or expected) time for completion."[13] This means students who earn a two-year degree in three years, four-year degree in six are counted as successful completers. Nationally, however, community colleges struggle to complete students in 150 percent time because the lives of community college students prohibit it. In one of the seminal texts that underpins the completion agenda's work, *Time Is the Enemy*, the difficulty is articulated well: "More students are working, and they are working more hours than ever before. Many can afford to attend only part-time, extending the years until they graduate."[14] However, with nearly 70 percent of community college students attending part time, the completion rate metric only sees the performance of these institutions from a lens of the few who are privileged enough to fit a nearly full-time schedule into their lives. Even more, the completion metric itself derives from a four-year college expectation and experience, where community colleges were developed for an entirely different experience. Imposing a metric that fits an economically privileged cohort of students on a community college system that was created for a different cohort tautologically marginalizes the students who are marginalized because they are marginalized. This is how the apparatus of white privilege works: Those who have the power and privilege to define direction have that power and privilege because of their being privileged in the past; their experiences are normalized and they become powerful enough to dictate direction of big systems; the marginalized remain marginalized as a result of that direction. History is always present.

This cyclical process is the very sort that characterizes the new white nationalism, and in the era of big data, definitional terms wield immense power while hiding that same power. O'Neil further illustrates how big data wields oppressive power accordingly. She writes:

> Many poisonous assumptions are camouflaged by math and go largely untested and unquestioned. This underscores another common feature of Weapons of Math Destruction (WMD). They tend to punish the poor. This is, in part, because they are engineered to evaluate large numbers of people . . . . The human victims of WMDs . . . are held to a far higher standard of evidence than the algorithms themselves.[15]

The current paradigm of big data can feed into, accelerate, and exacerbate inequities discussed in earlier chapters and so is a tool that does the work of the new white nationalism.

The completion agenda and big data definitions have placed significant pressure on those institutions that have missions of providing access to education through open door admissions practices. Those institutions have as their central mission to disrupt the social stratification through education. Yet, they are measured in the same way as Ivy League colleges, many of which were literally built in times that overtly benefited white privilege. The origin of the completion agenda, as a result, stems from well-intended desires. However, the data that the completion agenda originated from—a scrutiny of completion rates as defined by IPEDs—is based on assumptions about student experiences that normalize white and middle-class identities. As a result, the well-intended completion agenda began with and built systems and directions off of a privileged lens—one that also necessarily views people and institutions that do not conform to that lens as having deficits rather than strengths. To their credit, manifold community college alliances, such as the Voluntary Framework of Accountability, American Association of Community Colleges, and Achieving the Dream, have advocated for new manners of defining the ways in which completion is counted. However, the federal definitions remain unchanged.

To be clear, public scrutiny of higher education is justified.[16] It is a fact, for instance, that the current generation of young adults will be the first in American history to be less educated than the generation preceding it. This fact must raise eyebrows and demands intervention. However, the reasons for the declines in the completion numbers and rates extend beyond higher education, as previous chapters have shown.

And this is the second data-based problem associated with higher education: The interventions required to enhance completion numbers and rates are not as simple as discovering new data solutions and pedagogy in colleges themselves.

THE HEART OF THE MATTER: WHITE PRIVILEGE EVEN IN THE EMOTIONAL REALM

At the origin of the completion agenda there is a foundational problem. If not dealt with, this foundational problem will pervade all higher education reform work and the social structures upon which they rely for the long-term future. It is a philosophical and structural problem that anti-racist Audre Lorde identifies in "Poetry Is Not a Luxury." Lorde argues that rich white males were privileged enough to set up Western civilization in their own image and ways of thinking, so those systems and structures have always resembled and benefited their own identities. This society, she suggests, founded and still founds itself on a Kantian dichotomy of head and heart, and dismisses the latter as being an unnecessary component of the work world. Lorde states that systems in Western culture privilege rational thought over emotional and in order to have a seat at the tables where major decisions are made, one has to amputate the emotional elements of oneself. In a world that was built to privilege the white male, however, it follows that there would be fewer obstacles and emotional slights experienced by white males than other identities because systems already cater to that identity. One of the major yet under-discussed privileges of whiteness in such systems, then, is that the mindsets of people who operate in them, despite race, already assume a rational approach. The systems themselves already privilege whites. Hence, whites are less likely to feel oppressed in even the most mundane of processes, policies, narratives, and moments. How institutions have been built by whites, tautologically, privileges whites. And so the work world is set up where whites and males have less emotional adjustments to make to remain comfortable in the work world. This is not the case for those marginalized. Simultaneously, intense emotions are constantly marginalized as important in the work world; and yet, the privileged, it would follow, would have less reasons to have intense emotional responses to a work world comprising of institutional structures in general that privilege them.

Marginalized groups must therefore learn how to survive in Western culture by amputating parts of their emotional being and assimilate into structures and systems, like higher education. These systems and structures, however, have histories as old as slavery, Native American genocide, aggressive patriarchy, and general class-based oppression. While it is true that the imagined borders of what counts as "American" have expanded since original higher education institutions were built (as early as the late 1600s), the institutions that comprise the country have built on top of the policies, practices, and mindsets of the past rather than eradicating them in order to ensure inclusion. The completion agenda itself is building on top of those same structures.

Hence, the systems do not change. People are forced to change. They are made to fit in with the systems with centuries-old histories.

The current reform movements in higher education could be enhanced if they utilized the nostalgia spectrum. Doing so would focus on equity, but especially the systemic, structured, and narrativized white privilege and power that has been baked into higher education. Lorde underscores that Western society minimizes the role of the heart in how work is done. For an enhanced completion agenda to manifest, the systems that have been built on years of privilege and exclusion need to be upended while recognizing that the new white nationalism is actively engaged in a movement to continue that same privilege and exclusion. In a completion agenda so focused on equity, a next, scaled step should be to consider the institutional racism that higher education has built itself on, and intentionally challenge the assumptions of rationality that have been the totems of higher education for centuries. Plenty of scholars in higher education are capable of pointing this necessity out. However, the focus in the current paradigm of completion has been to assimilate minority students into a structure that would have actively marginalized them decades and centuries ago.

To expand, 2019 marked the third consecutive year in which college completion rates rose. Indeed, the data provides encouragement that the approach higher education has taken to the completion agenda has increased outcomes at the aggregate and disaggregated levels. But *how* the retention and completion numbers across the country have been enhanced is not altogether obvious. To draw connection between projects implemented at a national level and increased outcome data may be problematic. Data use typical of the current paradigm minimizes the effect that changing college employees' mindset has on completion and equity. It minimizes the role of people and maximizes projects as the reason for the positive change. Here is where Lorde's analysis of how Western culture emphasizes linear modes of thinking is most helpful. Lorde wrote, "For within living structures defined by profit, by linear power, by dehumanization, our feelings were not meant to survive."[17] The more that American culture believes higher education must rely on projects and outcomes, the less professionals in higher education talk about innovation, human interaction, emotions, and mindset to manifest the change desired. John R. Swallow notes this same sentiment:

> Those elements of humanity interact and coexist everywhere in life, including in the classroom. The best college teaching has always included both rational argument and emotional insight. That combination—especially the emphasis on the emotional insight—is more crucial than ever in college classrooms today . . . . Whether as part of college teaching or part of the campus experience, we cannot avoid the emotions present in students or ourselves. Sometimes we idealize the academic environment as one where only rational thought takes place. But to expect that human interaction on deeply meaningful topics—race, mental health, assault, or other sensitive issues—can rely solely on rational argument is irrational.[18]

The focus on only the measurable has led to a problematic approach. Perhaps Swallow's points, however, expand beyond the classroom. Perhaps the humanity needs to be injected into the systems, structures, and narratives of higher education. Perhaps the scaled projects within higher education's walls, such as mandatory orientation, accelerated learning, and streamlining admissions processes are all wonderful tools, but they have only added on top of a system that privileges whiteness without disrupting it. For if one steps out of the metric-, tuition-, and consumer-driven paradigm, many unanswered questions arise with regard to the data presented to stakeholders in higher education regarding completion. Some questions that should be asked regarding the positive numbers we see happening in the completion agenda are:

- Is it possible that discussions about the necessity of completion, and employees' mindsets and their thinking has had impact on their day-to-day work?
- In the work being done at community colleges, is the very discussion about completion having an impact on those numbers?
- What about how people think, how they feel, the immeasurable truth that changing people's perspective may have a meaningful impact?
- Why is it that in our discussions of improvement, assessment, and completion, that a fundamental aspect been lost, which is that of how people commit to (or do not commit to) institutional goals that are aligned with national goals?
- If the emotional and philosophical is of importance, what happens when entire paradigms of accountability, which require course assessment and institutional assessment, do not account for the human aspect?
- At base, what are we measuring and are we sure why?
- Is it possible that in our projects and assessment of them, we are neglecting the most important element of the student experience—relationships?
- What if funding models were changed at federal and state levels to enhance the institutional capacity for students to have relationships with more employees?

The conclusion that projects—and not the mindset change—created better outcomes for students, results, circularly, from the origin of the thinking: an explicit acceptance that only rational and measurable projects can be the reason for change. For "our own values and desires influence our choices, form the data we choose to collect, to the questions we ask."[19] Although there is often talk about the importance of people and the culture of a college in the current national paradigm, there is no focus on people and culture of colleges at the conferences or literature that pervades the work of the completion agenda. This is because it is very difficult to measure a shift in how people think and draw a direct line to positive outcomes. However, there is reason to believe that mindset shifts affect behaviors and that these behaviors result in better interactions with students. Herein is a major conundrum for our thinking. The paradigm of placing new initiatives on top of old systems and measuring them accordingly is limiting our understanding of what could best benefit students while leaving arcane and oppressive the systems, structures, and narratives upon which higher education was build intact. It is very possible, then, that interventions that could dismantle the new white nationalism are simply ignored. There is a tension here that can be exploited if the people making decisions at the top of institutions would allow frame-breaking approaches of how we do our work. For minor and immeasurable changes in people may collectively lead to better student outcomes. But such decisions require bravery. They require full understanding of how the new white nationalism has and continues to function and governing boards committed also to the vision of dismantling it.

In the interim, major interventions of the completion paradigm are project based—course and program assessment, creating curricular pathways, intrusive advising facilitated through technology, and required orientation. This project-based approach, typical of other sectors of American society, leads to easy and methodical measurement of effectiveness. The issue here is not that higher education is applying what many academic professionals would call "a business model to higher education." Rather, it is that the focus on project-based, measurable initiatives in any sector necessarily denies the role of people and feelings in the workplace and nation in general.

In the process, the focus on projects also potentially reinforces funding deficits for higher education the previous chapter highlighted as problematic: For a course's quality is generally a result not of its structure as indicated through assessment; rather a course is good because there is an excellent instructor teaching it. It is not only that majors are grouped and presented in a particular fashion that leads to completion, it is also that good advising exists in which students interact with an employee at the college correctly. It is not that the courses are sequenced transparently so students can select from them easily that leads to student choices for course selection being enhanced, but that the faculty teaching courses engage students, have mindsets to reach out to them on a personal level, and then tell them the courses to take next. It is not that institutions tout pedagogy and professional development, it is that they are intentional about both. It is not only that institutions need to include adjuncts in the heart of their institutions to ensure the entire class offerings are high quality, it is also that the stakeholders of higher education need to get serious about the very economic model underpinning colleges. Currently there is a general acceptance that 50 percent of courses at community colleges are taught by adjuncts who are uncertain if they will be teaching at the same institution the next semester and are woefully underpaid. Engagement with students is what we know leads to their success because it makes them *feel* connected to the institution they attend. To make a significant change in outcomes, a radical but simple paradigm shift is required: Fund public higher education so that institutions can hire the best faculty and staff with the intention of engaging students at low-tuition costs. Simple. Not rocket science.

It is simple to rationalize away feelings and relationships as fundamentally important to a higher education system that touts itself to be about rationality. But make no mistake: feelings and relationships are already part of higher education's story. They simply privilege a history of whiteness and marginalization of other identities. Centering feelings and emotions will be a revolutionary approach to higher education and through it the nation itself. Both would ultimately resist the new new white nationalism.

FURTHER EXPLANATION OF WHITE PRIVILEGE AND THE TYRANNY OR RATIONALISM

People who have been marginalized and experienced generational trauma are required enter into spaces that have traditionally been reserved for whites. In doing so, they have to amputate part of themselves. Well-meaning people may not understand the realities of how people different than themselves feel about entering into spaces where they are made to hide their feelings about marginalization or having to hide parts of their full selves daily. As a result, it is possible to theorize that on college campuses there are well-meaning, privileged people and marginalized people who are proverbial well-intentioned ships passing in the night. The space between these ships is where the struggle between anti-racism and the new white nationalism must be waged. That space is occupied by the minds of the well-intentioned privileged, complacent whites who have not yet fully understood their privilege.

The necessity of being empathetic to the complacent white as well as those marginalized cannot be underscored enough. The same cohort that makes up the youngest faculty members in higher education today grew up watching cartoons like Bugs Bunny where African American stereotypes pervaded the screen and were normalized.

Whether working in higher education or another sector, the imagined constructions of what different races look, behave, and think like are at least influenced by the mediated narratives about race that were consumed at younger ages. For those notions of race to be dismantled requires intentional work. However, many working whites who grew up with these stereotypes being shown to them believe, complacently, that such images, pervasive during their childhood, are not part of their subconscious. Likewise, many minorities have internalized these stereotypes and believe whites have internalized them. Intentional liberation from subconscious bias, whether against another race or one's own is an imperative part of having a mindset toward enacting a culture in colleges where employees

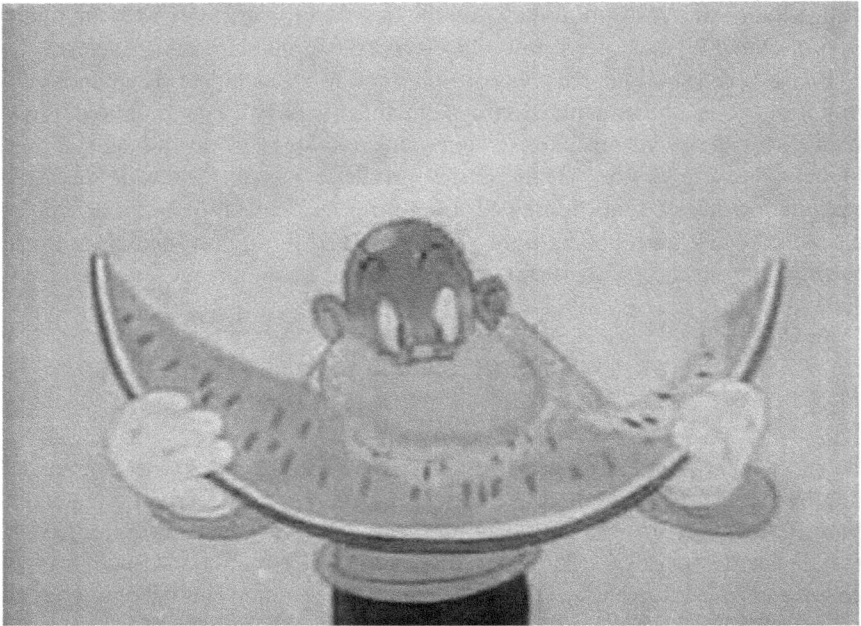

**Figure 4.1   The still captured from Looney Toon's "Scrub Me Mama with a Boogie Beat"
portrayed African Americans as watermelon eating, lazy Americans who lived in a town
called Lazy Town (Darrell Calker. (1941) Scrub me Mama with a Boogie Beat, USA,
1941).** These cartoons were shown on television, shaping young American minds through
the late 1980s. Images like these establish templates about race in young children's minds
that are replicated over and again in everyday interactions. Hence, it is not enough to
believe that all people who work in colleges and agree with the philosophy of anti-racism
have fully understood the work and implications of such a stance.

and students can engage in trusting environments. Yet, engagement, trust,
and safety have not been underscored as significant elements in the current
completion paradigms.

There is no doubt that American social and political systems have histories
that established whiteness as a norm, and there are sinister, individual players
operating at high levels as new white nationalists. The current paradigms of
data can accelerate and exacerbate inequities discussed in earlier chapters if
definitions are not challenged and feelings are not injected into the discourse.
The insertion of people over projects is the paradigm drama of our time.
However, higher education is being sucked into it in ways that may be detri-
mental for the overall cause of democracy and equality.

It is imperative, therefore, that those on the right-hand side of the nostalgia spectrum take care to nuance arguments about historic oppressions,

institutional racism, prejudice, and vision for the future if they are going to manifest changes to entire systems and outcomes for students and the nation. The battle against the new white nationalism's inertia is a battle of mindset. Those who believe in the power of higher education and the ability to transform America through it need to consider that the systems that have been constructed in colleges have been built upon for centuries. They must also recognize that those oppressions have operated on even the complacent and privileged. It is clear that the new white nationalist individuals operating in new ways understand that mindset is where the battle is.

Those who have anti-racist value systems and who are leaders of the institutions, making decisions about equity, must understand our role. The work of infusing emotion into the rational may indeed be the most important work of the completion agenda. For without it, the condition of American society will continue to move toward a rationalized version of measurement and rationalization only. And the risk is to further exacerbate the very inequities that spurred the completion agenda in the first place. In that same vein, the next chapter illustrates how well-meaning policy adjustments that are proposed and at times implemented by one sector of American society without considering the origins of scrutiny or oppression that caused the need for such policies can reinforce the same results over and again.

NOTES

1. John Kennedy, "Full Text of Moon Speech." *NASA Website*. Accessed August 23, 2019, https://er.jsc.nasa.gov/seh/ricetalk.htm. Retrieved June. 2, 2019.

2. Ibid.

3. Mitchell Michael, Michael Leachman, and Kathleen Masterson, "State Cuts Have Driven Up Tuition and Reduced Quality." *A Lost Decade in Higher Education Funding* (Washington, DC: Center on Budget and Policy Priorities, August 23, 2017).

4. Mitchell Michael, Michael Leachman, and Kathleen Masterson, "State Cuts Have Driven Up Tuition and Reduced Quality." *A Lost Decade in Higher Education Funding*, (Washington, DC: Center on Budget and Policy Priorities, August 23, 2017).

5. Moreover, a funding shortfall hits community colleges, those institutions of higher education that were built to enhance learning for marginalized groups, especially hard: Community colleges are generally without endowments, their annual budgets are constructed on shoestrings, and in a paradigm of accountability and efficiency, the "do more with less" slogan has become the norm. Yet, more and more the slogan is becoming known as do less with less.

6. Cathy O'Niel, *Weapons of Math Destruction* (New York: Penguin Books, 2017), 3–7.

7. Carol S. Dweck, "Mind-Sets and Equitable Education." *Principal Leadership* 10, no. 5 (2010): 26–29.

8. National Student Clearing House, "Six Year Outcomes." December 2018, http://www.ccdaily.com/2018/12/completion-rates-rise/.

9. Paul, Rozen and Edward Royzan, "Negativity Bias, Negativity Dominance, and Contagion." *Personality and Social Psychology Review* 5, no. 4 (2001): 296–320.

10. James Baldwin, "Sonny's Blues." In *The Oxford Book of American Short Stories*, edited by Joyce Carol Oates (New York: Oxford University Press, 2013), 485.

11. Craig Steven Wilder, *Ebony & Ivy: Race, Slavery, and the Troubled History of America's Universities* (New York: Bloomsbury Press, 2013).

12. Gene Wise, "'Paradigm Dramas' in American Studies: A Cultural and Institutional History of the Movement." In *Locating American Studies. The Evolution of a Discipline*, edited by Lucy Maddox (Baltimore: Johns Hopkins University Press, 1999), 165.

13. Integrated Postsecondary Education Data System, "IPEDS Glossary." Accessed November 12, 2019, https://surveys.nces.ed.gov/ipeds/VisGlossaryAll.aspx.

14. Complete College America, *Time Is the Enemy* (Washington, DC: Complet College America, 2012), 3.

15. Cathy O'Niel, *Weapons of Math Destruction* (New York: Penguin Books, 2017), 3–7.

16. Jamie Merisotis, *America Has Fallen Behind Globally* (Washington, DC: Lumina Foundation, February 18, 2019), https://www.luminafoundation.org/news-and-views/america-has-fallen-behind-in-the-global-education-race.

17. Audre Lorde, "Poerty Is Not a Luxury." In *Sister Outsider: Essays and Speeches*, (Berkley, CA: Crossing Press, 1984), 38–39.

18. John Swallow, "Why We Must Balance Emotion and Intellect." *Inside HigherEd.* July 10, 2018, https://www.insidehighered.com/views/2018/07/10/students-today-need-colleges-value-emotions-well-intellect-opinion.

19. Cathy O'Niel, *Weapons of Math Destruction* (New York: Penguin Books, 2017), 3–7.

Chapter 5

Contain the Minorities: Policies to Ensure a White Nation

In dark holding cells, children wrapped their shivering bodies in thermal Mylar blankets. Forcefully and indefinitely separated from their parents, they served as the Trump administration's symbols of deterrence against Mexican and Central American immigration. These children, these symbols of deterrence, ranged from infancy to seventeen years of age. Some were pregnant, all were fed literally scraps, all prohibited from bathing. Influenza contractions increased. Other diseases threatened as a result of the filth they were forced to sleep in.[1]

News reporting about these children revealed the Trump immigration policy to be simultaneously reminiscent of slave-holding practices where children were severed from their parents and internment camps that America held Japanese citizens in during World War II.

In 2019, 55 years after the Civil Rights Amendment was signed into law, 156 years after the Emancipation Proclamation, and 75 years after the last internment camp was abandoned, practices that were seemingly of a bygone era were brought to the fore under the guise of Making American Great Again. The phrase, invoking nostalgia for the past, was indeed one that had implications for the reality of the present: human rights were violated in policy enacted by the White House, supported by the congressional majority, and celebrated by a broad swath of the American public.

Six hundred miles away from the border, the first debate among candidates to become the democratic nominee to run against Donald Trump in the 2020 race for the United States president took place. Twenty-three democratic candidates took the stage over two different nights to debate their policy plans and visions for America. Under the bright lights in Detroit, Michigan, a city with its own racial past, the twenty-three democratic candidates bantered back and forth as they do. In the process, they underscored the importance of higher education in creating a socially just nation. It is easy to compartmentalize the discussions of higher education from those of immigration. However, doing so would set a discursive frame that would limit understanding of how these issues all intersect with one another.

Of debate was not immigration by itself, or higher education by itself. Rather, of debate was the very idea of what America could be. Of debate was the role of the new white nationalism versus anti-racism. Of debate was where the borders of the imagined nation of America would or should be drawn, and which people should be considered citizens of those nations.

On the second night of that democratic primary debate, many candidates discussed community college as playing a pivotal role in elevating the marginalized to a better life. Bernie Sanders touted free community college as a catalyst for transformation in the social stratification that pervades American society. His College for All Act would distribute $47 billion to eliminate college tuition and fees at public colleges. Senators Kamala Harris, Kristen Gillibrand, Tulsi Gabbard, and Tim Ryan all cosigned Sanders's bill. Mayor of South Bend, Indiana, Pete Buttigeig claimed: "Community college should be free only to those who cannot afford it, but government should not foot the bill for the children of the elite."[2] Joe Biden believed that by closing a tax loophole, community college could be free. Andrew Yang and Senators Elizabeth Warren and Corey Booker had their own plans that focused on reducing the cost of higher education for all.

In contrast, President Donald Trump proposed deep cuts to the Department of Education to follow on his $250 billion dollar recommended slashing of higher education funding in 2018. And at the very same moment that these politicians were debating, Alaskan governor Mike Dunleavy proposed to cut state funding for the University of Alaska system by $135 million or 41 percent. This put 1,300 faculty and staff jobs on the chopping block, not to mention a significant portion of the academic programs that comprised the higher education system in the state. This was a frontal assault on higher education that, according to the *Chronicle of Higher Education* was "unprecedented." Of the cuts, Dunleavy said, "The state . . . can no longer afford to continue down the path of oversized spending, outsized government, and out-of-line priorities."[3] And in this statement, Dunleavy revealed one of the dangers of the return-on-investment paradigm: In an era where efficiencies are touted—especially by many politicians—as equating to good educational practice, it is altogether unclear what the "priorities of the nation and state regarding higher education" are. For as assistant professor of higher education at University of North Carolina at Wilmington, Kevin McClure, noted, "it's easier to say we can't be all things to all people than to identify a vision and articulate what the purpose of higher education is going to be."[4] Remember, too, as state governments cut higher education under the guise of not being all things to all people, the overall effect is an increase in tuition, thereby making higher education even more inaccessible. Although Alaska represented one of the highest one-time cuts that a state-wide higher education system experienced, a series of states have had similar budget slashes in the preceding five years—Arizona, Florida, and Wisconsin among them.

The dichotomous polls of the nostalgia spectrum were thus clearly visible that week in July 2019. On the one hand, policies supporting free community college, which twenty-four states in the nation have offered in varying capacities, viewed higher education as a site with the potential to enact social justice in the country at large. On the other, return on investment language was used to justify cuts in funding that equated to making higher education inaccessible except for only the elite, a return to the raced and classed paradigm of the past. At the same time, debates about immigration amounted to whom civil rights were guaranteed under the Constitution. All the while, brown people were being held in what equated to cages at the Mexican-American border. At the most basic of levels, the commonality among these debates about education and immigration was that minority access to spaces was being discussed and decided upon by a privileged few. In this way, access for minorities would be made on terms determined by the privileged. Moreover, with slashes in state and federal funding for higher education being coupled with cages and walls being erected on the Mexican-American border, the spaces of debate—America and colleges—were underpinned by a struggle to define the borders, imagined and physical, of the nation.

Ultimately, those politicians touting free community college or different ways of supporting students through loan forgiveness clearly intended to enact a transformative policy to allow access to education. However, analysis of what is often considered to be the most radical of higher education policies in the second decade of the twenty-first century, free community college, may reinforce white privilege if it is not coupled with funding higher education institutions themselves. Indeed, policies like free community college and loan forgiveness are important and helpful. But they must be coupled with monies and support to shift the very institutions that have consistently practiced in the same capacity over the past centuries. Without funding higher education institutions in new ways, policies like free community college will not address the privilege and power that is at the center of higher education and the oppression necessitating such policies in the first place.

Despite where on the nostalgia spectrum politicians sit, there is a single and simple truth that underpins current approaches to educational funding in the political arena: The focus is on reducing tuition, load debt, or cutting institutional funding altogether. These foci, to put it simply, seem popular because they are easy-to-understand and clean in communication. But they do not sufficiently address the complexities of enhancing students' lives through education.

For instance, a free community college policy does not necessarily provide access to higher education for more people. Rather, it simply shuffles students around from four-year to two-year colleges. A study completed by Christopher Avery, Jessica Howell, Matea Pender, and Bruce Sacerdote notes:

> To have a positive effect on college attainment, a free community college policy would need to draw four new students who would otherwise not have enrolled in any postsecondary education for each student who would move from a four-year institution to a two-year institution . . . however, researchers found the number of students who went from no postsecondary enrollment to two-year colleges was about the same as those who went from four-year to two-year institutions . . . free community college programs wouldn't have a great effect on low-income students, who may already qualify to attend tuition-free with federal Pell Grants . . . a free community college policy would induce many students to change their choices of colleges, with 15% of students who would otherwise not enroll in any college and 6-7% of students who would enroll in four-year colleges switching to two-year colleges.[5]

The outcomes and graduation rates, and so the overall social transformation those politicians who support free college initiatives desire, will not necessarily be enhanced through free community college. Hence, the policy of free community college while well-intended, is misguided in the problem it is trying to solve.

The nostalgia spectrum as a tool that conceives of intent and aligns it against outcome is, therefore, helpful in examining the policy of free community college. Mike Krause, executive director of the Tennessee Higher Education Commission and Student Assistance Corporation, which administers the most highly enrolled of the free community college initiatives in the nation, notes that "low-income students might not know what Pell Grants are or how to receive them." He adds that free community college may not be the answer to increasing access to higher education that many politicians and stakeholders external to higher education believe it is.[6] Krause further argues that an intentional campaign to increase knowledge of Pell grants is necessary for access to higher education to manifest in the ways that well-meaning politicians desire. This, coupled with allocation of dollars to support community colleges' infrastructures of student support, would most definitely assist in increasing completion numbers and degree attainment for minorities and low-income whites on a national level. According to National Clearinghouse data, less than 50 percent of students who began their studies at college have completed their degrees. While many look at this number and see deficit, there is a way in which to look at that same number as opportunity. For it also suggests that the manner in which to increase completion rates is not only through free access to college. That less than 50 percent of students earn a college credential six years after initially enrolling provides a significant opportunity to reimagine the completion agenda itself and its relation to policies about new money being delivered to higher education.

Transformation can occur if there was recognition that the students already enrolled in college need support. To enhance outcomes for students requires both access and, just as importantly, better infrastructure at colleges to serve those already attending or who will attend. Providing more students with access to education through free community college without also funding for institutions to improve retention rates through scaled attempts at human interaction will produce the same graduation rates for higher education in total. Forcing more water through a leaky pipe does not fix the pipe. To fix the leaky pipe requires expert hands to have the best tools possible in plugging the holes. Moreover, a leaky pipe does not require more water to spit out more water—it merely needs some fixing. The metaphor is apt. Making community college free will not necessarily increase access to better lives through education on the scale and as efficiently as desired. Infusing community colleges with more funding will assist to hire full-time employees with whom students can connect at will. It really is that simple.

In a sound-bite era where mainstream news coverage includes covering Twitter feeds that are limited in their capacity to delve into the complex, the American public is often satisfied with the surface solution, considering it to be the best explanation for improvement. However, the surface solution of free community college does not address the actual problems of retention and completion in community college.

There is a single commonality between the politicians like Dunleavy cutting significant funds from higher education and those seeking to implement free access to community college: Both approaches allocate not enough dollars to higher education *institutions* to make the radical changes that politicians and stakeholders desire and are seeking. Likewise, tuition escalates, and the pilots of free community college have shown little increase in the access provided to populations who have been underserved. Although the intent of free community college proponents is diametrically opposed to the politicians who seek to significantly cut funds, they both suffer from a tendency to come up with solutions to problems without delving deeply into understanding what the problems actually are. In each case, the marginalized remain marginalized because the infrastructures to support student success are not built at the colleges that are trying to implement them. Rather, the infrastructures remain, as the previous chapters showed, based on paradigms of the exclusionary past that emphasized enrollment and not completion. Offering free community college or loan forgiveness, moreover, does not necessarily require a change in mindset of the white or privileged. For the spaces erected for whites and the privileged in these policies remain untouched. Hence, they do not necessarily lead to a transformative change linked to social justice and democracy. Rather, these solutions are characteristic of a privileged, albeit very well-intended, point of view that develops from and with the inertia of the new white nationalism.

THE NEW WHITE NATIONALISM AND FUNDING HIGHER EDUCATION INSTITUTIONS

Proof of the inertia of the new white nationalism and its relationship to reduced funding of public institutions is evident as a pervasive character-istic of the new white nationalism. Indeed, in "Partisanship, White Racial Resentment, and State Support for Higher Education," Barrett Taylor et al. illustrate that underpinning policy decisions and rhetoric regarding higher education funding is a clear connection to what I call the new white national-ism, and what they call white resentment.

> Drawing on the racial backlash hypothesis and quantitative analyses, we show that party control of state government and racial representation in higher edu-cation jointly explain state appropriations [toward higher education]. Unified Republican governments spent more than Democratic or divided governments when White students were overrepresented. Republicans spent less other-wise. These results suggest that partisan attitudes toward racial representation in higher education may shape state government support for colleges and universities.[7]

Herein is the importance of the nostalgia spectrum. On the one hand, are those who see a changing demographic in higher education and, seeing such shifts, work to defund higher education. They are the agents of the new white nationalism. On the other hand are those on the right side of the nostalgia spectrum touting free community college but not fully seeing the potential outcomes their arguments are making. In the middle are the voters, many of whom are complacent and may be persuaded to champion funding cuts as their knowledge about budget and the like is limited to what they hear from their representatives: "Some political actors might take positions on higher education in an effort to win electoral support by stirring negative partisanship and White resentment . . . . The consequences for higher educa-tion might be irrelevant when policy positions are intended to win votes."[8]

Moreover, there is an effect on voters who want to send their children to college. Whites, according to the Barret et al., are often happy to see the cuts to higher education that politicians make, but these reactions are not based on full understanding that those cuts may mean higher tuition for them. Finally, Barrett et al. show that cuts to higher education cannot be explained by economic models based on logic. After examining the variables, they conclude that whites with authority to make decisions often choose to reduce funding for institutions where students of color are being educated. Hence their actions are explained only by prejudice. Academics, the study claims, have a responsibility to underscore and highlight racism and power and privilege when it is being utilized. Ultimately, Barrett et al. show that the cutting of higher education funds in certain states is a result of active agents of the new white nationalism. Those agents must be resisted.

For truly substantive and transformative change to occur requires that there is pervasive revelation about where the problems facing higher education actually reside. And there must be commitment to subsequent disruption. Collectively, however, leaders in higher education and the stakeholders associated with it on the right-hand side of the nostalgia spectrum are not asking the right questions. The questions that need to be asked are simple ones, and yet they can easily be dismissed as some would find them to be uncomfortable:

What if the remnants of white power and privilege were confronted head-on in the discussions, policy decisions, and funding models that are currently impacting higher education?

What if American higher education was funded in a way that truly could transform the stratifications in American society for good?

But funding higher education in line with a transformative higher education system may require a redistribution of dollars that would disrupt the status quo. And this is where the rub is for politicians and mainstream America: Whenever there is an opportunity that would be offered to the marginalized, there is a sense of loss that catalyzes resistance and outrage from the privileged. Allocating dollars to educational spaces that are imagined to be for minorities is not an American tradition. In fact, in the past decade, we are seeing the opposite. From immigration to education, the new white nationalism allocates dollars to isolate minorities from the imagined (and in this case, physical) borders of the white nation. However, racialized spaces are part of an American tradition and the new white nationalism seeks to reinforce rather than diminish the borders between those spaces. If the example of immigration is not clear enough, another one regarding American prisons may be helpful:

Saving Futures, Saving Dollars notes the disparity between annual federal spending on students and inmates, and the findings are staggering; the United States spends $12,643 to educate one student for one year versus the annual cost of $28,323 to house one inmate. "If the nation made a comparable investment in effort and dollars in schools as it does in jails and prisons, the return would be decreased levels of criminal activity and incarceration as well as significant and life-changing impacts on the individual," the report notes . . . . Equity plays a large role in the connection between education level and crime rates; African Americans and Latinos are overrepresented in the criminal justice system. It is no coincidence, the report notes, that these same groups are disproportionately relegated to the nation's most troubled and low-performing schools.[9]

Clearly, funding goes toward structures and systems that relegate minorities to spaces away from whites. And as higher education threatens to become more integrated, the political arena, whether through cutting funding or focusing on individual tuition, is doing little to support higher education in a way that would disrupt this American dilemma.

Subsequently, the new white nationalism works in a way where even well-meaning politicians, shaded by their own privilege, misunderstand the problems confronting social justice and higher education. Their solutions feed the new white nationalism by not confronting the institutional racism underpinning the institutions themselves.

Claims such as these are often not received well by those who have yet to learn how white privilege operates. In *Possessive Investment in Whiteness*, Lipsitz argues that whiteness is a form of property that legally, financially, culturally, and socially benefits white people. He writes that "the artificial construction of whiteness almost always comes to possess white people themselves unless they develop antiracist identities, unless they disinvest and divest themselves of their investment in white supremacy."[10] Whiteness and class privilege offer tangible advantages to those who "own" it because the ideology characteristic of it tends to rigidly define minorities based on its own terms. White privilege underpins complacency toward the reality that the tenants of white nationalism have been tacitly reinforced through segregationist practices for centuries. In the twenty-first century, however, overt attempts at isolationism appear as something other than white nationalist in nature. Immigration policies that place children in cages at a national border, severe cuts to higher education funding which equate to significantly limiting access to college education, do very little to challenge the white, middle class, and elite. Those who are complacent and content with their lives can watch idly as such policies are developed and the new white nationalism subsequently gains momentum.

AMERICA'S SEMMELWEIS PROBLEM:
WHAT CAN BE DONE?

Small tweaks can have large-scale effects on the inertia of the new white nationalism. To demonstrate this, I want to digress shortly. In 1846, Hungarian doctor Ingaz Semmelweis set out to understand why five times as many women who gave birth in doctors' offices were dying than those who gave birth through midwives. Semmelweis studied the midwives' practices carefully and compared them to the practices of his own doctors. He noted, first, that midwives had their patients birth children on their sides. So he had his doctors do the same. The death rate did not change. He noted that when there was a death in his clinic, a priest would ring a bell, and theorized that this bell-ringing may startle the other patients so much that they would die. However, when the bell-ringing was ordered to stop, no change in death rates occurred. He then noted that his doctors would use the same instruments on the dead as the living, and when moving from patient to patient, did not wash their hands or instruments. In contrast, midwives did not perform autopsies on the dead and also spent time washing their hands and instruments prior to any procedure. As a result, he ordered his doctors to begin washing their hands and instruments with both soap and chlorine before and after every procedure. Lives were saved.

Seeing the effect this minor adjustment had on patients and their children, Semmelweis attempted to spread his discoveries throughout the European medical community. One would think such a small change would be welcome by the medical community and a subsequent death rate decrease would be witnessed. However, Semmelweis was demonized in the broader medical community when he shared his findings. His counterparts believed that underpinning his observations was an implicit blaming of doctors for infecting a broad swath of those who died. They also believed that such a message could not be true because doctors were the ones who healed. They did not create illness. Instead of looking at the results and implementing a small change, the medical community held fast to its current practice out of pride and a general unwillingness to change their thinking.[11]

Those privileged by race and class often suffer from a Semmelweisian syndrome, unwilling to consider that they play a role in the new white nationalism simply by not resisting it. Many of higher education's stakeholders, including politicians who hold the purse-strings, are those privileged by race and class and may suffer from a Semmelweisian syndrome. Moreover, it is possible that, higher education stakeholders are not seeing the power a small shift in thinking may have in literally changing lives. There is hope if this is the case.

As James Weldon Johnson's underscored over a century ago, mindset is the easiest and hardest of human capacities to change. Johnson's entire novel

Autobiography of an Ex-Colored Man rests on the premise that how we perceive the world makes it what it is. Of an overt racist who is honest about his prejudice, the main character thinks to himself:

> [The overt racist's] position does not render things so hopeless, for it indicates that the main difficulty of the race question does not lie so much in the actual condition of the blacks as it does in the mental attitude of the whites; and a mental attitude, especially one not based on truth, can be changed more easily than actual conditions.[12]

In Johnson's novel, the narrator explains how the world either remains static or changes based on the desire and ability to reimagine current conditions. Because the power dynamics continue to privilege whites in America, one way in which major structural change must occur is through the privileged's point of view. If the privileged can be convinced that their point of view is privileged, and they thus operate from a different point of view, radical change can occur. Johnson made this observation in 1912. Martin Luther King made the same observation in 1963 and throughout his prominence. Countless other thinkers from Frederick Douglass to Sherman Alexie explain the same. Their common theme: fundamentally, racism is a white problem that whites must be accountable for, and make changes in the mind, policy, practice, and narratives that establish power in the current days. The fact that systems of power and privilege have not shifted since these great thinkers spoke out loud and the movements they espoused took root is evidence of how powerful the inertia of complacency is.

Higher education's complex "problems" can be solved through a relatively simple approach, much as Semmelweis offered the medical community: Change the mindset about higher education so that institutions *and* students are funded at higher levels. And to fund institutions at higher levels may not require more money, but a reallocation of dollars to institutions that have generally been on the bottom of the priority list.[13] A reframing of how community colleges are situated in America and the zeitgeist based on what they can do, rather than what they cannot would allow a different discussion about what their value is, and a new thought regarding how to fund them.

More clearly, a reallocation of dollars at a small percentage from public, four-year colleges to community colleges would make a drastic difference in community colleges' success. Couple this reallocation with an intentional change in cultural imagination of the hierarchical spaces community colleges hold in the mainstream, and there could be a significant move toward accomplishing the completion agenda goals *and* more substantive social justice across the nation.

The imagined spaces of community colleges, nations, prisons, and more are clearly racialized. Even the most seemingly benign representations of how the world is imagined demonstrates that borders between and among spaces in our imaginations are racialized but can change.

The figure here, for instance, contrasts the manner in which the world is traditionally represented on maps and globes with what geographers and cartographers know to be a more realistic and true representation of what the world looks like. Africa, in the traditional representation hung in classrooms and offices throughout the world, appears much smaller than it should. In contrast, America appears much bigger than it should. Further, given that

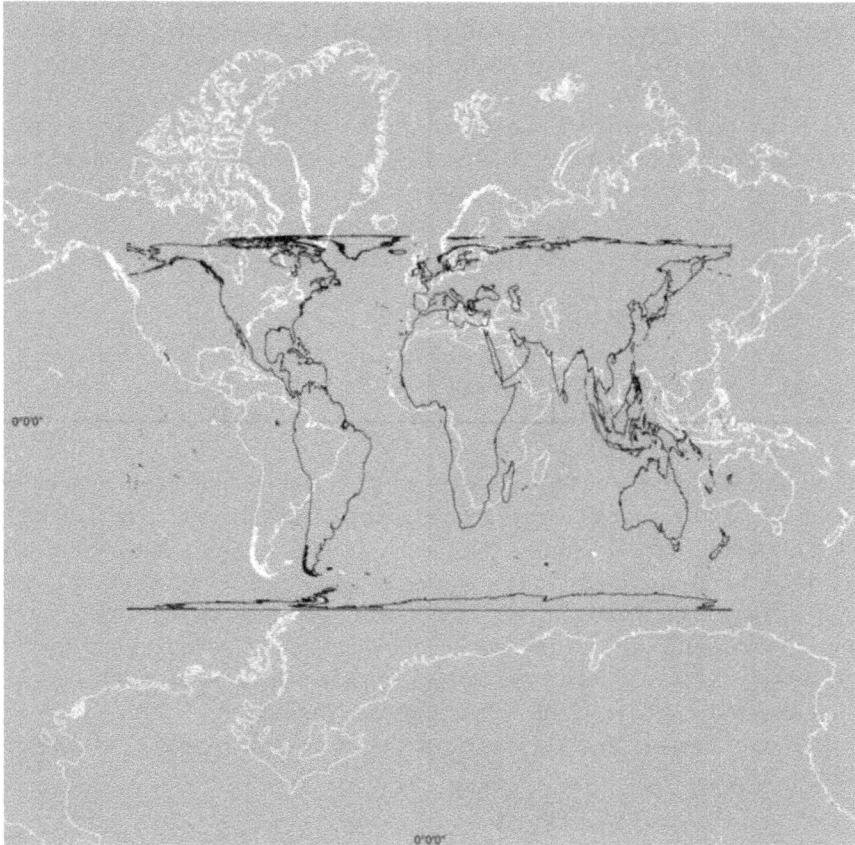

Figure 5.1 The distortions of maps stem from the imaginations of those who draw them. They are racialized, but then also become part of the general understanding of real-world geography (Nandi, 2017).

Earth is a sphere rotating through space, what appears on the top of a map and bottom is and was a completely arbitrary choice.

The nostalgia spectrum assists in articulating why the misrepresentations of geographical space and decisions about what appears as top and bottom, traditionally called North and South, exist. Simply, Europeans were the first cartographers. It is common for one to perceive themselves as the "normal" or dominant culture. It was for this reason that Aristotlean and Ptolemaic philosophies put the Earth at the center of the solar system. Similarly, European cartographers placed their own countries at the top of the pages on which they drew. The maps they drew, the first widely dispersed of the entire world, became the originals that were handed down generation to generation, with minor adjustments made over time. However, these same maps project dominance of European and American points of view and stem from a white supremacist outlook on the world. It is no coincidence that these maps were drawn at the same moment slavery and colonization were widespread; at the same moment whites proclaimed themselves civilized and black and brown bodies heathen. Even with the knowledge that these maps distort geographical reality and are associated with racist pasts, they remain in elementary schools as a result of complacency toward change. The manner in which policies from immigration to funding higher education based on racialized hierarchies of space and complacency in general is no different.

RECASTING THE NARRATIVES AND
BORDERS OF COMMUNITY COLLEGES

Making transparent how the imagined borders of different spaces across the globe and within social systems are racialized allows for potential disruption of the mindsets that adhere to the rigidity of how such borders are drawn. Michelle Singletary's article in the *Washington Post*, "Community College Should Be a First Choice, Not a Last Resort" underscores the possibility in and necessity of transgressing borders in social and cultural institutions like the news media in order to redraw the imagined borders of another social institution, in this case, higher education. She writes:

Repeat after me: My child is not a failure if he or she starts out at a community college.

And then I need you to stop saying, "Community college is like the 13th grade"—meaning a continuation of high school. This expression is derogatory and disparages students who attend a community college as a more affordable option than starting their college career at a four-year university.[14]

The article also goes through the many other reasons that community colleges should be the first choice for students, indicating that there are strengths to be built upon:

- Smaller classes
- Better bonds with advisors
- Great education

Here Singletary hones in on the elements that are fundamentally important in student success—connection and education. Singletary celebrates the characteristics of community colleges in today's higher education landscape, and ultimately argues, in a publication that is typically read by the very same families who often overlook community colleges, that community colleges should be a first choice for all, not just marginalized students. Singletary's article is in line with what may be a very simple yet radical solution to increase higher education's efficacy: reimagine the place of community college in the mainstream, imagined nation. And the way to do this is to change the minds of privileged citizens by illustrating the benefit of community colleges—and doing so by meeting the privileged where they are.

But policy and funding must operate symbiotically with a resituating of the role of community colleges in American higher education. An example of the hold the imagination has on race, space, and education was on display during the 2019 democratic presidential primary debate. Senator Kamala Harris criticized Vice President Joe Biden for his aversion to busing minority students to affluent schools when he was a senator in the 1960s. She argued in favor of this practice, referencing her own experience of traveling to Thousand Oaks Elementary School in Northern Berkeley from her home. Professor of History at Dartmouth University, Matthew Delmont, writes eloquently of this exchange and contextualizes the debate between Harris and Biden as resulting from a difference in generations and their experiences of integrating schools. Immediately following the debate itself, uninformed, national controversy ensued for a week. What was missing from the mediated debate was why busing was necessary in the first place. Berkley's approach to busing,Delmont explains, is and was so successful where other cities' busing initiatives were not because of how it was implemented:

Unlike many cities that placed the burden of busing on black students, Berkeley implemented a two-way busing plan that involved black, white, Asian American, and Mexican American students. The plan quickly changed the racial demographics of the city's schools. Thousand Oaks Elementary was 95 percent white and 3 percent black in 1963. When Harris started kindergarten in 1969, Thousand Oaks was 53 percent white and 40 percent black, and in no elementary school in Berkeley did any racial group comprise more than 60 percent of the students.[15]

Despite that busing as a topic is rife with the potential to discuss a matrix of issues that were and still are at the forefront of national political debate—race, poverty, education—the mediated coverage of the controversy between Biden and Harris limited itself to whether or not Biden's views as a young senator were prejudiced in nature. Near the end of that week, after the flurry of accusations, national media concluded that Harris and Biden's views on busing were similar in supporting voluntary transportation of students to public schools they were not zoned for. However, the discourse failed to explain the racism underpinning the economic, social, political, and educational structures that require busing as an intervention in the first place.

In short, desegregation is often touted as an excellent idea so long as the privileged are not too bothered by the mechanisms to make it happen. And even then, it has not always been well received. Rather, whites have been traditionally resistant to minorities entering what they consider their spaces. As an example:

> White parents in New York City organized in the late 1950s to oppose plans to bus black and Puerto Rican students from overcrowded schools to white schools with open seats. The parents used euphemisms such as busing and neighborhood schools to maintain segregated schools without explicitly saying they did not want their children to go to school with black or Latinx students.[16]

Hence, resistance to busing did take on white supremacist ideals in the 1950s. As late as 2019, busing of African American students to schools with demographics overly white were met with significant and resistance in Howard County, Maryland, a site generally considered to be quite liberal.

Still, underpinning the notion of busing students from one school zone to another for integration purposes is an assumption that systems can seek diversity, so long as minority children go back to their neighborhoods in which they live once the dismissal bell rings. Hence, with regard to space, borders, race, and education, there is an implicit yet uniform acceptance that the better schools are found in neighborhoods where more elite families live; that minority students must be the ones with their lives disrupted through busing for the benefit of desegregation; and that poorly-funded schools should remain poorly-funded. Busing, like funding individuals and not institutions for higher education, developed as a product of white nationalist practices of social segregation and white superiority. That condition of American reality was simply reinforced in August 2019 as immigration and education were being discussed at a national level. However, never is or was there discussion about potentially disrupting whites' lives and spaces for the purposes of diversity and social justice. More specifically, there was little movement to cease the imprisonment of Latinx children at the border; funding public, open-access institutions in new ways; nor the flipping of policies such as busing on their head to make white students go to schools with minority student populations while funding *those* schools at higher levels. In any and all of these cases, space, education, funding, and social stratification were revealed as part of a matrix resulting in social segregation of races that supports the new white nationalism. Injecting the discourse and policies that with notions of inverting the assumptions that whites be disrupted never occurred, but it could have been the first step toward a true anti-racist discussion and mindset shift. Instead, the debates, proposed policies, and narratives themselves mainly fell into traditional and predictable discourses that would do very little to disrupt for the greater good of anti-racism.

The new white nationalism is baked into the systems of our time so well—from politics to funding to how mainstream media discusses politics, culture, and society—that segregation, both current and in the resulting future is often met with a shrug of the shoulders and claims that it is a product of our system. That shrug of the shoulders is the equivalent of white complacency that does the work of the new white nationalism.

WHAT IS THE ACCOUNTABILITY ERA
HOLDING US ACCOUNTABLE FOR?

There is a self-fulfilling nature to the notions of funding community colleges at the same or lesser levels as before; not addressing the racism in such funding decisions; and, in general, the acceptance that higher education's woes result from higher education's decisions that it makes for itself.

That is, it is clear that the causes for tuition escalation and what are considered to be lackluster data points regarding higher education's effectiveness stem from a matrix of social systems. However, it is not clear if the constant questioning of higher education's value and the metrics leading to new national policy proposals about higher education stem from a legitimate or manufactured concern. For instance, a national Gallup poll in 2019 revealed the public confidence in higher education had been reduced more "any other U.S. institution that Gallup measures."[17] Between 2015 and 2019, articles in the *Washington Post*, *U.S.A. Today*, *The Atlantic*, *Post*, *InsideHigherEd*, and numerous books and televised news stories have characterized the cost of tuition, coupled with graduation rates, as a crisis. It is fitting to ask, however, whether or not there is indeed a crisis in higher education, or if the crisis has been manufactured through the discourse characterized by racial privilege.

Higher education is indeed facing a multitude of issues that, at the aggregate, amount to what could be called a crisis. However, I suggest this crisis is one of political and cultural imagination, not one reflective of higher education institutions' deficits. The imaginative deficit originates from the limitations the new white nationalism has placed around the imaginations of political authorities. A new paradigm of higher education reform should originate by challenging the very foundational assumptions regarding race, space, and funding that underpin higher education in general.

Currently, the questions driving national higher education reform movements are:

- How can higher education complete more students equitably?
- How can higher education be more affordable?
- Why is higher education so costly for individuals and state and federal governments?

These are the wrong questions. A grander approach to higher education reform could be achieved by beginning with more aspirational questions that may spur significant innovation and disruption. Examples of these kinds of questions would be:

- Are the current funding models for higher education aligned with the completion goals set for it?
- What assumptions underpin the current paradigm of accountability?
- Why is there a heavy distinction between the prestige of elite and open access institutions and how does funding for those institutions exacerbate that distinction?
- What if the higher education system could deliver on the American promise?
- What does a higher education system capable of delivering on the American promise of democracy look like?

There was a moment in American history where big questions that drew straight lines between higher education and greater American ideals of social justice were asked. One of the most revolutionary, politically driven, and innovation-sparking, actions taken regarding higher education in America was President Truman's Commission on Higher Education. The commission's charge was simple: On July 13, 1946, President Truman charged the members of the commission "with the task of examining the functions of higher education in our democracy and the means by which they can best be performed."[18] Understanding the significance of asking the proper questions to find transformative solutions, the commission predicated its findings on the notion that the system of higher education is not static, but dynamic. It argued that the system of higher education writ large may have to change significantly to meet national, democratic goals. In fact, one of the commission's primary findings was that "if the higher education system continued the funding status quo, the Commission members understood that [the charge of the Commission and its] aim was probably not achievable."[19] The commission culminated in a six-volume report with a recommendation that the community college system, which already existed, be expanded upon, and that the federal government support that expansion by funding both students and *institutions*. Within a decade of the commission report, what had been a very few community colleges in the nation proliferated to over 1,000, offering low-cost, college access to a variety of identities who were up until that point, marginalized from higher education.

The Truman Commission was, in no uncertain terms, transformative. It challenged the very structure of higher education. And it recognized the importance of funding models that were different from the norm. It is time to build off that good start, which was initiated nearly *eighty* years ago.

Now, in 2021, the nation requires a paradigm shift. For truly transformative work to be done with regard to completion as well as the ongoing project of equality and democracy, new ways of thinking need to be adopted. And the thinking has to include but extend beyond cutting funding for higher education, reducing individual debt, and providing full tuition for individuals. One of the most effective places to start in such transformation is to examine the past decade of reform and some of the thinking that has underpinned it.

In the past two decades, manifold researchers and national collegiate organizations have revealed simple practices that lead to student success. From Byron McKlenny to Vincent Tinto, from Achieving the Dream to American Association of Colleges Universities, from the American Association of Community Colleges to the Community College Research Center, there is a singular tactic identified as resulting in better outcomes for students: The human connection between students and employees is of paramount importance to completion. David Putnam's book *Our Kids: The American Dream in Crisis*, shows the same. In it, he illustrates that the single, most telling factor of a student's ability to succeed in higher education is not whether a curriculum leads to a job or whether student support services are faster-paced or technology-driven. Nor is it whether or not college is free. Rather, the most telling success factor for all students is that each student has one person, a single person, on a college campus with whom they connect and can check in with for advice. Putnam, in line with the great thinkers in higher education, argues that the community college system is the single site that has the ability to transform the national social stratification that is making the American dream more and more impossible. He writes:

Despite their mixed record, community colleges have real promise as a means of narrowing the opportunity gap by providing poor kids with a realistic path upward. To serve that role, they need more funding, improved student support services, better connections to local job markets and to four-year institutions, and a lower dropout rate. The best community colleges in the country, such as Miami Dade College, have taken up this challenge with gusto. As two experts on community colleges, Arthur Cohen and Florence Brawer, conclude "The community colleges" potential is greater than that of any other institution because their concern is with the people most in need of assistance. . . . . If the community colleges succeed in moving even a slightly greater proportion of their clients toward what the dominant society regards as achievement, it is as though they changed the world.[20]

Community colleges can change the world, Putnam writes. And the manner in which they will do so is through focused attention on students. But the funding necessary to make this connection real for all students is simply not there for many community colleges in the current educational paradigm.

The funding for community colleges as well as the resources devoted to human connections in the past decade of the completion agenda are few.[21] In short, the completion agenda and the policies and narratives about funding for higher education have yet to deal with the proverbial elephant in the room: The bulk of higher education employees who interact with students on a day-to-day basis, the faculty, are transient, do not have offices in which to meet students, and are paid at salaries that require them to be pulled away from teaching on one campus in order to teach at another or work at a full-time job elsewhere. That is, nearly 50 percent of all courses are being taught by adjuncts at community colleges. When half of the workforce interacting with students every day is transient, potentially without a job semester-to-semester, and without time and space to interact deeply with students, the level of engagement that leads to student success is simply limited. Such a workforce would be perceived as unacceptable in K–12 where the majority of the teachers are full time. And yet, the funding models that support higher education remain the same, or worse yet, continue to be cut. If there were to be a national movement in which stakeholders really engaged with the goal of increasing student achievement, the focus would be on how to fund community colleges in a way that made the student experience, not just the tuition, better. The reliance on part-time professors paid at a pittance contradicts the goals of student success. And yet the only way to increase the number of full-time faculty and staff for that matter is through increased funding. Higher education policy must be supported with institutional support.

The reliance on part-time instructors bares out in student responses to their experience at college. Students' perceptions of engagement with community college employees are in deficit in the following areas:

- Discussing grades or assignments with an instructor,
- Talking about career plans with an instructor or advisor,
- Discussing ideas from readings or classes with instructors outside of class,
- Working with instructors on activities other than coursework.

To be clear, the issue is not that the professionals in the classroom are adjuncts. The issue is that the funding models for community colleges perpetuate a system where there is unpredictability in these teachers' lives with regard to the courses they will teach and also lack of resources in terms of pay and simple necessities for meeting space and teaching materials. These real issues affect student success and the potential performance of institutions themselves with regard to student engagement.

According to the New Century Foundation's *Restoring the American Dream*, it is clear that community colleges can do more with less expenditures than their counterpart four-year institutions. Community colleges spend a third of what their public four-year counterparts do per pupil. And still, national averages show that community colleges garner one-third of the dollars four-year public colleges garner per pupil.[22] Of course, it makes sense that if an institution requires less money per student to complete its mission, it should receive less. However, it is difficult to marry initiatives at national and state levels demanding higher graduation numbers and rates with static funding models. Moreover, in states like Maryland, where 46 percent of the higher education population attends community colleges, funding those institutions at 25 percent of their counterpart four-year public schools seems counterintuitive to state and federal goals.[23] If the goals of the completion agenda are to complete more students, and nearly half of college-going students attend community colleges, the paradigm of funding must be challenged. Maintaining funding models for community colleges and four-year colleges in the same way as decades previous denies that the paradigm has shifted from enrollment-based to completion-based signifiers of quality. Likewise, it utilizes a funding model predicated on white power and privilege demonstrated in chapters 2 and 3, and so delivers that institutional racism upon which the higher education systems at large has been built.[24]

It thus is time for the nation to take the next step in the student success movement by examining what worked in the first decade of the completion agenda, and where there is room for improvement. While the first decade of the completion agenda has manifest in good results with regard to credentials, it has also yielded some interesting and important discoveries. The main one being that while structure and focus on administrative matters in individual colleges is important, the classroom and interaction with students is more important. To manifest quality experiences for students requires a recasting of priorities in the completion agenda and advocacy at the state and federal levels regarding policy and funding so that human connection can be the norm in community colleges.

While community colleges were asked to make drastic changes, the same entities calling for change—federal and state governments—have not creatively looked at their role in how to increase those institutions' effectiveness. In fact, nonsensical data requirements were increased, mandates passed down, and funding overall was decreased. Moreover, while the projects that are being implemented in community colleges throughout the nation have worked to make the entry experience streamlined for students, it has not challenged state and federal agencies to make that same process easier for families. Application, financial aid, and registration experiences are confusing and arduous, generally because there is a need to ensure data is captured for the federal and state governments' reports. These data will theoretically be utilized to oversee the efficacy of financial aid monies' distribution. But the data captured in the reports are not utilized in any recognizable capacity except to ensure compliance—not effectiveness. According to Wesley Whistle, former education policy advisor:

> Institutions are both burdened by a complex data submission process and students and families receive incomplete information as consumers. It would be one thing if data collection was burdensome for institutions and the federal government delivered highly useful and valuable information in return to all stakeholders. Or if the data collection process required little effort that produced little actionable data. But right now, we are living in the worst of both worlds—meaning that the data collection process we have is both overly-complicated and delivers subpar data in return.[25]

For all the talk of value and the accountability, return on investment and needs to enhance outcomes, there is, in short, neither at the national or state level. Moreover, the processes that institutions must set up in order to collect and then deliver the un- or mis-used data become the very obstacles that colleges are spending time and money finding innovative ways to navigate students around quickly. And in the whirlwind developed the most central component to ensuring student success—the interaction with the student—is lost. Herein is a self-fulfilling prophecy in this paradigm of big data and accountably that serves only as a barrier to students: More requirements to prove effectiveness and value have led to more accountability requirements, which have led to more data requirements, which lead to more obstacles, which lead to innovation going to negotiating those obstacles required for reporting the data. In the meantime, the student-to-employee relationship is overlooked in the innovation.

Just as O'Neil warns in *Weapons of Mass Destruction*, the questions being asked and the data that is pulled continue to marginalize because they are not addressing the actual problems confronting higher education. The ultimate result is the reification of racialized spaces that serve the new white nationalism.

The next chapter showsthat the very conditions of power and privilege characteristic of higher education and society at large remain unchallenged.

NOTES

1. Lizzie O'Leary, "'Children Were Dirty, They Were Scared, and They Were Hungry.'" *The Atlantic*. June 19, 2019.

2. Democratic National Debate. June 27, 2019.

3. Katherine Mangan, "'Unprecedented in Our History': One State Is on the Verge of Slashing Higher-Ed Funding, Leaving Public Colleges in a Panic." *Chronicle of Higher Education*. July 1, 2019.

4. Lindsay Ellis, "This 5-Word Phrase Has Become a Mantra for Slashing College Budgets." *The Chronicle of Higher Education*. July 3, 2019.

5. Christopher Avery et al., *Policies and Payoffs to Addressing America's College Graduation Deficit* (Washington, DC: Brookings Institution). Accessed October 23, 2019, https://www.brookings.edu/wp-content/uploads/2019/09/Avery-e t-al_conference-draft.pdf.

6. Madeline St. Amour, "Study Minimizes Impact of Free Community College." *Inside HigherEd*. September 9, 2019.

7. Barrett J. Taylor, Brendan Cantwell, Kimberly Watts, and Olivia Wood, "Partisanship, White Racial Resentment, and State Support for Higher Education." *Journal of Higher Education* 91, no. 1 (2020), 858–887.

8. Ibid.

9. "Crime Rates Linked to Educational Attainment, 2013 Alliance Report Finds." *Alliance for Education*. September 12, 2013, https://all4ed.org/press/crime-rates-lin ked-to-educational-attainment-new-alliance-report-finds/.

10. George Lipsitz, *Possessive Investment in Whiteness* (Philadelphia: Temple University Press, 2006).

11. NPR. "The Doctor Who Championed Hand-Washing and Briefly Saved Lives." *Morning Edition*. December 12, 2015, https://www.npr.org/sections/health -shots/2015/01/12/375663920/the-doctor-who-championed-hand-washing-and-saved -women-s-lives.

12. James Weldon Johnson, *Autobiography of an Ex-Colored Man* (New York: Sherman French & Co., 1912).

13. In *College Completion Glass: Half Full or Half Empty*, Tiffany Beth Mfume argues that the data on completion is not as dire as often presented. She argues that higher education is the singular most transformative experience any individual can have, and that even if a student does not complete, their lives are often changed through what they do get.

14. Michelle Singletary, "Community College Should Be a First Choice, Not a Last Resort." *Washington Post.* July 16, 2019.

15. Matthew Delmont, "There's a Generational Shift in the Debate Over Busing." *The Atlantic.* July 1, 2019.

16. Ibid.

17. Stephanie Marken, "A Crisis in Confidence in Higher Ed." *Gallup.* April 12, 2019.

18. "Higher Education for American Democracy a Report of the Presidents Commission On Higher Education Vol I–Vi." *American Congress.* Accessed September 23, 2019, https://archive.org/stream/in.ernet.dli.2015.89917/2015.89917 .Higher-Education-For-American-Democracy-A-Report-Of-The-Presidents-Commis sion-On-Higher-Education-Vol-I---Vi_djvu.txt.

19. Clairn Gilber and Donald Heller, "The Truman Commission and its Impact on Federal Higher Education Policy from 1947 to 2010." Accessed November 3, 2019, https://ed.psu.edu/cshe/working-papers/wp-9.

20. David Putnam, *Our Kids: The American Dream in Crisis* (New York: Simon and Schuster, 2015).

21. There has been significant resistance to the completion agenda based on manufactured fears that the quality of an education will be reduced as a result of a focus on ensuring students earn a credential. Such concerns are manufactured because the professional faculty who are in charge of the courses being taught are the ones entrusted with evaluating students and learning accordingly.

22. The Century Foundation, *Restoring the American Dream* (Washington, DC: The Century Foundation, April, 2019).

23. Richard Kahlenber, "How Higher Education Funding Shortchanges Community Colleges." *The Century Foundation.* Accessed November 3, 2019, HYPERLINK "https://tcf.org/content/report/how-higher-education-funding-shortchanges-commun ity-colleges/?agreed=1" https://tcf.org/content/report/how-higher-education-funding-shortchanges-community-colleges/?agreed=1.

24. In those areas that have moved to performance-based funding models, where completions are dictating state and county funding, the higher education institutions that have historically suffered because their student demographics include more students who must work full-time or live paycheck to paycheck continue to suffer. In either case, basing community college funding models of a past that was predicated on enrollment and also exclusionary in nature is problematic. The funding models of the past do not align with the values and benchmarks of success in other ways that are worth mentioning, even if not associated with the new white nationalism. For instance, there is innovative work being done in reducing developmental education requirements for students. This strategy alone is excellent for students, but bad for community college revenue and enrollment, and so the state funding that is

often associated with both. For instance, in 2000, it was typical for community colleges to have three developmental education disciplines: reading, writing, and math. In each of these disciplines, it would be typical for there to be up to three courses leading to credit level. As such, a student may have to take twenty-seven credits in developmental education, which could amount to approximately $3,000 of tuition at a community college prior to reaching credit-level. Reimbursement from the county and state would make this a $9,000 revenue proposition for the institutions. With the national reform of developmental education, however, the number of developmental education courses that students are typically required to take is one in each discipline, reducing the overall enrollment to nine credits and revenue in tuition to $1,000 and $3,000 with county and state contributions included. As higher education does what is better for students, its bottom line suffers, meaning less money to hire employees to interact with students. And in states where an enrollment-based funding model maintains, institutions that show progress in completion are actually punished fiscally. As higher education moves in innovative, paradigm-shifting places, federal and state governments funding higher education remain in arcane and static models that are literally punishing the innovation.

25. Wesley Whistle, "How Higher Education Data Reporting Is Both Burdensome and Inadequate." *Third Way*. November 1, 2019, https://www.thirdway.org/report/how-higher-education-data-reporting-is-both-burdensome-and-inadequate.

Chapter 6

Trust in the Age of Compliance

This is a story about civil rights violations, politicians' lies, the media that projects those lies, and the general deterioration of public trust institutions that results. It is a story that shows higher education's ability to address equity and social justice is hamstrung by compliance efforts, many of which are mandated to ensure public trust in education.

THE UNRAVELING OF TRUST IN POLITICS
IN THE LATE TWENTIETH CENTURY

In late 1978, Bill and Hillary Clinton and their friends, Jim and Susan McDougal, purchased 230 acres of undeveloped, tree-filled land on the Lake of the Ozarks. The foursome, power brokers in Arkansas politics and legal circles, intended to divide the land into four plots and build and sell a vacation home on each. They named the land and incorporated their partnership under the name Whitewater Development Corporation.

Once the plots of land were ready for sale, the interest rate on borrowing to purchase property had escalated to 20 percent, beyond what potential vacation home purchasers were willing to pay. The land remained, as a result, undeveloped.

The foursome, however, continued to rise in the Arkansas power structure. A year after purchasing the Whitewater land, Bill Clinton ascended from state attorney general to governor of Arkansas. The Clintons and McDougals remained friends and gained in political power, relying on each other for information and favors in their professional worlds. Ultimately, the Whitewater land was a net loss for both the Clintons and McDougals. But the McDougals suffered significantly more financial injury than the

Clintons. The discrepancy in net losses between the two families despite similar investment cultivated questions about the nature of the McDougal and Clinton relationship. Investigations into the irregularity of the business deal also led to unproven allegations that Bill Clinton pressured David Hale (a former banker and judge ultimately found guilty of bank fraud) to approve an illegal $300,000 loan to Susan McDougal in purchasing the Whitewater land. Although Hale did not originally implicate Clinton in his detailed testimony, when questioned by federal authorities, he did so. Many of Clinton's political adversaries saw Hale's testimony as indicative of a quid pro quo relationship between the Clintons and McDougals. Fourteen years after purchasing the land, and while still governor of Arkansas, Bill Clinton announced his candidacy to be the forty-second president of the United States.

Running against a popular and first-term president, George H.W. Bush, Clinton at first seemed to lack any chance of winning at all. However, at the beginning of 1992, the economy began to sour sharply, and Bush made a series of unforced, political errors. On March 8, 1992, the *New York Times* published an exposé on Clinton's Watergate venture. The exposé, written by Jeff Gerth, outlined what claimed to illustrate an elaborate financial and political fraud carried out by the Clintons during their tenure in Arkansas politics.

Although the race for presidency took place under the cloud of a Watergate scandal, Clinton ultimately won the White House. Once Clinton became president, the Watergate scandal permeated the political and legal spheres of Washington, DC. The Republican-dominated Congress established a series of committees to investigate any potential wrongdoing that the Clintons may have engaged while in Arkansas. In order to quell any concerns, Clinton established an Independent Council to review his involvement in the Whitewater scandal. The Independent Council, led by staunch Republican Ken Starr, extended its investigation into a variety of tangential events involving both Clintons. Starr's report culminated in the drafting of two articles of impeachment, stemming from President Clinton lying under oath about a sexual encounter in which he engaged with an intern at the White House. There was no mention of the Whitewater scandal in the articles of impeachment. And Gerth, who wrote the original article on Whitewater, was ultimately found to have lacked credibility and valid sources in a number of stories with national reach, the Whitewater scandal included.[1] On December 19, 1998, the House of Representatives voted to impeach President Clinton and he was later acquitted in the Senate. In the end, the Watergate scandal illustrated the power of media to push Congress into action, and how that action may align more with a partisan divide than national ideals of democracy, equality, or justice.

In that same year, the nation was just beginning the machinations to elect the42nd president of the United States.[2] As the nation went to the polls on November 7, 2000, electoral and popular votes poured in and it was clear that Vice President Al Gore would win the *national* vote. At 8 p.m. eastern time, the major television networks projected Florida, which was the pivotal state in the *electoral* vote count, to be Gore's. By 10 p.m., the networks retracted their projection. However, a few hours later, Florida was called to be Bush's. Gore then conceded to Bush. Again, however, more votes poured in, mainly in favor of Gore, and the state was too close to call. As a result, Gore retracted his concession.

That twelve-hour period marked another national example where politics and media intersected in setting a false narrative for leadership of the country.

Americans woke up the next morning, still uncertain of who the next president would be. It would be another full month until Florida, which held the deciding electoral votes, would sway toward George W. Bush. That single month and the decisions within it were among the first of the new century that can be directly linked to a significant destabilization and erosion of civilian faith in American media, political, legal, and judicial systems.

This destabilization has everything to do with the new white nationalism: The battle for Florida's electoral votes comprised of a contest to include or exclude votes cast by American citizens. Images of election officials holding up ballots with hanging chads to gymnasium panel lighting yet endure. And in those images are concrete examples of the political, legal, and media complexes converging on Florida citizens' ballots wherein voting was transformed, not for the first time, from a constitutional right into a grab for political power. Days past. Then a full week. Ire increased.

And then Katherine Harris, Florida's secretary of state, certified the recount vote based on a state-mandated deadline. This certification occurred despite that not all Floridian votes were yet counted. Of concern for many Americans and the Gore team was that Palm Beach, Broward, and Miami-Dade counties had not yet finalized their vote counts when Harris certified the state's electorate. Importantly, all three of these counties comprised of high percentages of black and brown citizens, a majority of them leaning democratic. Miami-Dade County was a majority Hispanic and African American, with only an 11 percent white population. Broward County was 42 percent Hispanic and African American. Palm Beach was overwhelmingly white, but heavily democratic.[3] When the Gore team sought legal intervention to ensure that these three counties' ballots be fully counted, the Supreme Court found 5–4 that Florida's electorate was legally sealed when Harris declared it so. One has to wonder if the Supreme Court's findings would have been the same if the counties where votes had not yet been fully counted were those the likes of Silver Springs or Chevy Chases in America—where the white and powerful live.

Studies since then show that the certified vote count of Florida may not have reflected the actual will of citizens. And certainly, the election of Bush did not reflect the popular vote. Underpinning the process of closing the 2000 presidential vote, then, was a political and judicial finding that many felt took away from minority American citizens' ability to elect a president. A national Gallup poll in December 2000 revealed that:

> Over a third of black Americans say they are "angry" and "bitter" about the election—the most of any subgroup to express those feelings—while two-thirds say that they feel "cheated" by the election outcome, that black voters were less likely to be counted fairly than white votes and that the vote count in Florida entailed fraud, not just errors.[4]

The nostalgia spectrum illustrates that the 2000 election was not an anomaly, however. The 2000 election marked only a new strategy used to repress black and brown votes. That strategy included invocation of the Supreme Court to conclude that not all votes need to be counted in order to seal a state's electoral votes—a strategy that seemed to run counter to the fourteenth and fifteenth amendments. Highlights on that list of restricting minority voting rights prior to the 2000 election are:

• Prohibiting African Americans and women from voting at all;
• Counting slaves as three-fifths a man in calculating state populations for sake of allocating the number of congressional representatives in the late 1700s;
• Poll taxes; and
• Poll tests.

It is hardly a coincidence, moreover, that the candidate who won the 2000 election was one who, in no uncertain terms, adopted the Southern Strategy to garner votes from his base. Only one year earlier, Bush supporters aligned against Senator John McCain by sending flyers out to South Carolina voters claiming that "McCain's adopted daughter from Bangladesh was really 'a Negro child' he fathered out of wedlock. The end result? Record high turnout, an 11-point Bush primary victory, and the stifling of McCain's momentum that effectively ended his chances at securing the nomination."[5]

In the Clinton impeachment and Bush election, the matrix of media, politics, power, and the legal system caused destabilizations of trust and they seemingly muted the voices of the voiceless. This destabilization of trust and work to silence minority voices became even more extreme by the time the 2016 election for the U.S. president came along.

THE NEW WHITE NATIONALISM OF THE TWENTY-FIRST-CENTURY ELECTORATE AND CONGRESS

After inserting himself into the 2012 presidential campaign through birtherism already discussed, Donald Trump launched his own presidential campaign to become the forty-fifth president of the United States in 2016. That campaign was characterized by extravagant manipulations of the voting public through injections of wild mistruths. Early in the Republican primary, Trump outlandishly claimed that opponent Ted Cruz's father assassinated John F. Kennedy. Later, after winning the nomination, presidential candidate Donald Trump publicly solicited Russian assistance in muddying the name of his political opponent, Hillary Clinton. Gazing into a live camera he said, "Russia, if you're listening, I hope you're able to find the 30,000 emails that are missing." Trump then went on to win the American presidency, just as Bush had, while losing the popular vote. In the 2000s, two of the three presidents to have sat behind the Resolute Desk in the Oval Office were not elected by a majority of the American voting public. Both of these presidents benefited from interventions outside the typical voting process to gain their seats.

As a result of Trump's many questionable decisions as candidate and president, the FBI launched an investigation into him and his inner circle to explore any ties he had with Russia. Like Clinton, Trump initiated a Special Council. However, that Special Council officially reported to the Department of Justice, headed by Attorney General Jeff Sessions, who supported the Trump campaign for president. When Sessions recused himself from oversight of the Special Council as a result of potential conflicts of interest, Trump said: "Sessions should have never recused himself, and if he was going to recuse himself, he should have told me before he took the job and I would have picked somebody else."[6] Trump ultimately demanded that Sessions resign. Sessions' public resignation stated to President Trump, "at your request, I am submitting my resignation."[7] Trump then replaced Sessions with William Barr, who had previously defended Trump's firing of then FBI director, James Comey. This firing was the precipitating event leading to official investigations into Trump's ties with Russia. Over a year passed as the Special Council investigated Trump's campaign and its ties to Russia. Throughout the process of the investigation, twenty-one people associated with Trump's campaign were indicted for working with Russian operatives to manipulate the election of 2016. As the Special Council was nearing its end, Trump met with Rod Rosenstein, assistant attorney general to Barr. Rosenstein said to an anxious Trump, "I give the investigation credibility . . . . I can land the plane." Much of the public, already weary of the potential for the Special Council's report to be given a fair and serious reading by the legal and political spheres of the day, saw this comment as evidence of a conspiracy happening in broad daylight. That feeling was solidified in spring of 2019 when the Special Council submitted its report to Barr, along with an executive summary. Within two days of receiving the report, Barr released his own executive summary. In it, Barr wrote, "I have concluded that the evidence developed during the Special Counsel's investigation is not sufficient to establish that the President committed an obstruction-of-justice offense."[8] However, when the Special Council's report was released days later, it became painfully clear that the Special Council's writing was not in alignment with what Barr claimed in his summary. The report stated:

> [T]he investigation established that the Russian government perceived it would benefit from a Trump presidency and worked to secure that outcome, and . . . the Campaign expected it would benefit electorally from information stolen and released through Russian efforts . . . a statement that the investigation did not establish particular facts [of outright collusion] does not mean there was no evidence of those facts.[9]

It was clear that Trump's attorney general's office worked to obfuscate the truth in order to ensure the Trump administration, already having been shown to be the epitome of the new white nationalism, would remain in power. The general shoulder shrug of Congress was telling of the power and the inertia of the new white nationalism: Not only does it slowly erode the ability to see racial discrimination even when in plain sight, but it chips away at people's ability to rely on what they see as reality.

In Bush and Trump's elections, then, there were potential violations of civil liberties. One of the main tenants of white supremacy, remember, is to ensure "white domination is complete and un-complicated by civil rights laws and voting rights for people of color." While the laws regarding voting rights are certainly on the books, the new white nationalism functions by circumventing those laws and using the three branches of government and media to do so. It is possible to see that the new white nationalism has been mainstreamed into politics, then. Indeed, Jim Rutenberg, Nick Corasaniti, and Alan Feuer write that "Republicans have used [the Southern Strategy] to roll back voting rights for the better part of the young century . . . . Republicans have pushed to justify laws that in many cases made voting disproportionately harder for Blacks and Hispanics, who largely support Democrats."[10]

FAITH IN THE AMERICAN DREAM

At the turn of the twenty-first century, the housing market was booming and interest rates for acquiring a loan to purchase a home were now at record lows. These low rates were available for adjustable-rate mortgages, meaning the rate today could be different tomorrow based on Federal Reserve dictates. For a two- to three-year period, the purchasing power of the dollar for property was at record highs. And neighborhoods that for generations remained the domain of the white and class privileged saw a diversification that they had never seen before. Hundreds of thousands of lower- to middle-class families toured lavish homes. Loan officers assured them that interest and home prices made it possible for them to literally buy their American dream.

In 2006, however, questions began to arise about whether the prices of homes reflected their actual value, or if the market was inflated to a false level. Later that same year, the lattice that undergirded the housing boom unraveled as it was shown "subprime" loans were the mechanism by which interest rates were reduced in the first place. These subprime loans were the ones most commonly distributed to buyers at this time, and when those subprime loans crashed, it resulted in economic disaster for the families who had seemingly earned their way into the American middle.[11]

Many families were left with no other option but to declare bankruptcy and abandon their dream homes. The housing market's collapse symbolized much more than an economic problem, however. This collapse told a story about for whom the American dream was a real possibility.

> Relative to comparable white applicants, and controlling for geographic factors, blacks were 2.8 times more likely to be denied for a loan, and Latinos were two times more likely. When they were approved, blacks and Latinos were 2.4 times more likely to receive a subprime loan than white applicants. The higher up the income ladder you compare white applicants and minorities, the wider this subprime disparity grows.[12]

In short, the housing market of the early 2000s allowed minorities access to the American Dream. However, that access was predicated on a false system of economics. And just as easily as that American dream was offered to these families, it was yanked away. Collectively, the victims of this crisis hold a mirror up to how the entire American housing market is built with the bones of the new white nationalism. That is, the economic and housing crisis of the early 2000s was really a correction of an American economic system that has always, except for that brief period of time in the early 2000s, engaged in the geographic isolation of races from one another. As such, the nostalgia spectrum allows one to examine this crisis as simply a return to American normalcy built on white nationalist principles of racial and economic segregation. The brief housing boom preceding the great recession allowed lower-class and minority families to transgress what had been hardened borders of neighborhoods. It was literally a fleeting dream.

Ultimately, the new white nationalism has desensitized a public to manipulations of truth and the security of social institutions all the while guaranteeing white power and privilege. Such destabilization, moreover, has led to a general lack of trust Americans have in political, social, and cultural institutions that comprise America.[13] A Pew Research Study in 2019 found that "many Americans see declining levels of trust in the country, whether it is their confidence in the federal government and elected officials or *their trust of each other* [emphasis mine]."[14]

What does all of this have to do with higher education and race in the twenty-first century, one may ask? Everything.

The 2000s has become characterized as an era where major American institutions, family lives, and general perceptions of reality have continuously been manipulated and thus impinged on the individuals' ability to make well-informed and autonomous decisions based on reliable information. It very well may be that American citizens have had an illusion of control for a majority of history. However, the events of the past three decades have been characterized by a disorienting barrage of false narratives and failure of institutions, all victimizing minorities and lower class.

ASSESSMENT AND ACCOUNTABILITY AS A REACTION TO A MISTRUSTING PUBLIC

There is little reason for the American public to consider that higher education operates in an ethically superior way than the political, mediated, or economic spheres—especially when individual higher education institutions have experienced scandals like the Varsity Blues admission debacle; Penn State and Michigan States' sex scandals; continuous fraternity hazing incidents surfacing in national media; and costs continue to rise. Likewise, there is every reason, especially after a housing crisis that revealed an economic system built on a flimsy foundation, for an American public to be weary that what they are paying for is indeed what they are getting. Mistrust of big purchase, life-changing items is understandable in this century. However, the thinkers about higher education have not contextualized the debates about higher education's value in the twenty-first century as related to a pattern of multiple institutions failing to protect citizens' rights and deliver on promises made to the public. Such contextualization provides insight into the actual problems that are facing higher education in the current moment. And it is with this context that the current assessment paradigm should be examined.

Although characterized as a means to improve teaching, assessment has generally been the manner in which accreditation agencies and state and federal governments claim that higher education has a mechanism to police what is happening in the classroom. And the classroom is generally what the American public that is attending or sending its family members to college care most about. Hence, it is no coincidence that the emphasis of academic assessment has become the mantra of higher education beginning with Clinton and through Trump.

Assessment of student learning, which ensures that faculty (1) communicate what will be learned in a course through outcomes, and then (2) collectively analyze students' abilities to reach those outcomes, is normal operations in higher education today. However, the philosophy of course assessment has permeated nearly all aspects of higher education institutions. All accreditors across the nation now require that courses, programs, institutions, strategic plans, and resources are measured in the same exact way: Set outcomes, implement plans to achieve those outcomes, assess whether those plans worked, adjust accordingly, and communicate about this process transparently. This approach to colleges ensures that outcomes/goals become aligned across different units and that accountability and efficiencies can be accomplished. While such an approach to higher education makes logical sense, it is possible that assessment sets undesired discursive frames around the very knowledge and processes being developed by the thinkers in higher education—and the result can have deleterious effects on the nation itself.

The assessment paradigm gained significant momentum in 202, about the same time as the housing crash, just as the nation was beginning to climb out of a two-year recession. Just years later, Richard Arum and Josipa Roska published *Academically Adrift*. The book sent shock waves through educational, political, and social circles. Using data from a standardized test called the Collegiate Learning Assessment, transcripts from twenty-four institutions, and surveys of students, the book concluded that higher education offered little to no value added in terms of students' abilities to write, think critically, or problem solve. Arum and Roska argue that higher education's curriculum often does not require a robust amount of reading or writing and this fact led to less than stellar results for student learning. Overall, public higher education was called out for inadequately preparing American college-going students for the work world. The book, in short, suggests that higher education is another one of those social institutions failing the American public, and that was not delivering on its promises. Moreover, the book was a harbinger of the the current paradigm regarding value, completion and metric-based approaches to learning we are currently in.

At nearly the same time, the Obama administration created a college score card that sought to increase transparency for students and their families about institutions' effectiveness in cost, graduation rates, and producing job-ready students. The score card was intended not only to provide students and families with information about the institutions they were considering for their futures, but also to put pressure on institutions themselves. In short, this information was created with an assumption—and perhaps a correct one—that some, if not many, higher education institutions failed to ensure that their academic programs led to workforce jobs. The assessment and scorecard, then, was an attempt to establish trust that was potentially already lost. However, the scorecard began with the assumption that colleges needed policing, and the paradigm was already set on a defense of higher education's shortcomings rather than a showcasing of its value.

Further, a scorecard does not necessarily solve the problems that the completion and assessment paradigms sought to solve. In *Making Colleges Work: Pathways to Success for Disadvantaged Students*, Holzer and Baum argue that "[j]ust making general information available is unlikely to significantly improve the college decisions of students from less-privileged backgrounds."[15] Moreover, assessments and scorecards cannot bolster public faith in the higher education system. Indeed, the public's faith in higher education has been on a sharp decline since the early 2000s despite the use of the scorecard. The assessment models that have been implemented as a means to ensure higher education delivers the knowledge, skills, and abilities for students prior to graduation have been ongoing for the first two decades of the twenty-first century, the same time period that the public has lost a significant amount of faith in higher education's ability to deliver those knowledge, skills, and abilities. As a result, one has to wonder, both in terms of public trust and in the learning that is to be supported through assessment models, if the current assessment paradigm is indeed serving higher education well. Perhaps the solutions dreamed up by well-meaning politicians and accreditors are not necessarily leading to desired outcomes. Perhaps the assessment paradigm, ironically, is having the opposite effect on academic and institutional effectiveness, and so public trust.

Assessment's goal of having faculty and administrators use data to discuss ways to improve is excellent, theoretically. However, implementing processes and procedures and even the sort of thought that goes into these models may not fit well with higher education. Perhaps the current approaches to assessment are too rigid and aggressive for a higher education space. For while assessment works as a robust model in other sectors, higher education has a single variable and luxury attached to its ultimate goal that other industries do not: time. The notion that learning of any kind can be reduced to an idealized unit of time is a generally accepted but a wholly untrue assumption. Still, assessment nearly calcifies this concept by asking faculty to develop and then adhere to outcomes that will be delivered to students in a semester, or over a period of a credential. Assessment focuses on the time-based achievement of goals.

Even the act of assigning students grades has itself rested on the idea that a course's end signifies a time for evaluation of a student. While there are elements of grading and assessment that will allow a snapshot of such learning, there is no way that either can glean the entire picture of what is learned or will be learned as a result of a class.

In fact, a recent study examined how well students performed throughout a semester when professors evaluated students without assigning grades. On a paper assignment, the professors would either assign grades only, grades and comments, and comments only on papers:

> [O]nly those who received comments did better on a subsequent qualitative task, which required creativity or problem-solving. The findings also indicated that comments supported intrinsic motivation, while grades weakened it. Grades may encourage an emphasis on quantitative aspects of learning, depress creativity, foster fear of failure, and undermine interest . . . . Other studies have found that [grades] reduce students' interest in what they're learning. They make students more risk-averse, less curious, and more prone to focus on their performance instead of the task at hand. Grades tempt students to cut corners, including by cheating. They position students and professors as adversaries. They make it harder for students to think for themselves.[16]

If grading, the very predicate for how higher education has evaluated students for over centuries, potentially stymies learning, the entire system of higher education and the assumptions upon which it rests needs to be reevaluated. Moreover, if grading reduces student performance, what does assessment do to the learning of both students and professors at entire institutions? As an administrator with significant experience in assessment efforts on campuses, I am convinced now more than ever that institutions may actually perform better if they are focused on values and innovation and looked forward more than backward through assessment practices.

Indeed, perhaps low scores on creativity, communication, critical thinking, completion, and equity, all of which catalyzed the assessment and completion paradigms, are not revealing that colleges are failing. Perhaps the low scores and the skepticism of colleges results from an approach to accountability that stifles students' and professors' innovation and ability to truly improve over time. Perhaps the accountability paradigm in higher education reveals a legitimate crisis in American trust of social and political institutions, and not a necessity for accountability. Perhaps the crisis is that the public has very little trust in the major societal institutions' ability to act in ethical and effective ways. However, if the crisis is about public trust lacking in institutionally ethical ways, the assessment paradigm will not fix this problem.

ASSESSMENT AND ACCOUNTABILITY AS SYMPTOMATIC TO A MISGUIDED AMERICAN PUBLIC

There are more pragmatic reasons for reconsidering the assessment paradigm in higher education. For instance, in all my years in higher education—from an adjunct professor to a tenured professor to three different kinds of administrative positions—I have never once been asked by a student or received a complaint from an interested party about the course outcomes or the assessments of those course outcomes. There have been no entities except for accreditors to ask for data on course or program outcomes. There have been no organizations clamoring for more assessments. And so let me ask a question that is asked in the assessment world over and again when it comes to curriculum. But let me ask it of the assessment paradigm: So what? So what for all the work higher education professionals have performed assessing curricula, key performance indicators, or program outcomes? Have we achieved, after two decades, a better system of learning for our students? Are we better off? And if so, in what ways? Or are we simply showing that we are accountable and compliant?

While there may be data to illustrate continuous improvement has occurred in pockets as a result of assessment, another question must be asked regarding continuous improvement: Continuous improvement toward what? It is clear, after two decades of the twenty-first century, that higher education must take its role as both the great equalizer and the protector of American democracy quite seriously. It must contextualize learning in the grander purposes of the nation, much like the forefathers of equality and democracy espoused. From Ben Franklin to Thomas Jefferson, the very underpinnings of democracy were believed to depend on an educated citizenry who could thereby stand up to oppressions and ensure civic liberty.[17]

If higher education professionals consider framing the assessment paradigm through the lens of national ideals as most of our missions espouse, we must also consider that the way we have implemented assessment on our campuses has also unintentionally ensured that disciplinary knowledge does not transcend into civic education. For instance, rarely does a biology class enter into the epistemologies of racism that underpinned the biological sciences in the 1800s. Similarly, medicine at the undergraduate level focuses on the knowledge necessary to pass a medical school's entrance exam, not sociological oppressions of health delivery that occur across the globe. When faculty are asked to write down the most essential knowledge, skills, or abilities that students should learn in a class, there is a tendency to think in terms of the course, not that course's place in the greater context of what it means to be an educated human being. Very easily lost in such discussions among faculty, and so outcomes on syllabi are foci on citizenship, equality, or democracy. Hence, this sort of narrowed approach to learning plays into the new white nationalism's desire to avoid a citizenry committed to values of equality, justice, and democracy. And yet, in an era where civil liberties are being eroded right in front of the public's eyes, intentional focus on citizenship is indeed a responsibility of faculty at most institutions: Dawn Michele Whitehead underscores that most colleges and universities claim to espouse global citizenship in their mission statements. However, learning outcomes of courses and majors rarely include language about citizenship; nor do institution's strategic plans.[18]

Proponents of assessment will claim that outcomes for courses or institutions can focus on citizenship, and so my argument is misleading. But my argument is much more foundational than that. It is hardly a coincidence that civil liberties are under an open assault in the same two decades that higher education has focused on assessment processes. In short, the paradigm of academic assessment is part of a greater paradigm in which big data and value are utilized in a way that unintentionally reduces focus on civil liberties, equality, and justice. Our culture has become so accustomed to supporting the concept that data and alignment of outcomes to goals are necessary that we do not see what parts of our society are truncated in the pursuit of such data and alignment. And so, despite that assessment is intended to demonstrate value and efficacy, it also may support the cause of the new white nationalism.

Indeed, the American Association of College and Universities argues that "too many institutions are marked by a helter-skelter approach to civic engagement. Rather than a cohesive educational strategy, happenstance and impulse more typically govern."[19] As idealistic as focusing curricular and institutional strategy on civic engagement may seem, doing so is only a slight shift in frame and mindset. If colleges' missions overwhelmingly make references to citizenship, democracy, and equality, which they do, then asking faculty to focus a single outcome of their courses on such areas of institutional emphasis aligns with the spirit of assessment. However, the success of such tweaks in the curriculum will not be measured by the methods adopted in current models of assessment. Rather, over time, they will be measured by how poorly behaving social institutions, which are led by the graduates of higher education, become better-behaving ones over time. Idealistic, yes, but actionable as well.

Moreover, the assessment paradigm measures only what can be quantified, and subsequently suffers from the very emphasis of the rational over the emotional that the previous chapters illustrated. Assessment thereby accepts a white, Western, and Americentric view of disciplines and the construct of knowledge; nostalgic constructions of disciplinary "truth" over inclusive; and so the new white nationalism's processes over the anti-racist.

While assessment models do allow an organizing and methodical framework, they may also erode the focus on the long-term missions of courses, majors, and institutions themselves—and do more harm in the process than good. In assessment, higher education has set up a system, much like the political, where outcomes may indeed be tangible at the end of certain cycles (the election of a president, number of graduates). But what happens in achieving those outcomes is just being revealed after two decades of those systems' implementation: A citizenry that is more and more disenfranchised, lacking trust, and subsequently disengaged with the social institutions that comprise America. In the case of higher education, moreover, assessment may even detract from the central purpose of higher education.

A significant restructuring and re-prioritizing of how higher education does its work is necessary if public trust will be regained. To be sure, a refocusing of higher education on citizenship, and so anti-racism throughout the curriculum is a call to action that requires disruption of our norms.

DISRUPTION AS THE NORM, AND CONTROLLING CHAOS

Higher education does not do well with disruption. Indeed, the traditional academic year, with a fifteen-week fall semester, winter break, fifteen-week spring semester, and summer has its roots in the early 1600s. That calendar was developed based on a Christian holiday emphasis, an agricultural rhythm to labor, and the fact that there was no air conditioning in summer. Academic success was not the reason that the academic calendar that exists today was created in the past. And yet, that calendar is firmly ensconced in the rhythms of all college-going families and higher education employees' expectations. Change is not the middle name of higher education.

However, if anything is clear over the past two decades, if not centuries, it is that stability is an illusion. American reality is more chaotic than most of us acknowledge in our day to day:

The banking industry has thrown America into fourteen recessions since the Great Depression, the last one spanning two full years. The political arena, since the turn of the decade, has resisted any semblance of stability. Constant upheaval has taken place under the guise of a culture war between progressives and conservatives. News cycles are constantly interrupted by chaos. News of gun violence has become like elevator music in the background. Political rhetoric is not taken seriously. American normalcy is chaos.

Employees who work at and students who attend institutions of higher education are affected by this chaos. In this era where significant public mistrust of big institutions is prevalent, making change at individual institutions poses complex problems for administrators. Heightened and intensified mistrust of national and state governments has indeed carried over into the governance systems at higher education institutions. Specifically, higher education institutions have within them, a decision-making process that is unique called shared governance. Shared governance allows input from many constituencies to occur about a variety of issues on campus, especially those that touch students, such as curriculum, orientation, or advising.

How higher education institutions will make decisions as mistrust has grown throughout American society needs consideration. This is one truth that has been grossly overlooked in the manifold external mandates visiting higher education.

Vincent Tinto offered a template for college administrators to consider when implementing large-scale changes in the name of student success. He wrote that colleges through the early 2000s had generally funded many small-scale but successful programs each year. In such an approach, there was very little institutional intention in leveraging the practices these boutique programs utilized to become norms on a scaled level. As a result, institutions had manifold pockets of excellence. These programs, serving around twenty students each, sap up intuitional resources, and their overall effect, when measured against the entire student population, was minimal. Tinto goes on to argue that in the era of completion and in the name of ensuring that all students succeed, the approach that colleges have taken to allocating what little resources they have equates to "tinker[ing] around the edges."[20]

Large-scale change for student success requires methodical and strategic use of resources and big decisions. And in order to implement them requires shifts in operations, mindsets of faculty and staff on campuses, and, often, vetting through governance systems on campus—systems that are often slow-moving and mistrustful of new initiatives. When broad-scale changes are considered in a national context of people having lost faith in their voices being heard, fear and skepticism abounds. And yet, the kinds of decisions that face colleges are not going away. As a result, shared governance systems in higher education campuses are facing a stress test for both the gravity and the pace of change.

Moreover, there are individuals on campuses who see their role as resisting change only to resist. While there are many who would criticize such individuals, they could also be seen as attempting to control their worlds in a country that is characterized by chaos. An Op-Ed in *The Chronicle of Higher Education* reflected on the shared governance model in higher education and how some individuals see resistance to change as the hallmark of their role on campus.

> Universities and many of us who work in them continue to react to the changing world at a snail's pace . . . . Many of my colleagues understand the power they have to stonewall proposals, filibuster new ideas, and engage in general foot dragging that effectively kills the ability of their organizations to react to the changing needs of society. One of my colleagues recently . . . suggested that the incredibly slow pace of change on his campus (which he mightily contributed to) was actually a good thing. He saw himself as one who holds the line against fads and the whims of the general public. Now, that's a real progressive attitude—and, I might add, a very arrogant one as well. The fact that this individual was considered by his colleagues to be a superlative academician makes his position even more sad.[21]

The above reveals a dynamic that exists on all college campuses. These people are committed and care. And to make systemic and meaningful changes through a shared governance system that has not been asked to make scaled changes requires an understanding that the people that comprise college campuses must have their fears and concerns addressed. They must also understand the consequences of slow action. What the Op-Ed in the *Chronicle* cited above illustrates is not that shared governance is a problem. Rather, it illustrates there is a general discomfort on college campuses with quick and broad change. After three centuries in which higher education has engaged in the protectionism of something as benign as the academic calendar, challenging white power and privilege will most definitely cause waves. Likewise, the shared governance model's slow pace is a means through which to slow social justice. The slower the pace for change, the more potential there is for the decisions that have oppressed in the past to remain in the present. Although the intention of some in the shared governance models may indeed be to ensure the right decisions are made, the outcome of slow pace may be to affect the very students who have been marginalized and oppressed for centuries. The students who are affected by this slow pace today will not benefit from the decisions made a semester or year after they graduate or drop out. As a result, the generational wealth gaps that were illustrated in chapter 2 will continue for those individuals and families as institutions wait for shared governance vetting to occur, or for the resisters to be convinced.

One of the great paradoxes of American higher education is that for nearly 300 years it has been both the bastion of innovation and all the while participated in the structural oppression of minorities. As shown in the previous chapter, the mantra of the completion agenda has been that time is the enemy of completion. While there is ample data to suggest that the more time students spend in higher education, the less likely they are to complete their degree, that same data really illustrates that the less time students spend in higher education, the less time life circumstances will prohibit students from attending college. Colleges can reengineer many of their systems to accelerate students toward completion and yet ensure academic rigor. Some of this reengineering, however, is delayed as a result of shared governance. And the more time spent delaying, the more students negatively affected by past practices are potentially not served, and the more inequality enacted. Time is the enemy of social justice, not just completion. Indeed, at a microcosmic level, shared governance that is not intentional and urgent invites the inertia of the past into the present.

Currently, there is a need to innovate with a sense of urgency with regard to equity and democracy through higher education. I am reminded again of Martin Luther King's "Letter from Birmingham Jail" in which he writes of the illusion of order in a chaotic and oppressive society. King noted of order and its relationship to social justice: "I had hoped that the white moderate would understand that law and order exist for the purpose of establishing justice and that when they fail in this purpose they become the dangerously structured dams that block the flow of social progress."[22]

Slowing down for the comfort of employees is not a valid rationale when students and the nation is to be served. King notes of a mindset that is complacent leading to a white supremacist structure:

> We know through painful experience that freedom is never voluntarily given by the oppressor; it must be demanded by the oppressed. Frankly, I have yet to engage in a direct action campaign that was "well timed" in the view of those who have not suffered unduly from the disease of segregation. For years now I have heard the word "Wait!" It rings in the ear of every Negro with piercing familiarity. This "Wait" has almost always meant "Never." We must come to see, with one of our distinguished jurists, that "justice too long delayed is justice denied."[23]

What King provides is a frame to consider the urgency and necessity of action. The paradox facing higher education and its stakeholders is that if they want to engage fully in the transformative work of completion, equity, and diversity, there must be recognition that disruptions, discomfort, and yes, even protests may occur. But leadership is what happens in those moments. Leaders of faculty, staff, and administrators must find a way to focus on equity and work with officials outside of academia to transform their thinking about the policies that serve as obstacles to institutional missions.

There have been manifold studies and initiatives considering the concept of time in the context of the completion agenda. However, these studies have focused on students' acceleration toward completion. They have not accounted for the inner workings of colleges and how time is an imperative consideration for how decision-making processes must be hastened. More studies and cases for success need to be created to this end.

Social justice has been delayed for too long by too many. Within the walls of community colleges and the meetings in which major decisions are made, there is a need to make less abstract the reality that delayed decisions equate to delayed justice. In the context of a national body politic where more and more oppression is visiting upon the oppressed, it is becoming more and more clear that higher education's role in enacting social justice is the moral imperative of our time. Governance systems need to be reimagined not necessarily in what they consider or in the sort of debates in which they engage. But they do need to be reimagined in the ways in which they facilitate rather than delay decisions. Moreover, in the context of a public that mistrusts nearly all institutions, administrators and governance systems on campus must work to ensure that both align the work of accreditation, effectiveness, social justice, and completion.

THE NEXT STEPS TO A NEW PARADGIM

Old ways of situating public higher education and simple solutions will not suffice to disrupt the new white nationalism. Hence, people on college campuses need to consider what it means when we wait. Recognizing that African American, Latinx, Native American, and Pell status students graduate at a significantly lower rates than their white, middle-class counterparts is a significant first step. That these gaps exist illustrates that higher education institutions are the very definition of racist institutions, however. Very few people in higher education, much less any other industry, desire to work at an institutionally racist organization. And most of us work at them. As a result, the first issue we must collectively acknowledge is that urgency is imperative. With each passing semester, a cohort of non-retained students is released back into a world that continues to reify the systemic oppressions that exist outside our walls.

In an era where higher education is indeed under assault, and also when the borders of the imagined nation are being hardened and protracted, higher education must embrace the challenge of opening those same borders. We must do so with urgency not just to meet our missions, but for the sake of the nation itself.

No matter what sector an employee at a college works, these are perilous times. The waiting to be told how colleges should react is a strategy that has not worked. We must pick up the mantel and demand a new approach to higher education by focusing on social justice. We must simultaneously demand a new paradigm in funding, different thinking, and understanding how to use the tool of the nostalgia spectrum for the benefit of all students. We must recognize that higher education is the most fundamental weapon against structural racism and the assault on civil liberties, which, the next chapter illustrates, is exacerbated in intensity each year.

NOTES

1. The story as well, upon further analysis, omitted significant information that would have contextualized financial decisions the Clintons made in a way that may have lessened the concerns about wrongdoing from the jump. Later, a similar pattern of using unchecked resources to send national politics into a tailspin was wintnessed in Gerth's story on Wen Ho Lee, a Chinese national studying nuclear warheads. In that story, Gerth suggested Ho Lee was a Chinese operative using his scholar status to spy on America. Ho Lee's career was put in jeopardy and his name sullied. Years later, of the fifty-one counts brought against him as a result of Gerth's reporting, only one stuck—and that one was related to how data was transmitted, not in how it was used. Gerth now claims that the articles of both Clinton's Watergate and Wen Ho Lee's nuclear research were problematically rewritten by editors, and this is why they contained erroneous material.

2. By late fall of 2000, Clinton was not viewed as such a pariah as the Gore team assumed at the beginning of the race. Clinton emerged from impeachment looking more like a victim of political gamesmanship than a perpetrator of crimes.

3. U.S. Census, 2010.

4. Gallup News Service, "The Florida Recount Controversy from the Public's Perspective: 25 Insights." Accessed December 10, 2019, https://news.gallup.com/p oll/2176/florida-recount-controversy-from-publics-perspective-insights.aspx.

5. Theodore Johnson and Leah Wright Rigueur, "Race-Baiting for the Presidency." *The Atlantic*. November 15, 2015.

6. Michael S. Schmidt and Maggie Haberman, "Citing Recusal, Trump Says He Wouldn't Have Hired Sessions." *New York Times*. July 17, 2017.

7. Sessions, Jeff. Resignation Letter. Accessed December 20, 2019 https://www .bing.com/images/search?view=detailV2&ccid=FmsL%2flei&id=ACEBFD23D371

4552D5953C9D7EB7218D9D5E7B07&thid=OIP.FmsL_leiMOOctw0vQ9QWxw
HaJl&mediaurl=https%3a%2f%2flegalinsurrection.com%2fwp-content%2fuploads
%2f2018%2f11%2fJeff-Sessions-Resignation-Letter.jpg&exph=2200&expw=1700
&q=jeff+sessions+resignation+letter&simid=607986490343686408&selectedIndex
=0&ajaxhist=0.

8. William Barr, "Executive Summary of the Mueller Report." March 24, 2019.

9. Robert Mueller, *Report on the Investigation into Russian Interference in the 2016 Presidential Election* (Washington, DC: Department of Justice, March, 2019).

10. Jim Rutenberg, Nick Corasaniti and Alan Feuer. "Trump's Fraud Claims Died in Court, but the Myth of Stolen Elections Lives On." *New York Times.* December 26, 2020.

11. The housing boom was underpinned a subprime mortgage scheme enacted by the major banks and insurance companies of the global economy. The entire economic system was inter-relational, and pulling one string would unravel the entire economy. Hence, when the Federal Reserve adjusted interest rates up, and the housing market fell, families who bought homes just years earlier, had more expensive mortgages, but homes of lesser value. They were literally paying mortgages that were well beyond their home value.

12. Badger, Emily. "The Dramatic Racial Bias of Subprime Lending During the Housing Boom." *Reuters.* August 23, 2013.

13. There are many more, to include a Senate refusal to allow the confirmation hearing of a Sumpreme Court judge elected by the sitting president because it was an election year—a political decision to ensure a seat on the Supreme Court, a lifetime appointment, would not be a centrist, but instead quite conservative; hearings for a Supreme Court judge in which political gamesmanship by both Republicans and Democrats illustrated a lack of desire to put a person on the bench who was a great legal mind, and a real desire simply to win.

14. Lee Rainnie and Andrew Perrin, *Key Findings about Americans' Declining Trust in Government and Each Other* (Washington, DC: Pew Research Center, July 22, 2019).

15. Harry Holer and Sandy Baum. *Making Colleges Work: Pathways to Success for Disadvantaged Students* (New York: Brookings Instititon, 2017), 123.

16. Beckie Supiano, "Grades Can Hinder Learning. What Should Professors Use Instead?" *Chronicle of Higher Education.* July 17, 2019.

17. Thomas Jefferson, "Letter to William Charles Jarvis." In *The Essentioal Jefferson* (Courier Corporation, 2008), 86.

18. Micele Dawn Whitehead, "Global Citizenship for Campus, Communities, and Careers." *AACU Perspectives.* September 2019.

19. Caryn McTighe Musil, "Educating for Citizenship." *Peer Review* 5, no. 3 (Spring 2003), online publication.

20. Vincent Tinto, *Completing College* (Chicago: University of Chicago, 2001).

21. Sam Miner, "Improving Shared Governance." *The Chronicle of Higher Education.* September 25, 1998.

22. Martin Luther King, "Letter from Birmingham." *African Studies Center, University of Pennsylvania.* Accessed August 1, 2019, https://www.africa.upenn.edu /Articles_Gen/Letter_Birmingham.html.

23. Ibid.

Chapter 7

The Attempted Coup, Black Lives Matter, and COVID-19

Masked citizens flooded American cities. They blockaded highway traffic, occupied City Halls, and chanted outside store fronts. They thrust Black Lives Matter signs into the air and demanded systemic change to a power structure built on centuries of protecting whites at the expense of nonwhites.

The origin of these protests was a tragically ordinary lynching of an African American by a white police officer. But these protests were different in their scale and intensity than any America had seen since the Civil Rights Movement. The demonstrations catalyzed by George Floyd's lynching continued for nearly three months, spanned across the globe, and catalyzed at least symbolic change in nearly every cultural, social, and economic sphere in the country. The protests did, however, stop. And the urgency for structural change is at risk of fizzling out.

There was a paradoxical variable that contextualized these Black Lives Matter protests, also. They took place during a globalized pandemic was exacerbated by people's physical proximity to one another. Those out in the streets demonstrating were risking their very lives by protesting; simultaneously, marginalized people were literally threatened everyday under a problematic power structure. Hence, not to protest was to accept that daily threat's continuation.

A similar paradox for scholars and social justice advocates to confront when situating and analyzing the significance of the summer 2020 protests is that they took place simultaneous to a 25 percent unemployment rate in America caused by the pandemic. With the constraints of a capitalist day and the labor it requires lifted off a great number of people in America, their potential to contemplate the severity of racial oppression was provided much more time and space than the many years previous. Spring and summer 2020, as a result, provides a window through which to study American and global

145

capitalism and how it obfuscates complacent America's understanding of systemic racism's violence under "normal" conditions.

The high employment rate also created anxiety among many citizens about the need to return to a "normal" workday in order to obtain a paycheck. This "return to normal," however, remains a dangerous mindset and possibility that confronts America in the context of any tragedy. For as I noted in *Sport in the Aftermath of Tragedy*, rhetoric and action of returning to normal following racial disruption is also a return to the same exact racist structures and systems that required such disruption in the first place.

Ultimately, the philosophies of the opposed poles of the nostalgia spectrum were revealed during the pandemic in 1) rhetoric, actions, policies, and practices surrounding the Black Lives Matter's protests and 2) the desire to return the economy to its pre-pandemic condition swiftly.

Finally, 2020–2021, with is concrete and immediate death-threatening events—multiple police lynchings, the insurrection of January 6, 2021, and the pandemic—revealed the success of the new white nationalism's decades-long infiltration of the political sphere and the subsequent movements to resist it.

To fully understand how the pandemic affected the unemployment rate and the everyday citizens across the country, it is necessary to paint a picture of how COVID-19, the virus causing the pandemic, affected global capitalism and everyday lives of people all over the world. Across the globe, governments forced mandatory stay-at-home orders and limited or prohibited gatherings of people, thereby forcing local businesses to temporarily close, or change their operations, to include laying off a broad number of workers. The result was that streets normally characterized by the clamor of traffic, vendors, and people finding their way to work resembled a dystopian movie. Entire ecosystems changed. Cougars walked the streets of Chile. Wild boar trotted down the alleys of New Delhi. Peacocks strutted the sidewalks of Miami. According to seismologists, the earth itself vibrated nearly 50 percent less than it had decades previous because traffic had, for the most part, ceased. Grocery stores, some of the only businesses that remained open, saw their food and product supply chain decimated. Every system and structure that ordered the everyday experience of the world was fundamentally upended, and in many cases, completely dissolved. Yet, the daily needs of the American consumer had to be met. Hence essential workers were asked to continue their duties. In America, essential workers were defined as laborers at grocery and big-box stores, online vendor warehouses, and mailrooms.[1] As a result, the shutdown of the economy affected a cross-section of classes and races in terms of who was unemployed. Yet it required lower-wage workers, many of whom were black and brown, to continue at their jobs.

In response to the economic crisis that coupled the pandemic, throngs of cars lined up in front of American city halls in a different sort of protest—one that demanded stay-at-home orders be lifted and to reopen the economy for the sake of businesses and out-of-work citizens. Even well-meaning people whose desire was to reclaim a paycheck tacitly accepted that people of color's bodies would be sacrificed more than whites' in the reopening. To clarify, 85 percent of restaurant workers in America were without a bachelor's degree, and the overwhelming amount of the lower-wage jobs in the restaurant industry were held by people of color.[2]

Further, at the height of the pandemic, decisions about whether or not American locales could open for business were left up to the fifty governors of states, forty-seven of whom were white. At times, those decisions were left open to business owners, nearly 80 percent of whom were white.[3] The push to reopen emphasized economics over racial justice, and so advocated a condition of normalcy characterized by the institutional racism that led to the inequities this book has already discussed. The new white nationalism's inertia put many of these governors in place, and they would operate without necessarily placing an anti-racist lens on the economy or how to reopen it. Some governors lifted stay-at-home orders as early as April 2020, when the virus was spreading across the country. The data was clear at that time that the virus infiltrated poor and minority bodies at higher rates than the white and privileged economically. The Center for Disease Control acknowledged "a disproportionate burden of illness and death among racial and ethnic minority groups" and listed a number of reasons why: multigenerational poverty, prisons being hot spots for the disease, and general bias in health. Indeed, as of June 2020, the death rate for African Americans was 250 percent higher than the white death rate for COVID.[4] Further:

> Race and place are clearly associated with the spread. While Black Chicagoans represent 29% of the city's population, they make up 70% of COVID-19 fatalities. In Washington, D.C., Black people are 46% of the population but 62.5% of COVID-19 fatalities. In Michigan, the heavily Black tri-county area of Detroit has quickly become the epicenter, accounting for nearly 85% of the state's COVID-19 deaths.[5]

In both the pandemic and the lynchings by police, then, the new white nationalism threatened the very lives of racial minorities in tangible and immediate ways. And in both, it was clear that the new white nationalism was working to establish not just an imagined nation of whites, but one that clearly and overtly established a hierarchy of races.

THE INFILTRATION OF THE NEW WHITE
NATIONALISM INTO LAW, ORDER, AND POLITICS

Many state and national leaders sought to ensure that the economy would be reestablished in the fashion it was prior to the pandemic, while squelching any clamor for racial justice simultaneously. This goal of the new white nationalists was clear and quick, as they understood that it is easier for the country to return to a state of "normalcy" characterized by institutional racism than to disrupt that return with an anti-racist stance.

In May 2020, the Proud Boys began a social media campaign to reopen the economy and organized protests to advocate for a reopening of businesses forced to shut down during the pandemic. The Proud Boys' social media campaigns led to significant demonstrations in cities like Detroit, Miami, Annapolis, and San Francisco. While these protests portended to be apolitical, many of those protesting carried guns, Confederate flags, signs with Swastikas, and banners expressing hatred for China and Asians in general.[6] President Trump echoed the Proud Boys' calls for reopening and conflated race, political party, and public health. Although he refused to take any federal position with regard to the economy and left that responsibility up to governors, he singled out democratic governors and their policies toward shut downs through social media. Of democrat governors Gretchen Whitmer of Michigan and Ralph Northam of Virginia, Trump wrote "Liberate Michigan," and "LIBERATE VIRGINIA, and save your great 2nd Amendment. It is under siege!" respectively.[7] In contrast, some Republican state governments aligned with the Proud Boys' and Trump's desires: Florida governor Ron DeSantis, Georgia governor Brian Kemp, and Arizona governor Doug Ducey, all of whom had connections to the Proud Boys, opened their states up to businesses and tourism a month prior to other states in the nation, stating it was a matter of personal liberty.

But the connection of the Proud Boys to high political office did not occur over night. Groups like the Proud Boys had, for over a decade, adopted new strategies for infiltrating politics by changing the way in which they operate:

> One of the qualities that makes the Proud Boys particularly dangerous is the friendly relationship they have been able to cultivate with the GOP. The Proud Boys' lack of overtly racist symbols has given them a level of access to the Republican mainstream (as well as a free pass for militant street activism) that the Alt Right can only dream of.[8]

Hence, it is hardly a far stretch to see the connection between these white nationalist groups and politicians' desire to reopen the economy. Through the summer and into the fall of 2020, many states with Republican leaders loosened restrictions on the number of people allowed in spaces, social gatherings, and resisted mask-wearing mandates. These stances must be understood in a broad context of which bodies were being protected and which sacrificed in a reopening of the economy. They must also be understood as taking their lead from the new white nationalist administration running the White House, and so supporting the new white nationalism in the process.

The new white nationalism can be examined by contrasting stance the White House took in responding to the pandemic, the insurrection at Capitol Hill on January 6, 2021, and the Black Lives Matter protests of 2020. The White House consistently supported the reopening of states in the context of the pandemic and riled up white nationalist groups against those governors who did not open. And when white terrorists attacked Capitol Hill, as noted in the introduction to this book, President Trump did nothing to stop them for six hours. When he appeared on camera to address the nation, he addressed those rioters saying, "we love you, you're very special." These white terrorists sought to defend the president who called peaceful Black Lives Matter protests "riot. . .s" and "domestic acts of terror." They aligned with Trump who called Black Lives Matter itself "symbol of hate."[9] In short, there was, through 2020–2021 a visible war between the oppositional poles of the nostalgia spectrum, and it was clear that the left-hand side, although it lost the presidency, was gaining in scale, intensity, and breadth in the political sphere, as the introduction of this book makes clear.

The tension between the left and right sides of the nostalgia spectrum was visible in how law, police, and protests were situated by politicians during 2020–2021 as well. As Black Lives Matter protests continued throughout the summer, Trump asserted a "law and order" stance, and made that stance a racialized hallmark of his presidential campaign. On Twitter, he wrote:

> The Democrats never even mentioned the words LAW & ORDER at their National Convention. If I don't win, America's Suburbs will be OVERRUN with Low Income Projects, Anarchists, Agitators, Looters and, of course, "Friendly Protesters."

Deputy national press secretary for the Trump campaign, Samantha Zager, noted that President Trump "condemned the violence [of Black Lives Matter], demanded law and order, and [had] taken action to protect our communities without hesitation."[10] Herein, the new white nationalism worked to reinforce and scare whites that black people needed to be tamed or else they would infiltrate white spaces and threaten white families. This stance informed Trump's reaction to citizens protesting against consistent lynchings of black people at the hands of the police. . It must be underscored, however, that there are yet major leaders in Congress who align Black Lives Matter protests with the treasonous, white supremacist attempted coup of America. Senator Marco Rubio, still in his seat, for instance, noted, "Now, are the left hypocrites? Absolutely. I remember what they now are calling 'insurrection,' they were justifying just this summer [when they supported the Black Lives Matter protests]."[11] Likewise, as noted in the introduction, nearly two-thirds of Republicans in the House of Representatives voted to delay and potentially overturn the sealing of the presidential election, another new strategy to limit the voting rights of American citizens that was touched on in the previous chapter.

The law and order stance that the Trump administration took regarding the Black Lives Matter protests, then, was a clarion call to suffocate racial unrest under the cloak of what looks like justice, but is really a tool of white power and privilege. Martin Luther King noted the same in his "Letter from Birmingham Jail" as he argued that the concept of "order" often usurps the concept of "justice," and that "order" is desired by those complacent whites who often claim themselves to be not racist:

> I had hoped that the white moderate would understand that law and order exist for the purpose of establishing justice and that when they fail in this purpose they become the dangerously structured dams that block the flow of social progress.[12]

Law and order often establishes a "negative peace" void of justice, King writes. Law and order is the rhetoric of white power and nationalism because in moments of racial tragedy and uprising it advocates for a return to the same law and order that existed prior to the unrest. Hence, the law and order position does little to disrupt or change conditions that need changing, and utilizes rhetoric of "returning to normal" as if that "normal" was benign.

. In the attempt to reestablish law and order over the Black Lives Matters protestors, Trump said, "when the looting starts, the shooting starts," a phrase used during the 1967 race riots. The phrase was re-tweeted and shared via social media indicating significant support by many Americans. Trump also called in armed forces and directed helicopters to hover in close proximity to protestors so they would be blown back by the force of their propellers. This order, according to the *New York Times*, was an effort "terrorize" protestors.[13] Clearly, the words and deeds of a new white nationalism were opposed to Black Lives Matter. The law and order of the new white nationalism was an overt attempt to force those protesting "back into their place" and also a battle for which kind of America would manifest in the future.

While distinction between and among the new white nationalist responses to the pandemic, protests of Black Lives Matter, and the January 6, 2021, insurrection are disturbing, they reveal the significant power that the complacent whites and privileged have in American society. And herein is where I distinguish myself between the current anti-racism arguments and my work. Our American systems make well-meaning people of all races victims to what is considered "normal." To a complacent white not well versed in history or racialized theory, "returning to normal" may seem benign. But it is anything but that. To a complacent white, attending a protest may seem like activist. It is not. To a complacent white, expressing disgust at lynchings or treasonous riots may seem like making a statement. It is not. The complacent white is often well meaning, but for active resistance of the new white nationalism to take place requires education through the nostalgia spectrum urgently. If 2020–2021 has shown anything, it is that the new white nationalism is strong, savvy, and active. And it will sacrifice non-white bodies for its own comfort, and use complacency as a weapon to do so.

GHOST SKINS: THE NEW INFILTRATIONS OF THE NEW WHITE NATIONALISM

The new white nationalists have been infiltrating spaces beyond the political in covert and strategic ways for decades. Understanding these infiltrations further situates African Americans' lynchings by police, the Black Lives Matter protests of summer 2020, and the January 6, 2021, white terrorism at Capitol Hill. For over a decade, the FBI warned police agencies that white nationalists known as "ghost skins" were encouraged and often succeeded in securing jobs for local and city police departments. "Ghost skins" are white nationalists who infiltrate new spaces of official institutions to perform the work of the new white nationalism. The underlying work of these ghost skins in police departments is "to disrupt investigations against fellow members and recruit other supremacist [in the department to the cause] . . . and covertly advance white supremacist causes."[14] While it is not known if ghost skins were responsible for or influenced the George Floyd lynching, it is clear that the agenda of white nationalism had infiltrated manifold police departments as verified by the FBI. At the time this book is going to press, moreover, ten Capitol police officers are under investigation for supporting the attempted a coup against the American government on January 6, 2021. During that attempted coup, these officers wore Make America Great paraphernalia and took selfies with the insurgents. Police officers from multiple out-of-state departments were also photographed at Capitol Hill and are under investigation. It is clear that one tactic of the new white nationalism is to infiltrate the law and order sector of America and in the process further white nationalist ideals in the guise of peacekeeping entities like the police. The white nationalist infiltration into police departments does not mean that all police are white nationalists. Rather, it means that a tactic of the new white nationalism is to infiltrate spaces of law and order to further its agenda.

The normative power structures that have an origin of whiteness were firmly in place by the time the modern police organizations took root. Dr. Gary Porter traced the origins of the modern police force to that of the slave patrol, which had the primary duty of: "controlling freed slaves who were now laborers working in an agricultural caste system, and enforcing 'Jim Crow' segregation laws, designed to deny freed slaves equal rights and access to the political system."[15] Clearly, American law enforcement, politics, and judicial systems have a nexus in punishing and surveilling the black body as a criminal to be tamed while protecting whites. This is a similar mindset that Trump played on when inciting whites' fears about Black Lives Matters protests. In short, the new white nationalism seeks to ensure the complacent white fears African Americans and potentially supports policies of segregation while dismissing horrific violence against black people. The strategy the new white nationalism adopts is to solidify the stereotype that African Americans are violent and scary. Ibram Kendi shows the hold this stereotype hason white imaginations:

> Black people are apparently responsible for calming the fears of violent cops in the way women are supposedly responsible for calming the sexual desires of male rapists . . . [the stereotype of the black] super predator [leads to the conclusion that Blacks] need tough laws . . . to civilize them back to nonviolence.[16]

The spate of black bodies lynched by police, white fear of black bodies that originates from the construction of the black criminality, even the White House response to Black Lives Matter protests all have an origin in ensuring black people "know their place" in a white nation.

LIES AND CHAOS AS THE NEW WHITE NATIONALIST STRATEGY

The new white nationalism sought to discipline other identities during the summer and fall of 2020 through exclusionary rhetoric as well.

In the context of a pandemic that originated in China, President Trump attached a decades-old stereotype of the Asian invader to t the virus had come within American borders. Trump called the Corona virus the "Chinese virus" and "Kung Flu." He also invoked memories of foreign terrorist and war acts against America in his rhetoric:

> This is worse than Pearl Harbor, this is worse than the World Trade Center. There's never been an attack like this. And it should have never happened.

Could've been stopped at the source. Could've been stopped in China. It should've been stopped right at the source. And it wasn't.[17]

Secretary of State Pompeo bolstered Trump's rhetoric by claiming he had "enormous evidence" the virus was manufactured in a Chinese lab. Dr. Anthony Fauci, director of the National Institute of Allergy and Infectious Disease, unequivocally showed the disease "evolved in nature and then jumped species."[18] Twisting science to fit into a narrative that creates a racialized hierarchy is a foundational principle of the new white nationalism. Indeed, "scientists have spotted distortions of their own academic papers in far-right internet forums" for decades.[19] In the more recent past, overt manipulation of facts has become a hallmark of the new white nationalism.

Such distortions have very real implications for health and safety (and trust as the previous chapter illustrated). During the months that the new white nationalists were making claims about COVID-19 being a weaponized anti-gen from China, the American Defense League showed that Asian Americans were the victims of an increased number of attacks, both physical and verbal across the country. Reports of acid being thrown at Asian Americans in New York, and families stabbed by white Americans were recorded among the nearly 1,200 hate crimes toward Asian Americans in the first two months of the pandemic.[20] Kristine Phillips, writing for *USA Today* chronicled incidents of hate crimes against Asian Americans in California alone and summarized them this way: "The theme: This virus is your fault."[21] During that time, the pandemic escalated because it was seen by some as a Chinese weapon rather than a disease, and, in some cases, as Trump claimed, a hoax.

Specifically, the anti-science approach to the virus coupled the lack of a federal plan to stem the spread of the virus. More and more people died. Refrigerator trucks sat outside of hospitals to hold the dead bodies morgues did not have capacity to. Meanwhile, the White House took very little urgent action to quell the pandemic. President Trump said of the virus on February 28, 2020, "It's going to disappear. One day, it's like a miracle, it will disappear"; then on March 10, 2020, "And we're prepared, and we're doing a great job with it. And it will go away. Just stay calm. It will go away"; and then on March 12, 2020, "It's going to go away"; then, on May 15, 2020, after 82,000 Americans had died, he said the virus "will just go away." Later, he suggested that Americans consider drinking disinfectant or finding a way to inject light into their bodies so the virus could not live there. He then claimed Americans should take Hydroxychloroquine, a medication that was later shown to have significant negative outcomes on life expectancy for those who contracted the virus. At the peak of the pandemic, he refused to take a leadership role: governors of each state were told by President Trump, "We will be backing you, but try getting [all the medical supplies and PPE] yourselves. Point of sales, much better, much more direct if you can get it yourselves" and to use their "own discretion" of how to reopen their states if they were shut down. One can imagine, however, if the disease was infiltrating white bodies more than any other, the national and congressional response would not only have been quick, but it would also have been organized as well. Instead, by January 1, 2021, over 350,000 Americans perished in the United States. Antithetical to nearly every other presidential response to tragedy, Trump sought division of citizens rather than unification. While there may very well be a psychological reason for his stances, it is also clear that the chaos he incited supported a white nationalist stance: white nationalists see chaos in general as a potential catalyst for drawing those who are complacent toward race relations to their cause.

> These far-right extremists . . . hope the chaos will drive more people to become frustrated by the status quo and begin pushing for more extreme political positions, spark political unrest or even begin agitating for more revolutionary measures to upend the current political system.[22]

Chaos was rooted in the manipulation of scientific fact as white nationalists eschewed proven methods of slowing the disease's spread. . Contrary to evidence, the new white nationalists, the White House, governors with relationships to Q-Anon, and the Proud Boys refused to mandate that masks be worn indoors and were among the loosest with restrictions on public gatherings. In the meantime, and as a result, the virus continued to threaten black and Latinx bodies more than whites'. Texas governor Dan Patrick, who opened his state's economy prior to many other states, overtly connected his decision to sacrifice lives to ensure a robust economy. He stated, "there are more important things than living and that's saving this country['s]" economy. By August 2020, when he re-opened the state, a disproportionate percentage and number of Hispanic and black people had died from COVID-19 .[23] The philosophy of placing minority bodies in danger to serve an economic engine is akin to that of slavery and Jim Crow.

The insidiousness of systemic racism's inertia and how it showed up in the context of the pandemic and racial strife can be crystallized through use of the nostalgia spectrum. The leadership of states that did not adhere to scientific truths about the pandemic was in line with historic approaches white power and privilege in particular states. That is, the first states to open their businesses during the pandemic were the same ones that had histories of extreme racism and associations with past and current-day lynchings.

Among the states that opened first during the pandemic were Louisiana, Arkansas, Mississippi, Georgia, Texas, and Florida.

Louisiana, Arkansas, Mississippi, Georgia, Texas, and Florida have recorded the most lynchings in American history according to a project carried out by the University of Missouri Kansas City Law School.[24]

Louisiana, Arkansas, Georgia, Florida, Maryland, Texas, Arizona, Oklahoma, Ohio, and California were in the top five states where unarmed black people were slain at the hands of police 2016–2019.[25] Many of these same states were the sites of police violence against black bodies that made national attention:

- Michael Brown was killed, unarmed in Ferguson, Arkansas, sparking the Black Lives Matter movement. The officer who shot Brown was acquitted.
- Tamir Rice, playing with a toy gun at twelve years old, was shot and killed by a Cleveland, Ohio, police man, Timothy Loehmann, who was acquitted.
- In Florida, George Zimmerman shot and killed an unarmed Trevon Martin. There was ample evidence it was a premediated and racialized killing. Zimmerman was acquitted based on Stand Your Ground laws.
- In Maryland, twenty-five-year-old Freddie Gray was killed after being arrested and thrown in the back of a police wagon without safety belts and taken on what police call a "rough ride," where the driver makes dangerous turns to injure the unsecured passenger. All charges were dropped against officers associated with the death.
- In Texas, Sandra Bland, pulled over for a routine citation, argued about the legitimacy of her being cited. She was arrested and put in confinement for such questioning. Days later, she was found dead in her cell. The officer in who arrested Bland faced no consequences, and the system in which she was incarcerated and found dead is still moving strong.
- In the midst of the pandemic and national protests about George Floyd's lynching, Rayshard Brooks was shot in the back and kicked in the back multiple times after being slain in Georgia.

Likewise, Georgia, Florida, Arizona, Oklahoma and Texas, in spring 2020, opened up their states earlier than others and by June 23, 2020, each had seen up to a 20 percent increase in the diseases' spread. Oklahoma was the site of President Trump's first campaign for reelection on June 20, 2020. His rally was labeled rife for potential spread of the virus because it was the first large indoor gathering in America since mid-March. Despite all the science that showed masks reduced the spread of COVID-19, President Trump did not require attendees to wear them. As people gathered, unmasked, they cheered when he labeled COVID-19 "Kung Flu" and threatened that protestors against racism in America would see "repercussions" if they did not stop. He then claimed that the liberals were "unhinged" for removing confederate names and statues because they were erasing "our history." Herein, the

Trump rally exhibited all the values of the new white nationalism, and in the process literally spread a disease that was killing marginalized people more than whites. The nexus of racism and minimizing the threat of COVID-19 while also spreading that disease was literally all traceable in the Trump rallies. Arizona was the next stop on Trump's campaign trail, which occurred on June 23, 2020. In the two weeks that followed these rallies, Oklahoma and Arizona saw 30 percent increases in their COVID-19 cases. In the federalized violence against Black Lives Matter protests, the infiltration of the Capitol Building, and in the approach to the pandemic, a common, new white nationalist theme arose: The white nation was being attacked, and the only recourse left was to protect whites and their children by infiltrating institutions of law and order. The outcomes of this strategy ran the gamut from squelching racial protests and hate speech on one extreme to lynchings, hate crimes, and a coup attempt in the Capitol Building on the other.

HIGHER EDUCATION, COVID-19, AND THE NEW WHITE NATIONALISM

As COVID-19 made its way from Asia to America, American institutions were planning for the possibility that they may need to pivot to a remote environment. In March 2020, higher education as a sector made broad and quick decisions to shut most of its face-to-face operations down.

The pivot required many faculty and students to shift mid-semester to remote learning even though many of them began in face-to-face modalities. Remote learning, however, provided a new way for the new white nationalism to infiltrate classrooms. Though use of what was called Zoombombing, white nationalists anonymously infiltrated synchronous online classroom sessions carried out through conferencing platforms. When new white nationalists gained access to these video conferences, they would disrupt the learning environment by yelling or displaying racist messages. In a remote environment, the only remedy professors had for ceasing these Zoombombs was to shut down the classroom itself for the day. As a result, with this new learning platform, the new white nationalism had a tool to halt the learning in colleges, a feat that they had long been attempting to achieve. Moreover, the new white nationalism found ways in which to use racially coded policy to marginalize international students. For instance, President Trump signed an order requiring that international students attend at least two courses *on campus* in fall 2020 to maintain their legal status. This law placed international students in the position of choosing to stay in America and risk exposure to the virus or having to return home. It was, in short, very similar to business owners demanding to open the economy so that their employees could go back to work and potentially expose themselves while doing so. That legislation was later rescinded after threats of law suits from educational institutions piled up.

The fight higher education was engaging with against the new white nationalism, however, extended beyond just Zoombombing. With the lynching of George Floyd and the subsequent protests, higher education was coming to a reckoning of its own, one that had to confront 300 years of institutional racism. Many higher education institutions' responses to the George Floyd lynching and protests, as one might expect, were considered lukewarm. Messages from college leaders pandered to the audiences of funders and audiences that comprised all quadrants of the nostalgia spectrum. "[F]ew explicitly mentioned black people, referenced the Black Lives Matter movement or included any concrete action items to address inequities on campus or in wider society."[26] But the accountability of the long-term oppression was coming forth and structural changes were necessary: "The number of Black professors hired by universities is paltry. Completion and debt rates show systemic inequities. The quad of the American college campus has racism at its root. It is a culture. It is a tradition." And the reckoning for all that past was upon the leaders of academic institutions.

> Now, in a moment of crisis for the sector, college leaders at historically white universities are being called to dig into their pristine grounds. Scholars and students are sharing stories of discrimination, pulling these institutions into the national conversation about the ingrained white supremacy of American systems, all amid a pandemic that could threaten lives—disproportionately those of people of color—on campus. Three weeks ago, those campuses were focused on the coronavirus. Now they are being pushed to reckon with racism.[27]

It is clear, however, that the manifold stakeholders of higher education hold sway over those institutions and their leadership. "Despite the meme that many colleges and universities are bastions of liberalism, most college presidents still have to serve constituencies from across the ideological spectrum as they try to walk a line between board members, faculty members, other employees, students, donors and politicians."[28]

Whether or not higher education reckons with its past of racism will be determined by whether or not leaders at the federal, state, county, and individual college levels see 2020–2021 as the harbinger and catalyst of great social, educational, and political change. Already, there is some indication that the federal government will continue with the status quo. Rather than considering the pandemic and the national movement toward anti-racism as full of imaginary potential, the American federal government took a stance that reproduced the very structures that underpin the new white nationalism. Specifically, in the first months in which the pandemic waged, the federal government allowed for relief dollars to funnel to higher education. The Corona Aid, Relief, and Economic Stimulus (CARES) Act, amounted to a total of nearly $2 trillion. The Brookings' Institution's analysis of the funding delineated between this package and the 2009 American Recovery and Reinvestment Act: "CARES is more appropriately thought of as relief—not stimulus."[29] In other words, the CARES act money was allocated to assist Americans live from one paycheck to another. However, the same Brookings Institute report warned that the people most in need of economic relief both prior to and because of the pandemic were least likely to benefit from the CARES Act. This outcome was not a surprise to most. What remains unclear is how the American government found such an immense amount of money in response to a singular moment of tragedy, and never considered spending a similar amount of money to eradicate the systematic poverty and racism that pervades the social structure in times of relative "normalcy." The reaction to this singular, albeit awful moment, resembles the manner in which nearly all tragedies in American history have been reacted to: Acknowledge the systemic failure, react in surprise at such failure, and then move on through stories of heroism after flooding the survivors of that tragedy with money. The reaction to tragedy is one where the government literally pays for the cycle of normalcy, and so systemic racism, to be returned to.

When all is said and done, after the pain and the sadness, we are where we always have been. The nostalgia spectrum teaches us that how we remember and situate America's 2020–2021 in cultural memory and official text will matter. The record we create in the present is also the memory of the future. And the nuances of economic hardship, cultural memory, levels of activism, and resistance to it are all telling of the sort of nation we will become.

NOTES

1. In both the police brutality and the pandemic, black, Latinx, and lower-class bodies were put on the line while white, middle- to upper-class bodies, save those in the medical field—another group of American heroes—suffered, but not as a result of systemic racism.

2. The Aspen Institute, *Reinventing Low-Wage Work* (Workforce Strategies Institute, 2010).

3. M'Balou Camara, Khaing Zaw, Darrick Hamilton, and William Darity Jr., "Entering Entrepreneurship: Racial Disparities in the Pathways into Business Ownership." The Samuel DuBois Cook Center on Social Equity, Duke University; The Institute on Assets and Social Policy, Brandeis University; The Kirwan Institute for the Study of Race and Ethnicity, The Ohio State University. Summer 2020.

4. Centers for Disease Control, "Provisional Death Counts for COVID-19." May 11, 2020, https://www.cdc.gov/nchs/nvss/vsrr/covid_weekly/index.htm#Race_Hispanic.

5. Andre M. Perry, David Harshbarger, and Carl Romer, "Mapping Racial Inequity Amid COVID-19 Underscores Policy Discriminations Against Black Americans." *The Avenue*. April 16, 2020.

6. Kassie Mille, "Anti-Lockdown Rallies Are Providing an Opening for the Proud Boys and Other Far-Right Extremists." *Southern Poverty Law Center*. May 12, 2020.

7. Jack Date and Alexander Millin, "Trump Uses Pandemic to Attack Virginia on Gun Control, But He's Done It Before." *ABC News*. April 22, 2020.

8. Kassie Mille, "Anti-Lockdown Rallies Are Providing an Opening for the Proud Boys and Other Far-Right Extremists." *Southern Poverty Law Center*. May 12, 2020.

9. Liptak Kevin and Kirsten Holmes, "Trump Uses Pandemic to Attack Virginia on Gun Control, But He's Done It Before." *CNN*. July 1, 2020.

10. Daniel Trotta, "Despite Trump's 'Law and Order' Rhetoric, Protesters Won't Back Down." *Reuters*. September 11, 2020.

11. Steven Lemongello, "Rubio Compares U.S. Capitol Storming with Black Lives Matter Protests." *Orlando Sentinel*. January 8, 2021.

12. Martin Luther King, "Letter from Birmingham Jail." *The Atlantic*. April 1963.

13. Thomas Gibbons-Neff, Eric Schmitt and Helene Cooper, "Aggressive Tactics by National Guard, Ordered to Appease Trump, Wounded the Military, Too." *New York Times*. June 10, 2020.

14. Kenya Downs, "FBI Warned of White Supremacists in Law Enforcement 10 Years Ago. Has Anything Changed?" *PBS News Hour*. October 21, 2016.

15. Gary Porter, *History of Policing in the United States* (Eastern Kentucky University), 2013.

16. Ibram Kendi, *Stamped from the Beginning* (New York: Bold Type Books, 2016), 9.

17. Ebony Bowden, "Trump Says Coronavirus Pandemic 'Worse Than Pearl Harbor . . . World Trade Center.'" *New York Post*. May 20, 2020.

18. Ashley Bowden, Connor Finnegan, and Jack Arnholz, "Pompeo Says 'Enormous Evidence' For Unproven Theory That Coronavirus Came from Lab." *ABC News*. May 3, 2020.

19. Amy Harmon, "Why White Supremacists Are Chugging Milk (and Why Geneticists Are Alarmed)." *New York Times*. October 17, 2018.

20. American Defense League, "Reports of Anti-Asian Assaults, Harassment and Hate Crimes Rise as Coronavirus Spreads." June 10, 2020.

21. Kristine Phillips, "We Just Want to Be Safe: Hate Crimes, Harassment of Asian Americans Rise Amid Coronavirus Pandemic." *USA Today*. May 10, 2020.

22. Kassie Miller, "White Supremacists See Coronavirus as an Opportunity." *Southern Poverty Law Center*. May 12, 2020.

23. Emma Platoff and Carla Astudillo, "Across Texas and the Nation, the Novel Coronavirus Is Deadlier for People of Color." *Texas Tribune*. July 30, 2020.

24. "Lynchings by State." *University of Missouri Kansas City Law School*, http://law2.umkc.edu/faculty/projects/ftrials/shipp/lynchingsstate.html

25. "Mapping Police Violence." *Mapping Police Violence Dashboard.* Accessed June 24, 2020. https://mappingpoliceviolence.org/states.

26. Lindsey McKinzey, "Words Matter for College Presidents, but So Will Actions." *Inside Higher Ed.* June 8, 2020.

27. Lindsay Ellis, "For Colleges, Protests Over Racism May Put Everything on the Line." *Chronicle of Higher Education.* June 12, 2020.

28. Rick Seltzer, "Why Presidents Say What They Say." *Insidehighered.* January 14, 2021.

29. Grace Enda and William G. Gale and Claire Haldeman, "Careful or Careless? Perspectives on the CARES Act." *Friday.* March 27, 2020.

Bibliography

Acosta Belen, Edna. "Reimagining Borders." In *Color-Line to Borderlands*, edited by Johanna Butler (Washington: University of Washington Press, 2001), 240–264.

Aho, Michael and Mark Levinson. "The Economy after Reagan." *Foreign Affairs.* Winter 1998.

Alliance for Education. "Crime Rates Linked to Educational Attainment, 2013 Alliance Report Finds." *Alliance for Education.* September 12, 2013, https://all4ed. org/press/crime-rates-linked-to-educational-attainment-new-alliance-report-finds/.

American Defense League. "New Hate and Old: The Changing Face of American White Supremacy." Accessed November 6, 2019, https://www.adl.org/new-hate -and-old.

American Defense League. "Reports of Anti-Asian Assaults, Harassment and Hate Crimes Rise as Coronavirus Spreads." June 10, 2020.

American Defense League. "White Supremacists Continue to Spread Hate on American Campuses." June 27, 2019, https://www.adl.org/blog/white-supremaci sts-continue-to-spread-hate-on-american-campuses.

Amour, Madeline St. "Study Minimizes Impact of Free Community College." *Inside HigherEd.* September 9, 2019.

Anderson, Benedict. "Imagined Communities." In *Nationalism*, edited by John Hutchinson and Anthony D. Smith (New York: Oxford University Press, 1994), 89–96.

Anti-Defamation League. "Alt Right: A Primer about The New White Nationalism." https://www.adl.org/resources/backgrounders/alt-right-a-primer-about-the-new -white-supremacy.

"Articles of Impeachment." *New York Times.* December 13, 2019.

The Aspen Institute. *Reinventing Low-Wage Work* (Workforce Strategies Institute, 2010).

Avery, Christopher et al. *Policies and Payoffs to Addressing America's College Graduation Deficit* (Washington, DC: Brookings Institution). Accessed October

23, 2019, https://www.brookings.edu/wp-content/uploads/2019/09/Avery-et-al_conference-draft.pdf.

Badger, Emily. "The Dramatic Racial Bias of Subprime Lending During the Housing Boom." *Reuters*. August 23, 2013.

Bahney, Anna. "College Grads Earn $30,000 More a Year Than Those with Just a High School Degree." *CNN*. June 13, 2019.

Baldwin, James. *I Am Not Your Negro*. (New York: Vintage Books, 2017).

Baldwin, James. "Sonny's Blues." In *The Oxford Book of American Short Stories*, edited by Joyce Carol Oates (New York: Oxford University Press, 2013), 483–515.

Barbara, Rebeka, "Organizing Against Koch Influence on College Campuses." *Facing South*. March 15, 2019.

Barr, William. "Executive Summary of the Mueller Report." March 24, 2019.

Barrouquere, Brett. "Richard Spencer Took Universities, Protesters by Storm; They Adjusted and Brought His Speaking Tour to an End." *The Intelligence Report*. Southern Poverty Law Center. (August 5, 2018), https://www.splcenter.org/fighting-hate/intelligence-report/2018/schools-out.

Berger, Peter and Thomas Luckman. *The Social Construction of Reality* (New York: Doubleday, 1972).

Berlant, Lauren. *The Queen of America Goes to Washington City* (Durham: Duke University Press), 1997.

Bienhart, Peter. "Trumpism Is the New McCarthyism." *The Atlantic*. June 16, 2020.

Blakemore, Erin. "How the GI Bill Promise Was Denied to a Million WWII Veterans." *History*, https://www.history.com/news/gi-bill-black-wwii-veterans-benefits.

Bowden, Ebony. "Trump Says Coronavirus Pandemic 'Worse Than Pearl Harbor . . . World Trade Center.'" *New York Post*. May 20, 2020.

Brooks, Mo. "Save America Rally Speech." *Rev.com*. January 6, 2021.

Brown, Adam. "The App That The Proud Boys Used To Celebrate Donald Trump's Debate Performance." *Forbes*. September 30, 2020.

Brown, Connor Finnegan and Jack Arnholz. "Pompeo Says 'Enormous Evidence' For Unproven Theory That Coronavirus Came From Lab." *ABC News*. May 3, 2020.

Burd, Steven. "Even at Private Colleges, Low-Income Students Tend to Go to the Poorest Schools." *New America*. May 18, 2017, https://www.newamerica.org/education-policy/edcentral/private-colleges/.

Burghart, Devin and Leonard Zeskind. *Tea Parties – Racism, Anti-Semitism and the Militia Impulse* (Institute for Research & Education, 2010).

Camera, Lauren. "White Privilege and the College Admissions Scandal." *US News and World Report*. March 13, 2019.

Caplan, Bryan. *The Case against Higher Education: Why the Education System is a Waste of Time and Money* (Princeton: Princeton University Press, 2018).

CBS News. "The Price you Pay, the Spiraling Cost of College." October 14, 2019.

Centers for Disease Control. "Provisional Death Counts for COVID-19." May 11, 2020 https://www.cdc.gov/nchs/nvss/vsrr/covid_weekly/index.htm#Race_Hispanic.

Chappel, Karen and Michael Tietz. "The Causes of Inner-City Poverty: Eight Hypotheses in Search of Reality." *Cityscape* 3, no. 3 (1999).

Chuh, Kandice. *Imagine Otherwise: On Asian Americanist Critique* (Durham: Duke University Press, 2003).

"CNN Newsroom." *CNN*. January 7, 2021.

Common Dreams. "Report Shows How Koch Brothers Bankroll 'Fox News of the Regulatory Policy World' to Help Push Polluter-Friendly Agenda." June 3, 2019. Accessed June 10, 2019, https://www.commondreams.org/news/2019/06/03/report -shows-how-koch-brothers-bankroll-fox-news-regulatory-policy-world-help-push.

Complete College America. *Time is the Enemy* (Washington, DC: Complete College America, 2012).

Congressional Research Service. "Membership of the 115th Congress: A Profile." Accessed June 1, 2019, https://fas.org/sgp/crs/misc/R44762.pdf.

Date, Jack Date and Alexander Millin. "Trump Uses Pandemic to Attack Virginia on Gun Control, But He's Done It Before." *ABC News*. April 22, 2020.

Delmont, Matthew. "There's a Generational Shift in the Debate over Busing." *The Atlantic*. July 1, 2019.

Democratic National Debate. CNN, Detroit, MI: June 27, 2019.

Diamond, Jeremy. "Trump Jokes after Rally Attendee's Suggestion to 'Shoot' Migrants at the Border." *CNN*. May 19, 2019.

Downs, Kenya. "FBI Warned of White Supremacists in Law Enforcement 10 Years Ago. Has Anything Changed?" *PBS News Hour*. October 21, 2016.

Dury, Richard, L. "Community Colleges in America: A Historical Perspective." *Inquiry* 8, no. 1 (Spring 2003), 1–6.

Dweck, Carol S. "Mind-Sets and Equitable Education." *Principal Leadership* 10, no. 5 (2010), 26–29.

Edna, Grace, William G. Gale and Claire Haldeman. "Careful or Careless? Perspectives on the CARES Act." *Friday*, March 27, 2020.

Ellis, Lindsay. "For Colleges, Protests Over Racism May Put Everything On the Line." *Chronicle of Higher Education*. June 12, 2020.

Ellis, Lindsay. "This 5-Word Phrase Has Become a Mantra for Slashing College Budgets." *The Chronicle of Higher Education*. July 3, 2019.

Enten, Harry. "Why Donald Trump Is Already the 2024 GOP Frontrunner." *CNN*, December 27, 2020.

Felder, Ben. "How Colleges Are Adapting to the Decline in Liberal Arts Majors." *PBS News Hour*. November 30, 2018.

Fieldstadt, Elisha and Ken Dilanian. "White Nationalism-Fueled Violence is on the Rise, but FBI Is Slow to Call it Domestic Terrorism." *NBC News* (New York), August 5, 2019.

Flaherty, Colleen. "Diversity Work, Interrupted." *Inside HigherEd*. October 7, 2020.

Foucault, Michel. *History of Sexuality* (New York: Vintage Books, 1990).

Foucault, Michel. "Truth and Juridical Forms." In *Power: Essential Works of Foucault. 1954–1974*, James D Faubion, ed. (London: Penguin 2002).

Franklin, Benjamin. "Letter to Samuel Johnson." *Founders Online*. Accessed November 5, 2019, https://founders.archives.gov/documents/Franklin/01-04-02-0009.

Friedman, Sach, "Is College Worth it?" *Forbes*. June 13, 2019.

Gallup News Service. "The Florida Recount Controversy from the Public's Perspective: 25 Insights." Accessed December 10, 2019, https://news.gallup.com/poll/2176/florida-recount-controversy-from-publics-perspective-insights.aspx.

Galston, William A. and Clara Hendrickson, "The Educational Rift in the 2016 Election." *PEW Research*. December 2016.

Garcia-Navarro, Lulu. "From the Tea Party to Trump: the GOP in the 2010s." *National Public Radio* (Washington, DC), December 29, 2019.

Gellner, Ernest. "Nationalism and Modernization." In *Nationalism*, edited by John Hutchinson and Anthony D. Smith (New York: Oxford University Press, 1994), 90–91.

Gilber, Clairn and Donald Heller. "The Truman Commission and its Impact on Federal Higher Education Policy from 1947 to 2010." Accessed November 3, 2019, https://ed.psu.edu/cshe/working-papers/wp-9.

Giuliani, Rudolph. "Save America Rally Speech." *Rev.com*. January 6, 2021.

Goldberg, Michelle. "This Is What Happens When You Slash Funding for Public Universities." *The Nation*. June 8, 2018.

Gramlich, John. "Federal Prison Population Fell during Obama's Term, Reversing Recent Trend." *Pew Research Center* (Washington, DC), January 5, 2017.

Gramsci, Antonio. "Hegemony, Relations of Force, Historical Block." In *The Antonio Gramsci Reader*, edited by David Forgacs (New York: Schocken Books, 2002), 189–221.

Grasgreen, Allie. "Liberal Arts Grads Win Long-Term." *Inside HigherEd*. December 14, 2014.

Hall, Stuart. "Gramsci's Relevance for the Study of Race and Ethnicity." In *Stuart Hall: Critical Dialogues in Cultural Studies*, edited by David Morley and Kuan-Hsing Chen (London: Routledge, 1996), 411–440.

Harmon, Amy. "Why White Supremacists Are Chugging Milk (and Why Geneticists Are Alarmed)." *The New York Times*. October 17, 2018.

"Higher Education for American Democracy A Report of the Presidents Commission On Higher Education Vol I - Vi." *American Congress*. Accessed September 23, 2019, https://archive.org/stream/in.ernet.dli.2015.89917/2015.89917.Higher-Education-For-American-Democracy-A-Report-Of-The-Presidents-Commission-On-Higher-Education-Vol-I---Vi_djvu.txt.

Hill Collins Patricia. *Black Feminist Thought* (New York: Routledge, 2000).

Holer, Harry and Sandy Baum. *Making Colleges Work: Pathways to Success for Disadvantaged Students* (New York: Brookings Institution, 2017).

I Am Not Your Negro. Directed by Samuel L Jackson. James Baldwin and Raoul Peck (Los Angeles: Magnolia Home Entertainment, 2017), DVD.

Institution for Education and Human Rights. *Tea Party Nationalism* (Kansas City, MO: IPRHR Press, December, 2010).

Integrated Postsecondary Education Data System. "IPEDS Glossary." Accessed November 12, 2019, https://surveys.nces.ed.gov/ipeds/VisGlossaryAll.aspx.

"Is President Trump's Rhetoric Racist?" *The Washington Post* (Washington, DC), August 12, 2019.

Jaschick, Scott. "Professors and Politics: What the Research Says." *Inside Highered.* February 7, 2017, https://www.insidehighered.com/news/2017/02/27/research -confirms-professors-lean-left-questions-assumptions-about-what-means.

Jefferson, Thomas. "Letter to William Charles Jarvis." In *The Essential Jefferson* (Courier Corporation, 2008).

Jenny, Jarvie and Brittany Mejia. "'Are We Going to Choose White Supremacy?' Voters of Color React to Trump's Comments." *LA Times.* October 1, 2020.

Johnson, James Weldon. *Autobiography of an Ex-Colored Man.* New York: Sherman French & Co., 1912.

Johnson, Theodore and Leah Wright Rigueur. "Race-Baiting for the Presidency." *The Atlantic.* November 15, 2015.

Kabaservice, Geoffrey. "The Old Tea Party May Be over, But the New One Is at its Peak." *The Washington Post* (Washington, DC), March 16, 2018.

Kahlenber, Richard. "How Higher Education Funding Shortchanges Community Colleges." *The Century Foundation.* Accessed November 3, 2019, https://tcf.org/ content/report/how-higher-education-funding-shortchanges-community-colleges/ ?agreed=1.

Kahn, Chris. "Majority of Americans Want Trump Removed Immediately after U.S. Capitol Violence- Reuters/Ipsos Poll." *Reuters.* January 8, 2021.

Kellner, Douglass. *Media Culture* (New York: Routledge, 1995).

Kendi, Ibrham, *Stamped from the Beginning* (New York: Bold Type Books, 2016).

Kennedy, John. "Full Text of Moon Speech." *NASA Website.* Accessed August 23, 2019, https://er.jsc.nasa.gov/seh/ricetalk.htm. Retrieved June 2, 2019.

Kerr, Emma. "Is College Worth the Cost?" *U.S. News and World Report.* June 17, 2019.

King, Martin Luther. "Letter from Birmingham Jail." *The Atlantic.* April, 1963.

Kronman, Arthur. *The Assault on American Excellence* (New Haven: Yale University Press, 2019).

Kronman, Arthur. "The Downside of Diversity." *The Wall Street Journal.* August 2, 2019.

Lemongello, Steven. "Rubio Compares U.S. Capitol Storming With Black Lives Matter Protests." *Orlando Sentinel.* January 8, 2021.

Levinthal, Dave. "How the Koch Brothers Are Influencing U.S. Colleges." *Time.* December 15, 2015.

Lipsitz, George. *American Studies in a Moment of Danger* (Minneapolis: University of Minnesota Press, 2001).

Lipsitz, George. *Possessive Investment in Whiteness* (Philadelphia: Temple University Press, 2006).

Liptak, Kevin Liptak and Kirsten Holmes. "Trump Uses Pandemic to Attack Virginia on Gun Control, But He's Done it before." *CNN.* July 1, 2020.

Lorde, Audre. "Poetry Is Not a Luxury." In *Sister Outsider: Essays and Speeches* (Berkley, CA: Crossing Press, 1984).

Lowe, Lisa. *Immigrant Acts* (Durham: Duke University Press, 2003).

"Lynchings by State." *University of Missouri Kansas City Law School,* http://law2 .umkc.edu/faculty/projects/ftrials/shipp/lynchingsstate.html

Mangan, Katherine. "'Unprecedented in Our History': One State Is on the Verge of Slashing Higher-Ed Funding. Leaving Public Colleges in a Panic." *Chronicle of Higher Education.* July 1, 2019.

"Mapping Police Violence." *Mapping Police Violence Dashboard.* Accessed June 24, 2020, https://mappingpoliceviolence.org/states.

Marken, Stephanie. "A Crisis in Confidence in Higher Ed." *Gallup.* April 12, 2019.

Massey, Douglass. "Residential Segregation and Neighborhood Conditions in U.S. Metropolitan Areas." In Smelser, N.J., Wilson, W.J. and Mitchell, F., Eds., *America Becoming: Racial Trends and Their Consequences*, Vol. 1 (Washington, DC: The National Academies Press, 2001), 391–434.

Matthews, Dylan. "The Tuition is Too Damn High." *The Washington Post* (Washington, DC), August 26, 2019.

Matthews, Patricia. "Academic Freedom in the Classroom: Students and the Trouble with Labels." Last modified December 2019, https://profession.mla.org/academic -freedom-in-the-classroom-students-and-the-trouble-with-labels/.

Maxell, Angie. "What we Get wrong about the Southern Strategy." *The Washington Post* (Washington, DC), July 26, 2019.

M'Balou Camara, Khaing Zaw, Darrick Hamilton and William Darity Jr. "Entering Entrepreneurship: Racial Disparities in the Pathways into Business Ownership." The Samuel DuBois Cook Center on Social Equity, Duke University; The Institute on Assets and Social Policy, Brandeis University; The Kirwan Institute for the Study of Race and Ethnicity, The Ohio State University. Summer 2020.

McGowan, Heather. "The Workforce Is Calling, Higher Education, Will You Answer?" *Forbes.* September 10, 2019.

McKinzey, Lindsey. "Words Matter for College Presidents, but So Will Actions." *Inside Higher Ed.* June 8, 2020.

Merisotis, Jamie. *America Has Fallen behind Globally* (Washington, DC: Lumina Foundation, February 18, 2019), https://www.luminafoundation.org/news-and-vie ws/america-has-fallen-behind-in-the-global-education-race.

Mille, Kassie, "Anti-Lockdown Rallies Are Providing an Opening for the Proud Boys and Other Far-Right Extremists." *Southern Poverty Law Center.* May 12, 2020.

Miller, Kassie. "White Supremacists See Coronavirus as an Opportunity." *Southern Poverty Law Center.* May 12, 2020.

Miner, Sam. "Improving Shared Governance." *The Chronicle of Higher Education.* September 25, 1998.

Mitchell, Michael et al. "A Lost Decade in Higher Education Funding." *Center on Budget Funding and Priorities* (Washington, DC), 2019. Accessed August 10, 2019, https://www.cbpp.org/research/state-budget-and-tax/a-lost-decade-in-hi gher-education-funding.

Mueller, Robert. *Report on the Investigation Into Russian Interference in the 2016 Presidential Election* (Washington, DC: Department of Justice, March, 2019).

Musil, Caryn McTighe. "Educating for Citizenship." *Peer Review* 5, no. 3 (Spring 2003), online.

National Public Radio. "The Doctor Who Championed Hand-Washing and Briefly Saved Lives." *Morning Edition.* December 12, 2015, https://www.npr.org/sections

/health-shots/2015/01/12/375663920/the-doctor-who-championed-hand-washing -and-saved-women-s-lives.

National Student Clearing House. "Six Year Outcomes." December 2018, http://www .ccdaily.com/2018/12/completion-rates-rise/.

Nietzle, Michael. "The College Profile of the 116th Congress' First Class.'" *Forbes*. December. 10, 2018, https://www.forbes.com/sites/michaeltnietzel/2018/12/10/ the-college-profile-of-the-116th-congresss-first-year-class/#446afe7d3bcc.

Neitzel, Michael, "Whither the Humanities: The Ten-Year Trend In College Majors." *Forbes*. January 7, 2019.

Niquette, Mark. "South Carolina Governor Backs Removal of Confederate Flag." *Bloomberg News*, https://www.bloomberg.com/news/articles/2015-06-22/south -carolina-officials-call-for-confederate-flag-to-come-down. Retrieved June 22, 2015.

Nitkin, David. "Ehrlich Calls Multiculturalism 'Bunk.'" *Baltimore Sun*. May 9, 2004.

Office of Management and Budget. "Executive Order on Combating Race and Sex Stereotyping." September 22, 2020.

O'Leary, Lizzie. "'Children Were Dirty, They Were Scared, and They Were Hungry.'" *The Atlantic*. June 19, 2019.

Omi, Michael and Howard Winant. *Racial Formation in the U.S.* (New York: Routledge, 1994).

O'Niel, Cathy. *Weapons of Math Destruction* (New York: Penguin Books, 2017).

Perry, Andre M., David Harshbarger and Carl Romer. "Mapping Racial Inequity Amid COVID-19 Underscores Policy Discriminations Against Black Americans." *The Avenue*. April 16, 2020.

Phelps, Jordyn. "Trump Defends 2017 'Very Fine People' Comments, Calls Robert E. Lee 'a Great General.'" *ABC News*, https://abcnews.go.com/Politics/trump-de fends-2017-fine-people-comments-calls-robert/story?id=62653478.

Phillips, Amber. "The Idea That Every Culture Is Equal Is Not Objectively True." *Washington Post*. June 20, 2017.

Phillips, Kristine. "We Just Want to Be Safe': Hate Crimes, Harassment of Asian Americans Rise Amid Coronavirus Pandemic." *USA Today*. May 10, 2020.

Picci, Aimee. "English Majors, Rejoice: Employers Want You More Than Business Majors." *CBS News*. October 28, 2019.

Pinsker, Joe. "Republicans Changed Their Mind About Higher Education Really Quickly." *The Atlantic*. August 21, 2019.

Platoff, Emma and Carla Astudillo. "Across Texas and the Nation, the Novel Coronavirus is Deadlier for People of Color." *Texas Tribune*. July 30, 2020.

Porter, Gary. "History of Policing in the United States." Eastern Kentucky University.

Postsecondary Value Commission. *Bill Gates Commission*. Accessed November 16, 2019, https://www.postsecondaryvalue.org/.

"Professor WatchList." Accessed June 1, 2019, https://www.professorwatchlist.org/.

Putnam, David. *Our Kids: The American Dream in Crisis* (New York: Simon and Schuster, 2015).

Quintana, Carolos. "U. of Virginia Bans Richard Spencer and Other Leaders of Violent 'Unite the Right' Rally." *Chronicle of Higher Education.* October 26, 2018.

Rainnie, Lee and Andrew Perrin. *Key Findings about Americans' Declining Trust in Government and Each Other* (Washington, DC: Pew Research Center, July 22, 2019).

Rao, Mythili. "Sherman Alexie: How Storytelling Can Create Social Change." *The Takeaway.* September 23, 2015.

Rathni, Nandi. "From Mercator's to Gall-Peters Projections, How the World Maps Vary and Change." *The Indian Express.* March 26, 2017.

Reeves, Richard and Christopher Pulliam. "No Room at the Top: The Stark Divide in Black and White Economic Mobility." *PEW Research Center.* February 14, 2019.

Reagan, Ronald. *1980 Republican Convention Address* (Detroit: MI, July 17, 1980), https://www.americanrhetoric.com/speeches/ronaldreagan1980rnc.htm.

Rose, Joel. "Leaked Emails Fuel Calls For Stephen Miller to Leave White House." *National Public Radio.* November 26, 2019, https://www.npr.org/2019/11/26/7830 47584/leaked-emails-fuel-calls-for-stephen-miller-to-leave-white-house.

Rozen, Paul and Edward Royzan. "Negativity Bias, Negativity Dominance, and Contagion." *Personality and Social Psychology Review* 5, no. 4 (2001), 296–320.

Santorum, Rick. *This Week.* August 20, 2005.

Scarborough, Joe. "Morning Joe." *MSNBC.* October 1, 2020.

Schmidt, Michael S. and Maggie Haberman. "Citing Recusal, Trump Says He Wouldn't Have Hired Sessions." *New York Times.* July 17, 2017.

Schoen, John. "Why Does College Cost so Much?" *CBS News* (New York), December 8, 2016. Accessed August 1, 2019, https://www.cnbc.com/2015/06/16/ why-college-costs-are-so-high-and-rising.html.

Seltzer, Rick. "Why Presidents Say What They Say." *Insidehighered.* January 14, 2021.

Sessions, Jeff. *Resignation Letter.* Accessed December 20, 2019

Singletary, Michelle. "Community College Should Be a First Choice, Not a Last Resort." *The Washington Post.* July 16, 2019.

Smith, Barbara, Gloria Anzaldua and Cherrie Morage, eds, *This Bridge Called My This Bridge Called My Back* (San Francisco: Persephone Press, 1981).

"Status and Trends in Racial and Ethnic Minorities, National Center for Education Statistics." 2019, https://nces.ed.gov/pubs2010/2010015/tables/table_24_1.asp.

Stokolos, Eli. "Trump Vow to 'Never Concede' Incites Mob of Supporters." *LA Times.* January 7, 2021.

Sturken, Marita. *Tangled Memories: The Vietnam War, the AIDS Epidemic, and the Politics of Remembering* (Los Angeles: University of California Press, 1997).

Supiano, Beckie. "Grades Can Hinder Learning. What Should Professors Use Instead?" *Chronicle of Higher Education.* July 17, 2019.

Swallow, John. "Why We Must Balance Emotion and Intellect." *Inside HigherEd.* July 10, 2018, https://www.insidehighered.com/views/2018/07/10/students-today -need-colleges-value-emotions-well-intellect-opinion.

Takaki, Ronald. "Multiculturalism: Battleground or Meeting Ground." In *Color-Line to Borderlands*, edited by Johanna Butler (Washington: University of Washington Press), 109–121.

Taylor, Barrett J., Brendan Cantwell, Kimberly Watts and Olivia Wood. "Partisanship, White Racial Resentment, and State Support for Higher Education." *The Journal of Higher Education* 91, no. 1 (2020).

Tchekmedyian, Alene and Brittny Mejia. "California White Supremacists Vowed to 'Reimagine' Racist Movements With New Look and Secretive Tactics." *L.A. Times* (Los Angeles, CA) October 25, 2018.

The Century Foundation. *Restoring the American Dream* (Washington, DC: The Century Foundation, April, 2019).

Thomas, Gibbons-Neff, Eric Schmitt and Helene Cooper. "Aggressive Tactics by National Guard, Ordered to Appease Trump, Wounded the Military, Too." *New York Times*. June 10, 2020.

Tinto, Vincent. *Completing College* (Chicago: University of Chicago, 2001).

Trotta, Daniel. "Despite Trump's 'law and order' Rhetoric, Protesters Won't Back Down." *Reuters*. September 11, 2020.

Trump, Donald. "Here's Donald Trump's Presidential Announcement Speech." *Time*. June 16, 2015, https://time.com/3923128/donald-trump-announcement-speech/.

U.S. Census Bureau (2010), Decennial Census by Decade." https://www.census.gov/programs-surveys/decennial-census/data/datasets.html

Variety Staff. "President Donald Trump Tells Hate Group Proud Boys to 'Stand Back and Stand By." *Variety*. October 1, 2020; Dana Milbank. "President Donald Trump Tells Hate Group Proud Boys to 'Stand Back and Stand By." *Washington Post*. October 1, 2020.

Victor, Daniel. "What, Congressman Steve King Asks, Have Nonwhites Done for Civilization?" *New York Times*. August 16, 2017.

Wagner, John and Seung Min Kim. "Trump Accuses Four Minority Congresswomen of Being 'Very Racist' and 'Not Very Smart.'" *New York Times*. July 22, 2019.

Weissman, Sara. "Is College Worth it? Yes, But Return On Investment Varies, Study Finds." *Washington Post*. November 13, 2019.

Whistle, Wesley. "How Higher Education Data Reporting is Both Burdensome and Inadequate." *Third Way*. November 1, 2019, https://www.thirdway.org/report/how-higher-education-data-reporting-is-both-burdensome-and-inadequate.

Whitehead, Micele Dawn. "Global Citizenship for Campus, Communities, and Careers." *AACU Perspectives*. September 2019.

Wilder, Craig Steven. *Ebony & Ivy: Race, Slavery, and the Troubled History of America's Universities* (New York: Bloomsbury Press, 2013).

Wise, Gene. "'Paradigm Dramas' in American Studies: A Cultural and Institutional History of the Movement." In *Locating American Studies. The Evolution of a Discipline*, edited by Lucy Maddox (Baltimore: Johns Hopkins University Press, 1999), 166–215.

Wise, Justin. "Steve King Asks How Terms 'White Nationalist' and 'White Supremacist' Became Offensive." *The Hill* (Washington, DC), January 10, 2019.

Index

About the Author

Michael H. Gavin has spent his career examining the impact of racism on people, policies, and the American promise. He is the author *Sports in the Aftermath of Tragedy* and has served as a high-level administrator for the past decade. In that role, he has spearheaded college-wide efforts to eradicate opportunity gaps that exist for students attempting to reach their goals.

www.ingramcontent.com/pod-product-compliance
Lightning Source LLC
Chambersburg PA
CBHW022319280326
41932CB00010B/1155